The
SIMPLIFIED
SHORT
BIBLE

A Short Chronological Summary
of the Old and New Testaments

Condensed, Organized, and Explained by

Peter J. Bylsma

BYBLIO
PRESS
Inspire, Inform,
and Transform

Byblio Press
11410 NE 124th St., #260
Kirkland, WA 98034 USA
1-321-425-5757
www.bybliopress.com
www.shortbible.com

Ordering Information: This book may be ordered by contacting the publisher at the address above. Special discounts are available on quantity purchases by corporations, associations, and others. For details, contact the publisher at the address above.

The views expressed in this work are solely those of the author and do not necessarily reflect the views of the publisher, and the publisher hereby disclaims any responsibility for them. Certain stock imagery © Getty Images.

www.shortbible.com
Maps created by David C. Hoerlein
Printed in the United States of America

ISBN: 978-1-964060-09-5 (sc)
ISBN: 978-1-964060-10-1 (e)

Library of Congress Control Number: 2024914358

CONTENTS

PREFACE

I began writing *The Short Bible* in the spring of 2020 when the COVID-19 pandemic began. I had studied the Bible for more than 50 years but I didn't understand how all its parts fit into one overall story. The Bible stories were like pieces of a puzzle that couldn't be put together because I couldn't see a picture on the box. Many people who want to read the entire Bible have not been able to finish it because it is so long and complicated in places, and they didn't have the time to read all of it.

After I published *The Short Bible* in 2021, it became obvious that an even shorter summary of the entire Bible was needed, and it needed to be written in simpler language. This **simplified version** was written for those who are at least 10 years old and can read English text. (Simplified versions of *The Short Bible* are being produced in other languages.)

As with the other versions of *The Short Bible* that have been published, I will donate 90% of all the royalties I receive through the Bylsma Foundation to nonprofit organizations that help people in need, promote justice in the world, seek and spread the truth, help others understand the stories and meanings of the Bible, and encourage those who need good news.

Peter J. Bylsma
April 2022

INTRODUCTION

The Holy Bible is a collection of 66 ancient documents written by many authors over a 2,000-year period. In the late fourth century, church leaders reviewed all available documents and decided on a final set that is now known as the *canon*. The books were then organized in their present order and translated into Latin. The Bible has two parts. The Old Testament has 39 books and spans about 1,500 years of history of the Israelites. The New Testament has 27 books and covers events in the first century AD in Palestine and in eastern Mediterranean Sea region.

Some of the documents ("books") are quite long, while others are only a few paragraphs. These books were divided into chapters and verses so readers can easily find specific passages. There are more than 1,100 chapters in the entire Bible, and it would take more than 2,000 pages to publish it in the format of a modern book. The names of all the books are found in Appendix A.

Part One of this book summarizes the Old Testament; Part Two summarizes the New Testament. A period of 400 years separates the events described in the two parts and is discussed in Chapter 14.

Various versions of the Bible have been written over the centuries. The earliest English version was created in the early 1600s by religious scholars working for King James of England. That began the creation of translations into other languages, and many translations and versions of the Bible now exist, including paraphrased versions that are easier to read and understand. (Appendix C has information about these versions.)

Contents of the Bible

The books of the Bible reflect various types of literature. These include narratives about various heroes, historical accounts, legal presentations, biographies, poetry, genealogies and census information, wisdom literature and proverbs, collections of short stories, parables, inspirational letters, and highly symbolic predictions about the future.

The Bible's content often lacks details that the reader might want to know. In contrast, some sections include many details, some of which are not important. The contents are not presented in sequential order, making it difficult to understand some of the main events. Most of the writings occurred when farming was the main occupation, so there are many references and metaphors using common items at that time (sheep, goats, soil, seeds, water, wheat, fish, vineyards, the desert). The stories often have rich symbolism, and dialogue is mixed in with a narration.

The Bible is a serious book that has little humor or romance. There are many sad parts, but there are also many heroes and victories. There are also major gaps in the Bible narrative that need to be filled so modern readers can understand the context of the stories.

Summary of Main Points

The Bible describes a loving and forgiving God that desires a relationship with human beings in the world where good and evil coexist. The term *God* describes a powerful force that has different forms, similar to how water has two other forms (steam and ice). The term *Lord* is also used as a word for God, and God has a Spirit form.

The Bible has a number of concepts that thread their way from the beginning of the story to the end.

- The world has a physical dimension that can be seen and an invisible dimension that is supernatural and spiritual that cannot be seen.
- Invisible forces have unusual powers. Some forces are good and loving, but others have evil motives that do bad things and try to destroy what is good.
- There is only one true and supreme force (God). Some people believe there are many gods, but these gods are not like the true God. While God's nature does not

change, God's methods are unpredictable, flexible, and often change. God's mind can change when hearing people's sincere requests ("prayers").

- There is life after physical death, and God decides what happens to a person after they die. God loves and forgives everybody in the world, so it is possible for everyone to enter some form of a happy life after they die. This applies to all people, no matter what they have done in their life.

- God is always good, merciful, forgiving, patient, and loving. God wants all people to live life a good life and gives people far more than what we deserve (this undeserved goodness is called "grace").

- God wants to have a loving relationship with everybody in the world. It doesn't matter what they look like, where they were born, or what kind of family or traditions they have.

- There are right and wrong ways to live. Obeying God's instructions and commands helps us deal with life's problems. Not following these instructions and commands can lead to severe struggles and a separation from God. With God's help, we can change our ways and do good.

- God has chosen people to show the world how life and relationships should look on earth. At first, God used individuals and families, then a special tribe of people (the Israelites) who lived in one area of the world (Canaan, now known as Palestine). When these people were selfish, disobeyed God's teachings, and did not live the right way, God sent them messages through brave people to remind them how they should live. When people in the tribe consistently disobeyed, God adopted everybody in the world to be part of God's family. God's people are called to love others and make sure life is fair (provide justice) for everybody.

- When relationships are broken or strained, some form of sacrifice is needed to heal the relationship. However, these sacrifices must be sincere — our motives and actions prove that we are sorry and want to mend the relationship.

- Life is unpredictable and often unfair. Our plans are interrupted by unexpected events beyond our control. God challenges our lives, hearts, and priorities in unusual ways that change our direction. In a world where good and evil coexist, good people suffer and evil people prosper. Faithfulness to God and how we respond to our circumstances are what matter the most. God's unlimited love, forgiveness, and grace are wonderful gifts to all people, even though none of us deserve them.
- God wants people to help those in need. God is especially concerned about foreigners and the sick, poor, abandoned, discouraged, and without support. Helping these people provides evidence that a person is obeying God.
- God's ways and desires for us are often different from the ways we normally react. For example, we are to love our enemy and depend on God and others rather than doing what we want or trying to do things by ourself.

Ultimately, the Bible is a long and complex love story. This love is not physical, emotional, or sentimental. Rather, it is the form of love that always supports, defends, and sacrifices for others and constantly seeks what is right and best for the world. The Bible urges everybody to learn from its stories and teachings and consider following this way of life.

Interpreting the Bible

Interpreting the Bible can be a challenge. In some cases, the author or character tells the audience what the story means. At other times, the author just tells a story without saying anything else, usually because the audience understood the point being made. So a reader needs to understand the setting to understand the full meaning of some stories.

Sometimes specific guidance is written to people in one location at a particular time, and it may not apply to those living in other areas or times — the guidance is not a universal truth for everybody to follow all the time. Correct interpretations are generally those that are consistent with the main themes running through all the documents.

While the biblical writings tell the world about truths related to good and evil, not everything that was written is literally true. The various authors used different ways to convey essential meanings, such as allegories, metaphors, exaggerations, and parables. Their audiences knew they were meant to make a point rather than to be taken literally or report historical facts.

The Nature of God

The Hebrew term *God* is a plural noun for a powerful force that has different forms, similar to how elements and compounds have different forms (solid, liquid, gas). The term *Lord* is used in the biblical writings as another word for God. The different terms for God were typically masculine pronouns (*he*, *his*, *him*) or the term *Father*. However, God is not a masculine deity and is neither male nor female. As a multidimensional force, God created both male and female humans in God's own "image," able to distinguish between right and wrong, possessing a soul, having self-consciousness and awareness of our surroundings, able to have meaningful relationships with God and others, and willing to love others in a sacrificial way.

God communicates with humans in many different ways. Although the events of the books took place centuries ago, there is evidence that God continues to communicate with people in all these ways.

1. The awesome beauty of the universe and its predictable cycles and "laws of nature" have inspired humans to see the planet and the worlds beyond as an orderly and beautiful creation that is not randomly designed.

5

2. God communicates using a "Spirit" that influences the human mind and emotions and provides direction to humans about their moral choices.

3. When humans take time to listen and seek direction, communication can occur through insights and an inaudible "voice" in the mind.

4. Sometimes communications are more direct — through dreams, visions, or messages from angels or "holy strangers."

5. On rare occasions, God disrupts the normal laws of nature to intervene directly in human activities, often affecting rare natural events at strategic times. These events are called "miracles."

6. Sometimes humans are inspired by the Spirit to speak the words of God to others in extraordinary and convincing ways.

7. Other believers provide godly advice and rebuke others by using their "spiritual gifts."

8. The Bible itself is available to study so we can learn about God's ways long after the events occurred.

9. Finally, God took on a human form and lived on earth, giving us the most concrete example of how we are to live and love one another.

God uses many different strategies and tactics to meet the overall goal of showing the world how to live. Many characters in the Bible speak for God, and some of them act and speak in unusual and bizarre ways. Different types of miracles occur. Punishment comes in different forms, sometimes in unexpected ways. While the intrinsic nature of God does not change, God's methods are unpredictable and often changing.

Organization and Contents of This Book

Part 1 summarizes the Old Testament, with chapter 13 describing unique books that don't fit into a chronological account. Part 2 summarizes the New Testament. A period of 400 years separates the events described in the Old and New Testaments, and chapter 14 provides information about what happened during this time.

A table of key terms (people, locations, concepts) that are mentioned in each chapter appears at the end of that chapter. If the term appears again in another chapter, it is **not** included again in that chapter. In some cases, more than one person or location has the same name. For example, there are several people who have the name Joseph, and they are listed separately in the chapter where they are first mentioned.

Appendixes at the end of this book provide the names of all the books of the Bible, a timeline of the key events that occurred, suggestions for further reading, an index of key names and subjects, the sections of the Bible that are quoted, how the chapters of this book align with the books of the Bible, and maps to show where the main events took place.

PART ONE

THE OLD TESTAMENT

CHAPTER 1

THE BEGINNING

The Creation, Evil Influences,
and the First Agreements

Before time began or anything existed, a multidimensional God was present in the universe. This God was all-powerful, existed everywhere, and knew everything. God's character was entirely good, forgiving, helpful, and kind, and God was constantly creating. God first created angels who were meant to adore the creator and help in God's work. God created light, then a physical world composed of an extraordinary number of stars and planets. On one unique planet, God created waters and dry lands that eventually yielded living organisms — plants and animals on land and in the waters that were all self-sustaining. And everything was good.

But some of the angels were jealous of God's power and wanted it for themselves. They rebelled, causing evil to enter the universe. All that was good now exists alongside corrupt forces that fight against what is good.

God then made the most important creation, the humans who were unique on the unique planet. God wanted to have a relationship with them, so God gave them some of the same qualities of God — creative, needing to relate to others, able to tell the difference between right and wrong, able to love others without any conditions, and willing to put other's interests before their own. The two human "images of God," male and female, joined together and produced children so the human race would continue and grow. God gave humans the entire planet and all its living things to enjoy. Humans were to care for the planet and obey certain rules to help them all be self-sustaining and maintain harmony. God believed all of this was very good.

At first, humans enjoyed a perfect and happy life on the planet and followed God's instructions. But at some point, the leading evil angel (an adversary called Satan) infiltrated their awareness, sowing seeds of doubt about how good life really was. Humans ended up believing the evil angel's lies and violated the rules God told them to follow. This disobedience and selfishness infected humans with an invisible disease called sin that coexisted with their invisible nature of goodness. Evil brought with it pain and made life a struggle.

God was angry that Satan harmed the very best creation. God had allowed humans to make choices about their lives and wanted a relationship with the humans, but only if the humans wanted that kind of relationship. God knew that with evil in the world, some would decide not to pursue a relationship with God and would instead follow their own path. And many people and angels chose to follow the ways of evil. But rather than destroy evil, God allowed evil to exist — eliminating all evil would mean killing all humans as well. So now we live in a world where God battles Satan and other evil forces until a time when one side will be victorious.

Nobody knows when, where, or how all these events happened. What we do know is that (1) a good force created the universe and all things in it, (2) humans make choices that can be either good or evil, and (3) God constantly reveals the benefits of choosing good. God helps people think and act in good ways and sometimes takes direct action to oppose evil in order for them to enjoy a better life and meaningful relationships with God and others. Yet evil forces still exist and want to disrupt the good. Most of the time, the influences of good and evil show up in the actions of individuals, organizations, and the way people live together in the world.

Adam, Eve, and Noah

The records of the earliest human activity describe the interaction of good and evil forces at play in the world. The first known couple, Adam and Eve, lived in a garden named Eden and had two sons. The older brother (Cain) killed his younger brother (Abel) due to jealousy. Cain was sent away from the family and started his own family somewhere else. Adam and Eve then had more children, who then had children of their own — eventually, there were thousands of people living on earth.

All the people on earth interacted with each other over time. But as the human population grew, life became increasingly violent and corrupt, bringing with it much pain and sadness. Eventually, there was so much evil in the world that God created a way to eliminate evil. God called Noah, a good man with a good family, to build a large ship (an ark) that could house his entire family and small numbers of all the known animal species. When the ship was finished, God caused heavy rains to fall for a very long time. This caused a massive flood and very high waters that drowned all the humans and animals that were left behind.

Eventually the rain stopped and the water level fell enough so that plants were exposed and started growing again. The ship eventually rested on high ground, and all the animals and family members left the ark and set up their homes again. Noah and his family followed the local tradition of burning an offering of thanks to a God they didn't know. A rainbow appeared, a sign that God would never again wipe out all evil on the earth.

Abraham and Sarah

About 4,000 years ago, God somehow told a man named Abram to move to Canaan (this area is now called Palestine). He lived with his wife Sarai in the city of Ur in southeast Iraq. Canaan was located on the eastern coast of the Mediterranean Sea and had very good soil. At that time, it connected the main trade routes of Africa, Asia, and Europe, so its people often interacted with those who lived in many parts of the world. Abram obeyed God and moved his household 1,000 miles to Canaan.

Eventually God told Abram that he would lead a specific tribe of people that was to act in a way that demonstrated to others how humans should live in the world. Members of his family and his descendants were to obey God's commands and treat others fairly. God made a promise to Abram: "I will make you a great nation and will bless you and make your name great. You will be a blessing, and all the families on earth will be blessed." God told Abram that his descendants would become as countless as the stars.

Abram became convinced that he should put his faith in this God. He had obeyed God and left his home for an unknown future, and God considered this to be a sign of righteousness (holy living). His name was changed to Abraham and Sarai became Sarah.

God eventually changed the promise to Abraham to a mutual agreement ("covenant"). Abraham's descendants would be very fruitful and rule the region as long as his descendants trusted and obeyed God. As a sign of the agreement, all of Abraham's male descendants had to be circumcised. This also applied to their servants and slaves from other tribes. This would distinguish those who followed their God from all others. Any male descendant who wasn't circumcised was making a choice to reject the agreement.

But after trying to have a baby for many years, Sarah couldn't get pregnant. This made it impossible for Abraham to have descendants. So Sarah told him to have a child with Hagar, their servant from Egypt. Hagar had a boy, and as he grew older, Sarah got very jealous and wanted a child of her own. She treated both Hagar and the boy harshly, causing them to leave home and go into the wilderness. An angel told Hagar that the boy's name was to be Ishmael and that his descendants would settle in the east and also be countless like the stars.

When Sarah was well past childbearing age, an angel told her and Abraham that they would have a child. They both laughed at the idea, but God said a boy would be born in a year and should be named Isaac ("child of promise"). Isaac was soon born in Beersheba, a desert-like town southwest of Canaan.

God Tests Abraham

When Isaac was still a boy, God tested Abraham's faith. God told Abraham to take Isaac to a distant mountain to be burned as an offering. Showing his faith in God, Abraham did as he was told. He and Isaac traveled to the mountain and took wood, fire, and a knife to make the offering.

As they climbed the mountain, Isaac asked his father where the lamb was that would be burned as the offering. Abraham said God would provide the lamb. Then Abraham built an altar and arranged the wood; then he tied up Isaac and put him on the wood on the altar. As Abraham was about to kill Isaac, he heard a voice saying, "Do not kill the boy. Since you were willing to kill your only son for me, I know you will obey me." Then Abraham saw a goat in a bush and used it as the offering in place of Isaac.

The voice continued: "Because you obeyed me, I will bless you and increase your descendants so they will be like the stars in the sky and the sand on the seashore. Every nation of the earth will be blessed through your descendants."

Isaac and Rebekah

When Isaac became a man, Abraham sent his senior advisor to Haran to find Isaac a suitable wife. Abraham had stopped there on his way to Canaan, and some of his relatives lived there (the city was located about 500 miles north in southern Turkey). The woman had to be a relative, have a gracious spirit, and be friendly to strangers. A very beautiful and honest woman named Rebekah had had these qualities, and her family agreed to let her marry Isaac. After they were married, they lived with Abraham and Sarah and their relatives near Beersheba for many years.

Esau and Jacob

Isaac and Rebekah also struggled to have a child for many years, but eventually they had twins. The first baby, Esau, was covered with red hair. The second baby was named Jacob and had smooth hair. Esau was Isaac's favorite child, and Jacob was Rebekah's favorite. One day Esau came into the tent very hungry and asked Jacob for some of the stew he had prepared. Jacob said he would give him the food if Esau would give him the rights of the firstborn son. Esau agreed to trade his substantial inheritance for the food.

When Isaac was dying and nearly blind, he asked Esau to hunt for food, then cook it so he could eat it and bless Esau as the firstborn son. Rebekah heard their conversation and created a plan to get Isaac to bless Jacob instead. She told Jacob to kill two young goats from the nearby flock so they could be cooked and served to Isaac before Esau returned from hunting. Jacob didn't' think this was a good idea—he knew his father could tell the difference between his two sons.

But Jacob did as he was told and Rebekah cooked the animals. She then had Jacob put on Esau's clothes so Isaac would think Jacob was Esau if they got close to each other. Jacob said he was Esau, and Isaac was confused when he heard Jacob's voice so soon after sending Esau out to hunt. When Jacob came close, Isaac felt and smelled the clothes of Esau, and asked several times if it was Esau. Jacob lied several more times, saying he was Esau. Because Isaac was nearly blind, he didn't recognize Jacob.

Eventually, Isaac believed Jacob's lies and blessed Jacob instead of Esau. In the blessing, Isaac said, "May God give you good soil and plenty of grain and wine. May people and nations serve you. Lead your brothers. Those who bless you will be blessed, and those who curse you will be cursed."

Right after Isaac gave his blessing to Jacob, Esau returned from the field. Isaac then realized he had been tricked when he heard Esau's voice. But Isaac didn't remove the blessing he had given to Jacob, and he didn't provide another blessing to Esau. This made Esau very upset —

he had lost both his birthright and father's blessing (both were typically given to the firstborn son). Esau plotted to kill Jacob, but Rebekah found out about the plan and sent Jacob away so he could be safe.

Jacob and His Family

Jacob moved to Haran where Rebekah had lived. On the way, he had a dream that his descendants would spread in all directions, and that through his descendants, all the families of the earth would be blessed. This was the same message God had given both Abraham and Isaac.

Jacob soon met a beautiful shepherd girl named Rachel in Haran. She was his cousin (the daughter of Rebekah's brother Laban). Jacob wanted Rachel to be his wife and he agreed to work for Laban for seven years to pay for her. But Rachel had a less attractive older sister, Leah, and the custom was for the oldest daughter to be married first. When Jacob finished working to pay for Rachel, Laban said he also had to pay for Leah. So Jacob worked seven more years to pay for Rachel.

As Jacob worked for Laban, he started his family with the two wives. Jacob loved Rachel more than Leah, which caused a division between the sisters. Leah had four sons — Reuben, Simeon, Levi, and Judah. Rachel wasn't able to have any children, which caused more tension between the two wives. Rachel was jealous of Leah and wanted children of her own. Rachel agreed to let Jacob have her maid Bilhah as another wife in order to have children who would be considered her own descendants. Bilhah had two sons, Dan and Naphtali.

As Leah watched Rachel's family grow, she decided to give Jacob her maid, Zilpah, as his wife. Zilpah had two sons, Gad and Asher. Then Leah had two more sons, Issachar and Zebulun, and a daughter Dinah. Finally, after all the years of not being able to have a child, Rachel had a surprise pregnancy of her own, and she gave birth to a son named Joseph.

After Jacob working off his debt for Laban's daughters, he worked six more years for Laban, and both sets of families prospered. Jacob then prepared to return to Canaan where he would inherit Isaac's property and develop his family and work his own way. Jacob had been very successful at raising healthy animals, which made Laban's sons jealous. Before returning to Canaan, Rachel stole some valuable idols from Laban's house. The family left without having the normal farewell party.

When Laban and his brothers discovered the theft and that Jacob's family had all left, they thought Jacob was trying to escape. Laban's family chased after Jacob and his caravan for a week. When they caught up with them, they confronted Jacob about the theft. He was surprised by their accusation and told Laban to search for any stolen items. He said that whoever had the idols would die (he didn't know Rachel had stolen them from Laban's house).

Rachel sat on the idols she stole, so Laban didn't find what she had taken, and Jacob felt unjustly accused. He had helped Laban become wealthy and hadn't been paid for six years. They finally agreed as cousins that they should support one another, and they left each other as friends.

CHAPTER 2

JACOB RETURNS TO CANAAN
Family Crises and a Move to Egypt

As Jacob traveled toward Canaan, he sent messages to Esau to say he was coming home and would share his wealth with him. Esau went to meet Jacob's caravan and Jacob sent him some animals as gifts to make Esau happy. On the way, Jacob met a stranger and wrestled with him for several hours, but neither could win. The stranger wanted to stop fighting, but Jacob said he wouldn't stop until he received the stranger's blessing. The stranger blessed him and said his name would be Israel.

When Esau and his men reached Jacob and his family. Jacob stood in front of his family and caravan when he met Esau and his men; Rachel and Joseph were last in the group. Jacob bowed to Esau to show him honor, but to Jacob's surprise, Esau hugged him and they cried in each other's arms. Esau then returned to his home in Edom and Jacob traveled to an area near the city of Shechem. When Dinah went into the city, she was attacked because she was so beautiful. Jacob's sons found out what happened and got revenge on the town by killing all the men in the city.

Jacob found out about these crimes and was very upset—everybody in the area would turn against them. When Jacob and his family move further south, the people along the way were afraid of them, and nobody bothered them.

Rachel later died while giving birth to another son, Benjamin. So Jacob had 12 sons and one daughter—these were the children of Israel: Reuben, Simeon, Levi, Judah, Issachar, Zebulun, Dinah, Dan, Naphtali, Gad, Asher, Joseph, and Benjamin.

Joseph and His Brothers

Jacob loved Joseph the most of all his sons and made him a coat with many colors. Joseph would tell Jacob about the bad things his brothers did, and they grew to hate him and picked on him. Joseph had dreams in which he was the boss of his brothers, which made them hate him even more.

One year, Joseph was sent to check on his brothers who were watching animals graze in better pastures. When the brothers saw him coming, they devised a plan to get rid of him. They tore off his colored coat, threw him into a deep pit, and sold him to foreign traders who took him to Egypt. The brothers then covered Joseph's coat with animal blood and took it to Jacob, who believed Joseph had been killed by a wild animal. Jacob became so sad that he cried constantly for weeks. Nobody could comfort him.

Joseph in Egypt

The traders sold Joseph to Potiphar, the leader of those who guarded the Egyptian king (Pharaoh). Joseph was so smart that Potiphar put him in charge of everything in his house. Joseph was also young and handsome, and Potiphar's wife tried to get him to love her many times. But Joseph resisted. One day when only Joseph and the wife were home, the wife tried to embrace him passionately, but Joseph ran out of the house. To get revenge, the wife told Potiphar that Joseph had attacked her but ran away when she screamed. Potiphar then threw Joseph into prison.

But Joseph was a leader in prison. He interpreted the dreams of some of the prisoners, and the events he predicted came true. One prisoner knew the king well and learned all about what happened to Joseph. When the man left prison and returned to serve the king, he told Pharaoh that Joseph could interpret dreams. When Pharaoh had dreams he could not understand, he had Joseph explain them. Joseph said he was merely a spokesman for his God, who was the true interpreter.

Joseph told Pharaoh that the dreams predicted seven years of very good harvests, but then seven years of a severe famine. Joseph suggested that Pharaoh hire somebody wise to create a system of store extra food during the years of abundance so that food could be used during the years of famine.

Pharaoh liked this plan very much and saw that Joseph had God-given wisdom. Pharaoh put Joseph, a foreigner who was only 30 years old at that time, in charge of the entire Egyptian kingdom — only Pharaoh had a higher position. Joseph carried out the plan to store food for the coming famine during the seven years of good harvests. While this happened, Joseph started a family with his Egyptian wife and had two sons, Manasseh and Ephraim.

Famine Brings Israelites to Egypt

The famine affected the entire region, including Canaan, and grain for bread was the only thing that would grow. People came from everywhere to Egypt to get food, and Jacob sent 10 of his sons to Egypt to get grain while Benjamin stayed behind. When the brothers arrived, they went to Joseph to buy grain because he was in charge of all food in Egypt. But Joseph's brothers didn't recognize him because he disguised himself when he saw them coming and because they all thought he was dead.

Joseph started questioning them harshly, accusing them of being spies who wanted information about Egypt. When he interrogated them about their family, they said their father and one brother still lived in Canaan. The brothers consulted privately among themselves, saying they were now paying a price for their sin of treating Joseph badly and selling him. The brothers didn't realize that Joseph could understand what they were saying because he know their language. Joseph was so full of strong emotions at seeing his brothers that he had to leave the room to cry in private.

When Joseph returned, he was gracious and sold them grain to take back to Canaan. He also gave them supplies for their trip home. But he kept Simeon behind in prison until all the brothers, including Benjamin, could return together. When the brothers stopped to feed their donkeys during the trip home, they found all the money they used to pay for the grain in their donkeys' feed bags.

Jacob was very worried when the brothers arrived home and told him what happened in Egypt. He didn't want Benjamin to return with them to Egypt — he didn't want lose Rachel's other son. When all their grain was gone, Jacob asked his sons to go to Egypt to buy more grain, and they took Benjamin with them.

When they all went to see Joseph, they reported that their father was still alive, and they introduced Benjamin as the youngest brother. Joseph was so overcome with emotion when he saw Benjamin that he again had to leave the room to hide his tears. After composing himself, Joseph returned and gave them all an amazing amount of food (Benjamin got much more than the others). Simeon was released from prison and was there, and all the brothers were amazed that they were being treated so well.

Joseph then played a trick on the brothers. He had his servant fill all their sacks with food and put their money at the top of the sacks. But the servant buried Joseph's silver cup in Benjamin's sack. After the brothers left town, Joseph sent the servant to catch them and accused them of stealing the cup. They denied taking anything that wasn't theirs. They all agreed that if anybody was found to have taken something, the person would become Joseph's slave. After a quick search, the servant found the cup in Benjamin's sack.

All the brothers were very upset and returned immediately to see Joseph. Judah, one of the older brothers, spoke privately to Joseph and told him how their father didn't want the youngest son to return with them to Egypt — he had already lost one son from his favorite wife and didn't want to lose the other. But Jacob allowed Benjamin to go to Egypt because it was a condition for them to buy more grain. Judah said that if Benjamin couldn't return with them, their father would certainly die. Judah then offered himself to be the slave in place of Benjamin.

At that point, Joseph couldn't contain himself any longer. He had everybody in the house leave, except for the 11 brothers. He cried so loud that all the neighbors could hear him. He then told his brothers his true identity, but they didn't understand him. He had them come closer and he talked to them quietly:

> I'm your brother Joseph. You sold me to men going to Egypt. Don't be sad or angry with yourselves; it was God who sent me before you in order to preserve your life. The famine has lasted two years and has five years to go. God sent me before you to preserve you as a remnant on earth and keep you alive. It was not you who sent me here, but God, who made me like a father to Pharaoh and lord of all his household and ruler over all the land of Egypt. Go home and tell our father that I am alive and that you shall all live in the land of Goshen, and you will be near me. You and your household will stay very poor if you don't come.

The brothers returned home and told Jacob all about the trip and how Joseph was alive and a ruler in Egypt. Pharaoh was glad to hear that Joseph's brothers had come to Egypt and invited Jacob and all his relatives to move to Egypt where life was good and where they all would live on the best land. Everybody moved to Egypt and brought all their livestock and possessions. God spoke to Jacob in a dream, saying, "I am the God of your father; I will be with you in Egypt and will bring you up to Canaan again."

Joseph rode to Goshen in his chariot to meet Jacob and the rest of the family when they arrived. They were given the best land, in the delta of the Nile River, and Joseph provided all the families with food.

CHAPTER 3

LIFE IN EGYPT

God Rescues the Israelites from Oppression

Jacob and his extended family lived in Goshen for 17 years. Before he died, he blessed his 12 sons and Joseph's two sons, Manasseh and Ephraim. After he died, Joseph's brothers worried that he would be mad at them for the horrible things they did to him. They asked him to forgive them and bowed down to him. But Joseph explained that he would take care of them, even though they treated him badly. God had turned all the bad things into something good.

Israelites Suffer in Egypt

The tribe of Jacob and his descendants were called Israelites and spoke the Hebrew language. They continued to prosper and grow in number after Joseph and his brothers died. But a new pharaoh didn't care what Joseph had done and noticed that the Israelites outnumbered the Egyptians. He decided to make the Israelites slaves and made them work in the fields and build Egypt's cities. When the Israelite population continued to grow, Pharaoh ordered the Egyptian nurses to kill all their baby boys. The Israelites suffered extreme hardships and cried out to their God.

Moses Is Born, Then Talks to God

One Israelite family with a boy and girl had another baby boy during that time. They were afraid the Egyptians would kill him, so they hid him for three months. But they soon realized they couldn't hide him any longer, so they put him in a basket and pushed it into the plants growing by the shore of the Nile River. His sister hid and watched to see what would happen to the floating basket.

Pharaoh's daughter was bathing nearby and saw the basket. She retrieved it and realized it contained an Israelite baby boy. He was crying and she took pity on him. The sister came to Pharaoh's daughter and said, "Should I get somebody to nurse him for you?" Pharaoh's daughter agreed, and the girl had the baby's mother nurse him until he could eat solid food. Then Pharaoh's daughter adopted him as her own child. She named him Moses.

As Pharaoh's adopted grandson, Moses became well educated and a good writer. When he got older, he found out he was adopted and who his real mother and father were. He grew to love the Israelites and he watched as they were treated harshly. One day he saw an Egyptian beating an Israelite worker. When Moses thought nobody was looking, he killed the Egyptian. But some Israelites saw what happened, and eventually Pharaoh heard about it. Pharaoh tried to kill Moses, but Moses escaped to Midian, a wilderness region several hundred miles away.

When Moses was in Midian, he married the daughter of Jethro and started a family. Moses took care of Jethro's flocks, and when he was at the foot of a mountain, an angel appeared to him in a bush that was on fire. But the fire didn't burn the bush, and Moses tried to figure out why.

Then a voice came from the bush. "Moses! Don't come any closer. Take off your sandals because you are on holy ground. I am the God of Abraham, Isaac, and Jacob. I have seen the pain of my people in Egypt and have heard their cries. I have come to deliver them and lead them to good land that is flowing with milk and honey. I will send you to Pharaoh so you will bring my people, the people of Israel, out of Egypt."

But Moses said to God, "Who am I to go to Pharaoh and bring them all out of Egypt?"

God replied, "I will be with you, and when you have brought them out of Egypt, you shall worship God at this mountain."

Moses responded, "The Israelites will want to know your name. What should I tell them?" God said to Moses:

Say I AM sent me. The God of our fathers — Abraham, Isaac, and Jacob — sent me. Tell the elders of Israel, "The Lord appeared to me and said, 'I'm concerned about you and what is being done to you in Egypt. So I will bring you out of slavery and lead you to Canaan, a land flowing with milk and honey.'" They will listen to you. Then you and the Israelite elders shall say to the king of Egypt, "The Lord, the God of the Israelites, has met with us. Please let us go into the wilderness so we can sacrifice to our God." But I know the king will not let you go unless he is forced to do it. I will then strike Egypt with many miracles, and after that, he will let you go. Egyptian neighbors will give you articles of silver, gold, and clothing to take with you.

Moses was still concerned about doing what God wanted him to do. He asked, "What if they won't believe me or listen to me? They may say doubt that you appeared to me."

The Lord said to him, "What is that in your hand?"

And he said, "A wooden staff."

Then the Lord said, "Throw it on the ground." Moses threw it on the ground, and it became a snake, frightening Moses. But the Lord said, "Grab it by its tail," and when Moses did that, the snake turned back into his staff.

The Lord then said, "Now put your hand inside your robe." When Moses did it and then took it out, his hand looked white like leprosy (a dreaded skin disease). Then the Lord said, "Put your hand inside your robe again." When he put in it and took it out, his skin was normal again.

The Lord continued, "If they will not believe you because of the first sign, they may believe because of the second sign. But if they won't believe after the two signs, take some water from the Nile and pour it on the ground. The water will become blood on the ground."

Moses made up more excuses about why he shouldn't go back to Egypt. He said to God, "I'm not a good speaker and I talk slowly. Please send somebody else." The Lord was angry with Moses's excuses and continued:

Who made your mouth? Who makes a person deaf or blind? I do! Now go! I will be in your mouth and teach you what to say. Your older brother Aaron is a good speaker. He is coming to meet you now. Tell him what I told you and he will speak for you. Take the staff so you can perform the signs so everybody will see God is with you.

Moses Returns to Egypt

Moses then met Aaron and they went back to Egypt. He explained what God told him and showed him the signs he could do with God's help. When they both arrived in Egypt, they met with the Israelite leaders. Aaron told them what God told Moses, and Moses performed the signs to the people. The people believed, and when they heard that God was concerned about them and knew what was happening to them, they bowed and worshipped their Lord.

Moses also performed all the signs in front of the new king. Aaron said to Pharaoh, "Our Lord, the God of Israel, says 'Let my people go so they can celebrate a feast to me in the wilderness.'" But the king didn't let them go — he couldn't afford to have so many workers leave.

Pharaoh then made the Israelites work even harder. He made them get their own straw for the bricks they were making, but they still had to make the same number of bricks. When they didn't meet enough bricks, the Israelite supervisors were beaten and the people were accused of being lazy. The supervisors were mad at Moses for coming back and making their work even harder.

Moses regretted coming back to Egypt because he had made things worse, not better. When Moses told the people again that the Lord promised to deliver them from Egypt, they didn't believe it would happen. Everybody could only think about how cruel their life had become.

The Lord told Moses and Aaron to go back to Pharaoh and tell him again to let the Israelites people leave. They told Pharaoh this many times, and each time they showed Pharaoh God's power in some form of affliction that hurt only the Egyptians. Each time, Moses said to Pharaoh through Aaron, that the God of the Israelites had said, "Let my people go so they may serve me." Each time Pharaoh agreed to let them leave, and each time Moses made the affliction stop by spreading out his hand. But each time when things got better, Pharaoh changed his mind and refused to let the people go.

These acts showed that the power of the Israelite God was much stronger than the magical powers of the priests of the Egyptian gods. Here are some of the things that happened.

- Moses and Aaron first struck the Nile River with their staffs and all the water turned into blood. They stretched their hands over all types of water, and they all turned into blood. The fish died and the water was polluted so the Egyptians couldn't drink it.
- Frogs invaded everything in the Egyptians' world and swarms of gnats, flies, and locusts fill the air.
- Moses and Aaron caused illnesses to kill all the Egyptian livestock, hailstorms killed all the crops and the animals and people who were outside, and skin boils that broke out on the Egyptians and their animals.

One last affliction convinced Pharaoh to let them go. God told Moses to have all the Israelites gather articles of gold and silver and clothing from their neighbors. Most Egyptians respected the Israelites and gave them what they requested. Then at midnight, God caused all firstborn children and cattle to die. But the Israelites would avoid this catastrophe if they followed certain instructions. They were to kill a young and perfect lamb at twilight, then spread some of the lamb's blood above the door and on the doorposts of their home. They were to roast a lamb and eat all of it very fast, along with bitter herbs and flat bread. The blood on the doors was a sign to God that the angel of death should pass over the family living inside, sparing the firstborn from death. The people were not to go outside until morning and were to burn any leftovers from this "Passover" meal. And they were to remember these events, repeating the steps they had taken, and make it a permanent annual celebration to remember how God saved them from slavery. That night, the Israelites did what Moses said they must do.

Moses had told Pharaoh, "My God says to you, 'Israel is my son, my firstborn, and will serve me. But you refuse to let him go. Therefore, I will kill your firstborn.'" And that night, it all happened the way God said it would. In every household in Egypt, except for the Israelites, the firstborn of the family and livestock died, innocent casualties of the ongoing war between good and evil.

Pharaoh was so upset that night that he ordered all the Israelites and their livestock to leave Egypt as fast as they could. The mass exodus involved about 600,000 men, along with their wives and children and their livestock. Some slaves and foreigners left Egypt with them. The descendants of Jacob had been in Egypt for more than 400 years, and now they were heading back to Canaan.

CHAPTER 4

THE ISRAELITES LEAVE EGYPT

God Sustains the Disgruntled Israelites and Gives Laws for Life

Moses led the Israelites south toward the Red Sea. They followed pillars of clouds during the day, and pillars of fire at night. Soon after they had left, they ended up at the edge of a large body of water. Pharaoh was keeping track of where the Israelites were going and wanted them to return to be slaves again. He knew they were close and backed up in the wilderness against the water. Pharaoh thought they could be easily captured, so he sent his army on chariots and horses to kill and capture them.

When the Israelites saw the Egyptian army approaching, they were afraid and got mad at Moses for bringing them out of Egypt. The people said that it would be better to live as slaves in Egypt than to die in the wilderness.

God told Moses to have the people start walking toward the water and to lift his staff and hand over the sea to divide the water so everybody could cross on dry land. Meanwhile, a pillar of clouds moved between the Israelites and the Egyptian army during the night to protect the Israelites from attack. Moses lifted his staff and hand above the water that caused a strong wind to blow that separated the waters and dried the ground. The Israelites then walked on the dry ground to the other side.

In the morning, the Egyptians chased after the Israelites in their chariots and horses using the same path through the water. After all the Israelites had crossed to the other side, Moses raised his staff and hand over the waters again, stopping the wind. The water quickly returned to its normal level and rose quickly around the entire Egyptian army. Every Egyptian soldier and horse drowned.

When the people saw the dead bodies floating in the water, they were stunned by God's power and believed Moses. They celebrated their victory and honored God who had freed them and conquered their enemy. The Israelites couldn't take credit for defeating the Egyptian army; only God was responsible for it.

Moses Leads the People in the Wilderness

As Moses led the Israelites into the wilderness, they experienced many hardships. They couldn't find enough water to drink, but God supplied water in miraculous ways. They were attacked by soldiers from a nearby tribe, but Joshua led the Israelites to victory. The land was getting rocky and could not produce food. When the people complained about being hungry and thought about the food they ate in Egypt, God had a sweet cracker-like substance (manna, or "bread") appear on the ground in the morning like frost and had birds ("meat") fall from the sky at night. The bread would only last one day (it would melt in the sun or rot by the next morning). On the sixth day of the week, there would be twice as much on the ground, and when it was cooked, it would last two days. Moses told the people that God wanted them to take what remained from the sixth day and not do any work on the seventh (last) day of the week. This established the tradition of the "sabbath," one day of rest at the end of the week.

When the Israelites were near Midian, Moses met Jethro again and rejoined his family. Jethro told him that supervising all the people was too big of a job for one person. He said Moses should be God's representative to the people and teach them about God's laws and how to live their lives. But Moses needed to pick good men who loved God and hated dishonesty to be leaders and judges who would provide good advice and handle minor disagreements. Moses should handle just the major problems. Moses took Jethro's advice and set up the system to make sure all the leaders were supervised properly.

When the Israelites camped at the foot of Mount Sinai, God made an agreement with the people. God told Moses, "Tell those in the house of Jacob and the sons of Israel: 'You saw what I did to the Egyptians. If you obey my commands and laws, then you will be my people. You shall be a holy nation to me, and I will keep you safe and healthy.'" Moses told the people what God had said, and the people agreed to obey.

The Major Commands and Other Laws

Then God came down to Mount Sinai in a cloud of fiery smoke that covered the mountain, and Moses climbed to the top of the mountain where he met God, who said, "I am the Lord your God, who brought you out of Egypt and slavery. I am a jealous God, putting the sins of parents who hate me on their children. But I will show lovingkindness to those who love me and keep my commands." Then God spoke these 10 commands to Moses.

> (1) I am to be your only God. (2) Do not make an idol or anything looking like a god, and do not worship or serve them. (3) Do not use or say my name carelessly — treat it with great respect. (4) Remember the sabbath day — keep it holy. Do all your work in six days, but on the seventh day, nobody in your household, including your slaves, animals, and visitors staying with you, shall do any work. (5) Honor your father and your mother so you may live a long life. (6) Do not murder. (7) Do not commit adultery. (8) Do not steal. (9) Do not lie against others. (10) Do not desire anything that belongs to your neighbor — not their house, their wife or servants, or their animals.

In addition to these 10 commands, God told Moses about many laws the people must follow. Most related to providing justice and making sure people live the right way.
• There were laws about owning slaves (if a person buys an Israelite slave, the slave must go free on the seventh year without any more payment).

- There were laws about personal injuries. For example, "a person who kills or kidnaps another person or curses his father or mother shall be put to death. And if there is a fight, the penalty is equal to what happened: a life for a life, an eye for an eye, a tooth for a tooth, a hand for a hand."

- There were laws about property rights and relationships. These include, "Anybody who makes a sacrifice to another god will be destroyed. Don't treat strangers badly, for you were strangers in Egypt. Do no harm to any widow or orphan. If you hurt them and they cry out to me, I will hear their cry and get angry."

- There were laws about money. "If you lend money to any of my people who are poor, do not charge interest. You must not delay the offering from your harvest. A tithe (10%) of everything from the land belongs to the Lord."

- There were laws about justice and the principles of correct living. "Don't join a wicked person and tell lies. If you meet your enemy's animal wandering away, you must return it to him. You must not take a bribe, for it blinds people from knowing the truth and can harm others. Be nice to foreigners — you know what it is like to live in another land. Harvest your land for six years, but on the seventh year, do nothing and let needy people eat from it."

God told Moses that an angel would guard them as they traveled toward Canaan. If the people obeyed God, they would defeat those who tried to stop them. They weren't to keep anything related to the gods of the tribes they conquered. They would control a vast region and keep it only for themselves because letting other tribes live among them would damage their way of life and love for God.

Moses came down the mountain and told the people what God said. The people listened and said they would follow God's commands and laws. Moses wrote down all the things God told him in order to preserve the commands and laws as reminders for others in the future.

More Trips Up the Mountain

God called Moses to the mountain again and took Joshua with him. They stayed for 40 days. God told Moses that the people should contribute some of their possessions to build a tabernacle where God would live with the people. In addition, a large ornate box (the Ark of the Covenant) was to be built to store sacred items that were collected along the way to Canaan. Other items were to be made for the tabernacle, and God gave Moses detailed instructions about how all of them should be made and used. Detailed instructions were also given about how priests should make sacrifices and how other acts of worship should occur. Moses's brother Aaron was to be the High Priest, and his sons were also to be priests. When God finished giving these instructions, Moses went down the mountain with two flat stone tablets that had the words of the 10 commands written on them.

When Moses and Joshua returned, they saw that some of the people had built a golden statue of a calf. It had been weeks since Moses and Joshua climbed the mountain and didn't come back, so these people thought they were dead and told Aaron to create the golden calf as the god they should follow. The people worshipped the calf and made sacrifices to it.

Moses was extremely angry when he saw the golden calf and the people dancing around it. Moses threw the stone tablets to the ground, shattering them into pieces. Moses had the golden calf burned to the ground. Then he told the people, "Those of you who live for the Lord, come to me!" Levi's descendants and many others gathered with Moses. Then Moses told the Levites to kill those who did not come forward. About 3,000 rebellious and disobedient men were killed. This was how the Israelites got rid of people who would cause problems as they traveled.

Moses then told those who worshipped the golden calf that they had committed a great sin. Moses asked God to forgive them. God was extremely angry, calling the people very stubborn in their resistance to change, and wanted to destroy them all. But Moses reminding God of the promise to make them a great nation. God then reconsidered and told Moses to continue leading the people toward Canaan.

Moses then went up the mountain a third time. He etched two more stone tablets with the 10 commands to replace those that were shattered. God told Moses again about the original agreement made with Abraham, Isaac, and Jacob: the Israelites were God's people and would be blessed and were to go into Canaan and obey God's commands and laws. When Moses came down the mountain after 40 days, his face "glowed." He then gave directions about how to build a tabernacle based on what God said it should look like. When it was finished, ceremonies were held to bless the priests who would work in it. When the ceremonies ended, a cloud covered the tent in the tabernacle, and God filled it. The God who had delivered and saved Israel was finally living with the chosen people.

More Rules for Living

God spent several more months providing Moses with many rules about how the priests were to conduct their religious affairs, how people were to worship, and how Israel — as the people of God — was to live as a community. Aaron and his descendants, all from the tribe of Levi, were officially made the priests. Other Levites worked to support religious activities.

Some of the rules were specific laws while others were general principles. God was holy, and the Israelites had been chosen to be a holy people, God's representatives on earth to show others how to live and glorify God. But since humans will always sin in some way, the people were to stand before God and repent, making sacrifices and burning offerings to show their sorrow and be cleansed of their sins. Offerings and sacrifices made in the tabernacle had to be high quality, using the finest grain and animals without any defects, which symbolized perfection.

Shedding blood was key in the sacrifice to mend a broken relationship between God and humans. God told

Moses, "The life of the body is in the blood." The blood was to come from animals, not humans. Through sacrifices and offerings, God forgave the people, separating them from their sins, restoring the relationship between God and humans. Related to this idea was a special Day of Atonement that was to observed once a year. It involved sacrificing one goat and having the High Priest put his hands on the head of another goat, confessing all the people's sins, and transferring the people's sins into that goat. This second goat was then released into the wilderness to symbolize that the people's sins were removed (a "scapegoat").

Moses gave detailed instructions about what to eat and not eat, what could be touched and not touched. The instructions were practical and helped maintain the people's health. For example, anyone with a skin disease had to be quarantined and practice social distancing from others — they had to move out of the camp, wear torn clothes, not comb their hair, and yell, "Unclean! unclean!" to others until they were healthy. New washing methods had to be followed, which were quite advanced for that time; when followed, these methods gave the Israelites an advantage in battle and how long they would live.

While most of these rules dealt with religious ceremonies and health-related matters, some rules dealt with the principles of morality and justice. For example, there were rules and penalties associated with specific crimes, and people were commanded to "love your neighbor as yourself." The rich and poor were both to be judged in the same way. Foreigners were to be accepted and loved just like everybody else, just as the Egyptians had welcomed the Israelites during the famine. A field was not to be harvested to its edge, and the poor and foreigners were allowed to eat the food at the edge as well as anything that fell to the ground during the first harvest.

A sabbath year was established that was similar to the weekly sabbath day. In the seventh year, land was not to be tilled, and the food coming from it was freely available to anybody who wanted it. Food from the sixth year was to be stored to last through the seventh year (similar to how manna was treated on a weekly basis). And every 50 years — the extra year after seven sabbatical year cycles — the Year of Jubilee was celebrated. The possessions of the poor that had been sold so the poor could survive had to be returned to the original owners.

The rules and instructions ended with reminders of the consequences of how people live. There are many rewards and blessings for those who obey God's laws and commands, but punishment occurs when people do not obey. If the nation of Israel breaks its agreement with God, it would lose their land, be scattered across the region, and become the slaves of its enemies. Yet even after people disobey, there is forgiveness and reconciliation when the people are sorry and apologize and start obeying God again. There is no permanent condemnation for those who disobey God — there is always a way to earn the benefits of the agreement again. God's nature is forgiving and extravagant when it comes to being in a relationship with humans, the most valued creation.

CHAPTER 5

LIFE IN THE WILDERNESS

Lack of Faith Extends the Journey Back to Canaan

When the Israelites camped at the foot of Mount Sinai, their population was several million strong, including an army of about 600,000 men.[1] The entire tribe of Levites took care of everything related to the tabernacle and was dedicated to God. The tabernacle was located in the center of all the camps, and Moses created rules about how to deal with sick people and thieves. Those who wanted to dedicate themselves to God for a limited amount of time took a Nazarite vow to not consume any form of a grape, not touch a dead person, and not shave their head (a sign to others that they had taken the vow).

One year after leaving Egypt, the people celebrated the Passover, and Moses gave the priests God's blessing to say to the people: "The Lord bless you and keep you. The Lord make his face shine on you and be gracious to you. The Lord turn his face toward you and give you peace."

---

[1] The very large numbers written in the scriptures may not mean the same as our understanding of numbers. It's unlikely that several million people could survive for long periods of time in areas where there was little water. The Israelites may have had a different method for counting people and animals, and the word "thousand" may not mean the same thing it does today (perhaps a 0 was added to some of the numbers, making 60,000 into 600,000, when some of the early stories were copied by others much later). The very advanced age people were said to have lived may reflect a different way numbers were used to measure time. Methuselah is said to be the longest living human and died at age 969 (see Genesis 5:7), but his age initially may have had a decimal point, which would have made him about 97 years old.

Crises on the Way to Canaan

The Israelites then started their journey toward Canaan, which was about 250 miles north. God was in the tabernacle, and when the cloud rose from the tabernacle, the Israelites moved on. Priests used trumpets made from animal horns to announce meetings, signal the time to move forward, prepare for battle, and celebrate offerings during their festivals.

After traveling 30 miles, some of the people started complaining about the food. They dreamed of the food they had in Egypt, especially meat, and were tired of eating the same food every day. God was upset with their attitude, which frightened Moses and made him think his job was too much for him. Moses told God, "I can't take care of all these people by myself; the burden on me is too much. Kill me now." God told Moses to gather 70 men around his tent, and the Spirit filled them so they would also become wise and help lead the people.

Spies Go to Canaan

When the Israelites approached Canaan, God told Moses to have one man from each of the 12 tribes travel into Canaan to gather information about who was living there and what kind of food was being grown. Moses told the 12 spies, "Go see if the people are strong or weak, few or many. Find out if the land is good or bad, if the soil is fertile or poor, and if there are trees. Determine what kind of towns they live in and if they have walls or fortifications. If you can, bring back some fruit of the land."

The 12 spies scouted the region thoroughly and returned after 40 days. They reported that land was excellent, but the people were strong and would be hard to defeat in battle. Ten spies said that occupying Canaan would be impossible because the cities were large and well defended and the different tribes had fierce fighters. The people were huge— the spies felt like grasshoppers compared to them.

But two of the spies, Caleb and Joshua, had a different opinion. They said, "God will lead us into the land if the Lord is pleased with us. If we don't rebel against the Lord and are not afraid of the people who live there, we will devour them. Their protection is gone if the Lord is with us."

The 10 doubters convinced the leaders that a successful invasion was impossible. They then started screaming at Moses and Aaron for leading them on a meaningless trip. They threatened to stone Caleb and Joshua and even considered replacing Moses with a leader who would take them back to Egypt.

God was very upset with the Israelites and said to Moses, "How long will they refuse to believe in me, even after everything I have done for them? I will strike them with a plague and destroy them."

But Moses argued that God's reputation would be spoiled because all the other nations knew what God had promised to do for the Israelites. "The nations will say you weren't able to bring your people into the land you promised them, so you slaughtered them in the wilderness. You are known as the God who is slow to anger, full of love, and forgiving our sin and rebellion. As a loving God, forgive the sin of these people, just as you have pardoned them every time since they left Egypt."

The Lord agreed with Moses. "I will forgive them as you have asked. But nobody who is at least 20 years old, other than Caleb and Joshua, will enter Canaan as I promised them. They will die in the wilderness. Their children will suffer for being unfaithful by working as shepherds in the wilderness for 40 years, one year for every day the spies explored the land. They will suffer for their sins and know what it is like to have me against them."

God told Moses to lead the people into the desert back toward the Red Sea. The 10 spies who stirred up the crowd caught a plague and died. After seeing that these spies died, and facing the prospect of 40 more years of wandering in the wilderness, the people repented. But many of their confessions were not genuine; they had repented only so that the trip toward Canaan would resume. Moses told them that they had to stay together and all go back into the desert, and that God would not be with anybody who left the group. But some of them insisted on moving north on their own to invade Canaan. When they did, they were defeated.

Moses Is Challenged

As the people prepared to head south, four men brought 250 highly respected community leaders to him and challenged his authority. One of the rebels was a Levite who questioned the priesthood authority of Aaron's family. Moses told them all to come back to his tent the next day. When they came back the next day, God told Moses and Aaron to step aside. Then Moses said to those who gathered near the tents, "If these rebel leaders die a normal death, then the Lord has not sent me. But if the Lord does something unusual, then you will know these men treated God with contempt." As soon as Moses said this, the ground split apart, and the rebel leaders and their households fell into an opening in the ground. Then the earth closed up, and they were all gone. Then fire burned the 250 other men.

The next day, the entire Israel community was angry with Moses and Aaron and complained that they had killed many of God's people. Leaders from each of the 12 tribes confronted Moses and Aaron. God caused a plague to infect the Israelites, and it only stopped when Aaron ran fast to make an offering. But by the time he had done this, thousands of people had died.

Moses Continues to Lead

When the Israelites moved into the wilderness, there was little water because so many people were living on the edge of the desert. The people started complaining again and wished they were dead or back in Egypt. God told Moses to pick up a long stick and tell the rock in front of them to produce water. When the people gathered by the rock,

Moses became impatient and hit the rock twice with the stick, producing a gusher of water. But Moses didn't honor God in the process and hit the rock rather than telling it to produce water. Because of his impatience, God told Moses and Aaron that they could not enter Canaan.

Moses led the people south through a valley controlled by some of their enemies, and the people complained again about the lack of water and bread and the miserable food. To punish them, God sent poisonous snakes, and many Israelites were bitten and died. The people confessed and asked Moses to have God take away the snakes. The Lord told Moses to make a bronze snake and put it on a pole, and anyone who was bitten could look at it and live.

Moving Toward Canaan

The Israelites then turned back toward a region east of Canaan where they were met by different enemies along the way. The Israelites won all the battles and took over the land on the east side of the Salt Sea. They camped east of the Jordan River across from Jericho, a large and mighty city.

Moses and the other Israelite leaders got ready to cross the Jordan River into Canaan. The number of soldiers in their army was about the same as when the Israelites left Egypt more than 40 years earlier. But only two of them were the same people, Caleb and Joshua, the two spies who believed God would lead them to victory in Canaan.

Then God gave Moses specific instructions about what the people should do when they entered Canaan.

> When you cross the Jordan into Canaan, drive out all its inhabitants, destroy all their images and idols of their gods, and demolish all their altars. Occupy and settle in the land, for I have given it to you. If you don't drive them out, those who remain will be stumbling blocks for you — they will give you trouble, and then I will do to you what I plan to do to them.

Since Moses was not going to enter Canaan, God chose Joshua to become the new leader of the Israelites. Moses gave instructions about how offerings and celebrations should occur in Canaan. He also recorded all the important events that had occurred and what God had said to him after the Israelites left Egypt.

Moses Gives His Final Words

Before the people crossed the Jordan River into Canaan, Moses spoke to them and summarized the main events that had occurred during the past 40 years. He stressed how important it was to honor God, keep the commandments, and obey the rules he had established — all of them were from God.

Moses also warned the people about the consequences of not being faithful. He knew their major challenge would be spiritual in nature. He told them:

> If you become corrupt and do evil in the eyes of the Lord, God will be angry, and you will quickly perish from the land. The Lord will scatter you among other nations, and only a few of you will survive. But if from there you seek the Lord with all your heart and all your soul, you will find God. Later, you will return to the Lord, who is merciful and who will not abandon or destroy you or forget the promises made with your ancestors. Hear, O Israel: The Lord our God is one Lord. You must love the Lord your God with all your heart, with all your soul, and with all your strength.

Moses gave more instructions about what should happen when Israelites entered Canaan. God would lead them to victory over the larger and stronger nations, and these nations must be totally destroyed. The Israelites were not to be terrified by the nations occupying Canaan because the "great and awesome" God was with them. They were not to make any treaties with the other nations and were not to show them any mercy. They were not to intermarry with the families of other nations because it would lead the Israelites to follow other gods. Anything related to another god had to be destroyed.

To keep the Israelites from getting arrogant about their success, Moses told them, "It is not because you are righteous or good that you will take possession of their land. Rather, it's because of the wickedness of these nations. After all, God considers us a stiff-necked people." The people were to love and obey God, not in a formal and routine way, but because God had first shown love for the Israelites in many ways. Love was at the heart of the relationship — it had to be shown by both God and the Israelites.

Moses told the people to remember God's goodness by reading the stories about how God delivered them from Egypt and all the other things that happened since then. Moses told them to surround themselves with reminders of that goodness and to obey God's commands. He gave them this message from God:

> Fix my words in your hearts and minds; bind them as a sign on your hands and foreheads. Teach them to your children, talking about them when you are at home and walking on the road, when you lie down and get up. I set before you a blessing and a curse. You will be blessed if you listen to my commandments, but you will be cursed if you do not listen to my commandments and turn away from me to follow other gods.

Moses told the people that God was just asking them to respect the Lord. "Walk in obedience, love and serve the Lord with all your heart and with all your soul. Observe God's commands and decrees I'm giving you today for your own good. This isn't too difficult for you. Today, I set before you life and prosperity, death and destruction. Choose life."

Moses told Joshua that the Lord was with him, had gone before him, and would never leave him. Therefore, he should not be afraid or discouraged. God spoke secretly to Moses and Joshua and said the people would indeed turn away from God. The past 40 years proved that the Israelites were naturally rebellious and stubborn, had short attention spans, would often forget, and took God's blessings for granted. God told Moses to write a song that people could sing when things got bad in the future. The song described how the good God left them because they were not faithful to God's commands. The Israelites would sing the song and remember why they suffered.

Moses saw Canaan from a hill east of the Jordan River. After he died, Joshua told the people to get ready to cross the Jordan River and enter Canaan.

CHAPTER 6

THE OCCUPATION OF CANAAN
Joshua's Victories Eliminate Most Areas of Idolatry

Many different "nations" of people lived in Canaan when the Israelites camped near Jericho, and the tribes did not get along with each other. Many of the cities had strong walls, and their leaders paid more powerful nations in order to avoid being taken over. The nations occupying Canaan believed in many gods that the people though demanded horrible things. For example, it was common for the people to think their gods wanted children to be killed as a sacrifice.

Israel Crosses the Jordan and Attacks Jericho

Joshua sent two spies to learn more about Jericho, the first city they would battle. They met a sinful woman named Rahab who informed them that everybody in Canaan already knew about the Israelites and their powerful God, and that they planned to take over all the land. Everybody was very afraid of them.

The spies were quickly spotted when they visited Rahab, and the city guards went to her house and told her to release them. But she hid them on her roof and told to the guards they were no longer there. The guards believed her and left to look for them. Then Rahab asked them to spare her and her family from the coming destruction — she had saved them and wanted to be saved as well. The spies devised a plan to ensure she did not die with the city was attacked. She then let the two spies down to the ground by a rope through a window in the wall, and they made their way across the river to Joshua.

The next morning, Joshua ordered the Israelites to gather at the Jordan River, which was at the flood stage in the spring. The priests carried the Ark of the Covenant to the edge of the river, and it stopped flowing soon after they put their feed in the water. (A huge section of rock had just broken off the hillside 15 miles upstream, causing a reservoir to form and stopping the flow of the river.) The people crossed the river and camped close to Jericho. The people were amazed by God's power.

Jericho's gates were closed as it expected a battle with the Israelites. But Joshua didn't attack. Instead, the Lord told Joshua to have the entire army march around the city once a day for six days. Priests led the parade and played their trumpets while other priests carried the Ark, with the army trailing behind. The army was silent as they marched. On the seventh day, they marched around the city seven times, and when the army heard one long blast of the trumpets, they all gave a loud shout. The walls of the city collapsed and the army rushed into the unprotected city and killed everybody except Rahab and her family members, who were all allowed to live with the Israelites. Joshua burned Jericho to the ground and cursed the city.

Word spread quickly in the region about what happened to Jericho. The different kings that controlled all the land in Canaan knew Israel's god was much stronger than theirs, and they lost the courage to fight. The Israelites attacked many other cities in the region, but if anybody kept valuables for themselves, the army would lose the battle and the thief would be killed.

The people of Gibeon saw they were doomed and tricked Israel into making a peace treaty with them. They posed as poor foreigners who offered to be Israel's servants. Joshua made a treaty with the Gibeonites, but he soon found out it was a trick. But he still honored the treaty — the Gibeonites were not killed, but for their deception, they were cursed to be servants for Israel.

The nearby kings combined their armies so they would fight against Israelites as one army. They attacked Gibeon, but Joshua and his army marched all night and surprised the invaders in the morning. The Israelites fought all day and defeated all the opposing armies at Gibeon, then pursued the retreating armies and killed the kings of the invading armies. Joshua and the army continued south and conquered many other cities, leaving no survivors. By the time he was finished, he had conquered the whole region, from central Canaan and all the areas south of them.

Joshua Directs the Attacks Northward

Then he and the army turned north. The nations in northern Canaan heard what happened to the armies in central and southern Canaan and banded together to fight Israel's army. In a surprise attack, the Israelite army routed the combined forces of some of the opposing armies, and then it defeated the massive chariot-led army of the large city of Hazor and burned it to the ground. Israel's army then pursued the retreating armies of the northern nations all the way to Phoenicia. Everybody was killed, but other than Hazor, no city was destroyed, for they would be used by the Israelites in the future. The Israelites kept all the livestock and valuables from the people for themselves. This ended all the fighting.

The Conquest Is Complete

It took seven years for Joshua to finish all the battles, and 31 kingdoms had been conquered in Canaan. Only those in Gibeon made a peace treaty with Israel, and they were Israel's servants. But some areas were not occupied, so people from other tribes still lived in the region. Joshua had essentially done what God and Moses had told him to do — eliminate Canaan's inhabitants who had cold hearts against the one true God. This allowed the Israelites to settle in the promised land, but they still coexisted with nonbelievers.

Joshua gave land to the 12 tribes of Israel according to the number of people in each tribe: larger tribes inherited more land. The armies of three tribes got land they wanted east of the Jordan River. The Levites were to be given 48 towns to live in within the land of each tribe and land outside these towns for their animals.[2] Six towns inherited by the tribe of Levi were designated to be "safe refuges" so people could seek safety if they accidentally killed somebody. The tribes designated cities and grazing areas for the Levites. Caleb, the only other survivor from the previous generation who crossed into Canaan besides Joshua, was given the city of Hebron. Shiloh was made the religious center where the Ark of the Covenant was kept and where national disputes were handled.

When Joshua distributed the land to the tribes, he was an old man. He gathered the tribes' leaders to remind them to stay faithful to the one true God and not to mix with the Canaanites who lived in the region. He reminded them that good things came to them because they obeyed God but that God would destroy them if they behaved in evil ways. The battles and cleansing of Canaan were meant to eliminate the powers of evil in the region, demonstrate to the world the power of Israel's God, and create a society of holy people who didn't compromise with evil. He told those present:

> Fear the Lord and serve God with all faithfulness. Get rid of any of the gods your ancestors worshipped in the past. But if serving the Lord seems hard for you, then you need to choose who you will serve, whether it's the gods your ancestors served, or the gods of the people who live in the land where you are living. But as for me and my family, we will serve the Lord.

The leaders promised to trust, serve, and worship the Lord, to follow God's commands and decrees, and not to mix with the Canaanite people.

---

[2] The 12 tribes that inherited land were Reuben, Simeon, Judah, Issachar, Zebulun, Benjamin, Dan, Naphtali, Gad, Asher, and Joseph's two sons, Ephraim and Manasseh. The Levi tribe received cities among the 12 tribes.

CHAPTER 7

ISRAEL STRUGGLES IN CANAAN

Tribes Separate, Abandon Their Faith, and Start Losing God's Blessing

Because of the distances and a lack of unity among the 12 tribes, there was no place for tribal leaders to make decisions or determine how to work together. As a result, each tribe developed its own ways for living in the area where they settled.

The tribes fought battles with those who were still living in the region. Several major cities were still controlled by the Canaanites because the Israelites in their area were not strong enough to defeat them in battle. In some cases, the local people rebuilt cities the Israelites had destroyed and became powerful again. Some Israelites became friends with the Canaanites and adopted their ways of living, including taking part in religious ceremonies to other gods. Intermarriage led to further deterioration of the Israelites' faithfulness to God's commands and religious rituals. Moses had warned the people about not doing these things, and the people had promised not to do them. But most people did whatever they wanted to do.

Over the next few centuries, the Israelites abandoned their faith in God so often that God took away the blessings that were promised to Moses and Joshua. This spiritual unfaithfulness, in which the people broke the promises they had made to stay faithful to God, led to them being dominated by others. Various Israelite leaders with faith in God helped the tribes overcome that domination and created times of peace and prosperity until the next round of unfaithfulness occurred.

Periodic Oppression and Victories

The Israelites were first attacked by their northern enemies that treated very harshly for eight years. Othniel, a judge and military leader from the tribe of Judah and Caleb's younger brother, defeated the armies, which started 40 years of peace. But the Israelites again did evil in God's sight, and a different tribe to the east invaded them and took control of Canaan for 18 years. Ehud, from the tribe of Benjamin, tricked and killed the foreign king and earned a military victory over that army. That led to 80 years of peace.

The region was then taken over by Canaanite powers based in Hazor, which had been rebuilt. The Israelite prophet and judge Deborah handled disputes among the Israelites while she watched the wicked things being done to her people. (Prophets spoke God's thoughts and teachings to the people and leaders, and they sometimes made predictions about the future.) God told her to contact a man named Barak, to say that the Lord wanted him to lead armies against the strong Hazor army. God promised Barak a victory, but he would only go if Deborah came with him. She agreed, and together they defeated Hazor's army when its heavy iron chariots got stuck in the mud after heavy rains came just before the battle; 40 years of peace followed their victory.

Gideon and Jephthah

Israel eventually became unfaithful again and did all kinds of evil things. Hostile nomads from Midian would sometimes raid the Israelites' food and animals. These periodic raids drove the Israelites to live in caves and the hills.

When the Israelites called to God for help, the Lord called Gideon, a young farmer, to lead them. A stranger told him that God would make him a mighty warrior, but he doubted this was possible. He had no training, was from a small village in the weakest tribe, and was the youngest in his family. He knew God had abandoned the tribes of Israel because of their continued sinfulness. But the stranger said God would be with him and would drive out all the Midianites.

Gideon wanted a sign to prove that God was with him. Several miracles occurred to prove to Gideon that God had chosen him to lead the army and would be victorious. He had more than 32,000 men in his army, but God told him that was too many—if he won the battle, people would not give credit to God. Through a series of tests to reduce the number of men in the army, Gideon ended up with only 300 men. With such a small army, if Gideon won a battle against all odds, only God would get the credit.

Gideon's men launched a surprise attack during the night, which caused confusion and panic among the enemy, which starting fighting each other. Many of them retreated and were chased by Gideon's men over a 40-mile distance, well beyond the Jordan River. More than 135,000 enemy soldiers and leaders were killed in this long battle.

After the battles, the Israelites wanted to make Gideon their king and his sons the succeeding kings. But he refused and said God was their king. However, he asked for a gold earring from everybody who took gold from the enemy. The people gave Gideon 43 pounds of gold, and he made an elaborate garment for himself and took it to his hometown. There it became a sacred garment that people revered more than they did God.

The victory brought the Israelites 40 years of peace. But when Gideon died, the Israelites started worshipping the local god, Baal. They forgot what Gideon and the Lord had done for them. After several judges led Israel through 45 years of peace, the Israelites starting worshiping Baal and other gods again, and foreign powers took over the region and mistreated the Israelites.

After 18 years of domination by the Ammonites in the east, the Israelites asked God to forgive their past sinfulness. They destroyed their foreign gods and served the Lord. Then they asked Jephthah to lead an army to defeat this foreign power. He was an illegitimate son who was mistreated by his half-brothers, and he ran away and lived with homeless men at the edge of the desert. He had become famous as a fearless warrior who led a gang of bandits. The Israelites said that if he won the battle, they would make him their leader.

Jephthah agreed and first tried to negotiate a peaceful solution with the enemy king about a land dispute, but that effort failed. Jephthah then went and destroyed 20 of the enemy's cities and led all of Israel for six years until he died.

Samson and the Philistines

Jephthah was followed by different judges who served another 25 years, but after that, the Israelites turned from the Lord and followed foreign gods. They fell under the domination of the Philistines, a strong tribe that occupied fertile land on the Mediterranean Sea. Their control over Canaan lasted 40 years.

An angel told a couple who lived near Philistine territory and were unable to have a child that they would have a son. He would be a Nazarite from birth — he would not consume any form of a grape, not touch a dead person, and not cut any hair on his head. The boy would deliver Israel from the Philistines. When the boy was born, they named him Samson.

Samson became famous for his great strength. But he was also impulsive and quick-tempered and lacked wisdom and good moral character. For example, he slept with strange women, married foreigners, and often broke his vow not to touch a dead body. He killed thousands of Philistines because of his bravery and great strength, and he ruled over Israel for 20 years.

Delilah

Late in his reign, Samson fell in love with a woman named Delilah. The Philistines asked her to find out why Samson was so strong, and they paid her to find out his secret. Delilah asked Samson several times how he got so strong.

Each time he lied about it, and each time Delilah told the Philistines what he had said. When the Philistines tried to capture him, he fought them off because he was still strong.

Delilah complained many times to Samson about how he had lied to her. She said he didn't love her and had made her look like a fool. She nagged him about it day after day until he got sick of her nagging. Sampson didn't realize what Delilah was trying to do, and he finally told her that his strength would go away if his hair was cut. Delilah told the Philistines this secret, and after she cut off his hair while he slept, God left him, and the Philistines easily captured him. They gouged out his eyes and made him a prisoner and forced him to grind grain.

Over time, Samson's hair grew longer and he regained his strength. When the Philistine rulers took Samson out of prison to make fun of him for a very large crowd, he his handler to put him between two pillars that held up the building so he could lean on them.

Samson then prayed to the Lord, "Please Lord, remember me. Strengthen me one more time and let me get revenge on the Philistines for my two eyes." Then Samson braced himself between the two center pillars that held up the temple and pushed the pillars with all his might. The temple collapsed and killed everybody in it.

Naomi and Ruth

During these troubled times, members of the Israelite tribes moved around the region. Migrations occurred because of fighting, famine, and to bring family members together. During one famine, a small family that lived in Bethlehem moved beyond the Salt Sea. The husband died and left behind his wife Naomi and two sons. The sons married Orpah and Ruth, two local women. When the sons died, all that was left was Naomi and her two daughters-in-law.

Naomi heard that God had provided food in Judah, but she wanted to go alone so Orpah and Ruth could get married again. Ruth insisted on going with Naomi and said, "Where you go, I will go; where you live, I will live. Your people will be my people, your God will be my God. Where you die, I will die, and I will be buried there. May the Lord deal with me severely if I let anything other than death separate us." She was giving up her former life and committing herself to the ways of the Israelites.

When Naomi and Ruth arrived in Bethlehem, Ruth said she wanted to work in the barley fields that were being harvested. She ended up working for Boaz, a wealthy landowner who was related to Naomi's dead husband. When Boaz saw Ruth in the field, he learned she was Naomi's daughter-in-law and was a hard worker.

Boaz told Ruth to work for him and watch the fields. Ruth bowed to Boaz and asked him, "Why have you noticed me and liked me, even though I am a foreigner?"

Boaz replied, "I've been told what you have done for your mother-in-law after your husband died and how you left your parents and homeland to come and live here with people you don't know. May the God of Israel reward you."

Ruth replied to Boaz, "May I continue to be favored in your eyes. You put me at ease by speaking kindly to me, even though I'm not one of your servants." Boaz gave her some food to take home, and Ruth explained to Naomi what happened that day.

Ruth continued to work for Boaz through several more harvests that year while living at home with Naomi. Eventually, they got married and had a son named Obed, who later became the father of Jesse, who had a son named David, who would become Israel's greatest leader. Ruth's status had changed dramatically because of her integrity and courage to change her allegiance.

Other Conflicts and Periods of Peace

There was a consistent pattern during these centuries. The Israelites would start out honoring God, but they would get comfortable, conform to the ways of the local customs and culture, and gradually forget to follow God. This led to oppression by others and led the people to experience the absence of God's blessings. When things got really bad for the Israelites, they would appeal to God for help, and different heroes emerged to defeat the oppressors. Their victories were due to God's power, not the power of Israel's armies. It was through human weakness and limitations that God's power and glory were revealed. God continued to be faithful and forgive those who called out for help, obeyed the rules for good living, and had faith. The victories restored peace (*shalom* in Hebrew) and justice until the cycle of decline started again.

CHAPTER 8

CROWNING A UNIFYING KING
Initial National Status Has Mixed Results

The different Israelite tribes fought among themselves and sometimes were angered when they were left out of battles where they would have gained something from a victory. The tribes also fought each other because some offense occurred between members of the different tribes. During these civil wars, the people of the various tribes stole from each other, including taking women from other tribes to be their wives. The tribes felt no loyalty to one another and were jealous of each other. There was no king, and each tribe acted in its own self interests.

Without a unifying king and a way to select the next king, the tribes of Israel had little prestige in the region. The Philistines posed the biggest threat to Israel—their army and economy were strong while Israel's was weak. Israel also had enemies to the north and east, and having the sea on their western border was not an advantage because Israel did not have any experience using large boats. They were surrounded by trouble and needed to defend themselves, but the 12 tribes were not working together in any way to do so.

Samuel, the Prophet and Judge

During this time, religious life in Israel was mostly neglected. The priests acted inappropriately and took advantage of those who came to the tabernacle in Shiloh to worship and make sacrifices.

A childless woman named Hannah came to the tabernacle one day and was crying passionately. For many years she wanted a child, and she made a vow to God: "If you give me a son, I will give him to you for all the days of his life." The high priest saw Hannah praying and asked her about her prayer. He told her, "Go in peace. May the God of Israel grant you what you have asked." She left encouraged and God granted her request—she had a son and named him Samuel.

Samuel worked and lived in the tabernacle as a boy and took his duties seriously. One night, he heard somebody call his name. He eventually learned that it was God calling him. God said that the high priest and his sons would be destroyed because they did not honor God as they should, and they later died in battle. Word traveled throughout Israel that Samuel, who was still a boy, was God's prophet.

The Philistines dominated and mistreated the Israelites for 20 years, and eventually Israel turned to the Lord. Samuel told the people to destroy their foreign gods and follow God. The people put away their other gods and served only the Lord. Samuel then gathered the Israelites together in a city and prayed for them. The Philistines heard about the gathering and attacked the Israelites. But God brought thunder to the region and the Philistines retreated. The Israelites chased and killed many of them, and the Philistines stopped invading Israel for many years.

Samuel was a judge and religious leader throughout Israel for the rest of his life. He traveled from city to city making legal decisions, liberated cities the Philistines had captured, and drove out Philistines who lived in other areas. There was peace between Israel and its neighbors while Samuel was the leader.

Saul, Israel's First King

When Samuel was old, the elders asked him to appoint a king to lead the nation — they wanted to be like the other nations that had a king. The Lord told Samuel that they were rejecting God as Israel's leader and that having a king would mean the Israelites would have to spend a lot of money and time and hire many people to serve the king and protect the kingdom.

When Samuel described what would happen if they had a king, the people didn't listen. They said they wanted a king and be like other nations. God told Samuel to appoint a king and that the next day, a man would come to town from the tribe of Benjamin (the smallest and least prestigious of all 12 tribes) who should be Israel's first king.

The next day, a tall and handsome man named Saul walked into town looking for his donkeys. Samuel met Saul and privately told him that he would become Israel's first king. Samuel blessed him and described things that would take place the next day that would confirm to Saul that he was the chosen one. Saul became a changed man, and everything happened the next day that Samuel had predicted. God's spirit filled Saul and he spoke the truth clearly. People who knew Saul were amazed at his changed personality.

Samuel then led a process with the leaders of all the tribes to select a king. They drew straws to pick one tribe, then did the same to pick one clan and again to pick one family in that clan and finally, one man within the family. This method of making decisions was often used as a way for God to make a decision. Eventually Saul was selected, and when he was brought before the people, he was clearly the best among those who were present. Samuel said to them, "See the man the Lord has chosen. There is nobody like him among all the people." The people responded loudly, "Long live the king!" He was 30 years old at the time.

Samuel then made his last speech to the Israelites and reminded them of their past. He said God loved them, and they were to love and honor God. But they wanted a king, and now they had one. As long as the people served and obeyed the Lord, everything would work out well. However, if they fell away as they had in the past, God's hand would be against Israel and its king, just as it had been in the past. Having a king was not going to save them.

Saul's Flaws

Despite his awesome physical appearance, Saul had personality flaws that ruined his chances for greatness. He was insecure and didn't think much of himself. He came from the smallest tribe and was always worrying about what others were thinking of him. It was clear to those on the battlefield that he lacked confidence in his military strategies. He lacked good judgment when dealing with others, was suspicious of others' motives, was jealous when others received recognition, and set up monuments to honor himself.

But worst of all, he disobeying God. He got scared and offered sacrifices too soon when it looked like he might lose a battle. Before one important battle, Samuel told Saul that God wanted him to completely destroy their people and all their possessions. However, after winning the battle, Saul spared their king, and his soldiers persuaded him to let them keep the best animals. When Samuel met Saul after the battle, Saul said that everything had been destroyed. But Samuel knew this wasn't true — he heard the sounds of sheep and cattle in the background.

Saul's excuse was that his soldiers kept the animals to use in sacrifices. Samuel was furious and said, "Does the Lord delight in your offerings and sacrifices more than obeying God? Obeying God is more important than the sacrifice of fatted animals. Rebellion is sin and being proud is evil. Because you rejected the Lord's word, God has rejected you as king." Samuel never talked to Saul again.

David Rises, Saul Falls

While Samuel mourned for Saul and Israel, the Lord had him go to Bethlehem and meet with Jesse, the grandson of Boaz and Ruth, to identify the next king. The first son that appeared to Samuel was Eliab, who had a very impressive physical appearance. Samuel thought this would surely be the man God wanted to be king. But God told Samuel, "No, don't consider his looks or height. God doesn't look at what people see, their outward appearance. The Lord looks at the heart."

Jesse brought seven of his sons to Samuel, who rejected all of them. He asked if there were any others, and the youngest was tending sheep. David was called and entered the room, very healthy and handsome. Samuel said that David was to be the next king. David was a good speaker, a brave warrior, a musician, and a poet. When Saul was tormented by evil spirits, his servants told him about David's ability to play the lyre (a small harp), which soothed Saul's spirits. Saul had him come as a visitor many times while David continued to be a shepherd of his family's flocks.

Goliath

When the Philistines threatened to raid Israel again, the two armies stood opposite each other on the hills above a valley. The Philistine army had iron and bronze armor and a soldier named Goliath who was nearly seven feet tall. He had heavy armor and weapons, which were perfect for hand-to-hand combat. However, his unusual size meant he had a deformity that made him slow and visually impaired, so he could be killed by somebody who used a different method.

Goliath went into the valley each day for more than a month and challenged Israel to send one soldier into the valley to meet him in a winner-take-all fight. The side of the loser would become the servants of the other. That way, there would be no bloodshed in a large-scale battle. Saul and his entire army were terrified by this challenge, and nobody volunteered to fight Goliath.

Several of Jesse's sons were with Saul at the battle site, but David was home tending sheep. Jesse had him to take food to his brothers, and when David arrived, he found out about Goliath's challenge. David volunteered to fight Goliath, but Saul said he had no chance against such a large and experienced warrior.

David told Saul, "I've been caring for my father's sheep, and when a lion or bear attacks a sheep, I kill it. If I can kill a lion or bear, I can surely kill this Philistine. He has defied the armies of the living God."

Saul agreed to let David fight Goliath. Saul put his heavy armor on David, but David said he couldn't fight that way. Instead, he would use the weapons he used as a shepherd: a wooden staff, a few smooth stones, and a sling. The stones, whipped fast and released by the sling, could travel at more than 100 miles an hour and were very lethal in the hands of a skilled slinger, even from hundreds of feet away. With God on his side and a lethal weapon in his hand, he went into the valley with confidence to fight Goliath.

When Goliath saw how small David was and that he had no armor, he mocked and cursed him. But David told him, "You fight me with a sword and spear, but I fight you in the name of the Lord Almighty, the God of the armies of Israel, whom you defy. So now the Lord will deliver you into my hands. I will cut off your head, and the entire world will know there is a God in Israel."

As Goliath moved closer for the attack, David ran forward, put one stone in his sling, and shot it directly at the giant, The stone hit Goliath in the forehead and knocked him to the ground. David ran up, grabbed Goliath's sword, and cut off the giant's head, lifting it for all to see. When the Philistines saw Goliath was dead, they turned and ran. The Israelite army chased them and killed them as they went.

Saul Pursues David

David became very famous, and Saul kept him in his household where David developed a very close friendship with Jonathan, Saul's son. David was very successful when he went into battle, which increased his popularity. Saul became jealous of David's fame when he heard the people after the battles say, "Saul has slain his thousands, David has slain his tens of thousands." Saul got increasingly paranoid and tried to kill David several times, but David always escaped. Saul sent him into battle, hoping he would be killed, but David always came back the victor.

Saul's daughter became David's wife, and she warned him that Saul wanted to kill him. David escaped and was nearly captured several times as Saul's men chased him around the region. David had several chances to kill Saul, but each time he chose not to because Saul had been appointed king by God. David knew that if he was to become king, he shouldn't make the process go faster by disobeying God's command not to murder. God's process would allow him to become king the right way. David hid in different locations and eventually moved to Philistine territory for safety.

Saul and his sons were eventually killed in a battle with the Philistines. He received no royal burial, and with their victory, the Philistines controlled all of Canaan. Saul's life was a tragedy. He rose from humble beginnings to a position of power and prestige, but his personal flaws, improper behaviors, and decisions to disobey God resulted in a loss of God's blessing and a disgraceful ending.

CHAPTER 9

KING DAVID AND KING SOLOMON
Flawed Characters Lead During Israel's Golden Age

When David heard of Israel's defeat and Saul's death, he knew it was his time to become king. He went to Hebron and was named the new king. But one of Saul's sons was crowned as the next king by other tribes. The families of both men had disputes for several years about who was the right king. Through a series of negotiations and fights between those backing each man during this civil war, David emerged as the king. He was 30 years old.

David Rules and Israel Expands

After he became king, David attacked and defeated the foreign powers that had occupied Jerusalem, and the city became known as the City of David (also referred to as Zion because of a hill in the city with that name). The city became the nation's political and religious capital, and with the help of the Phoenicians, a large palace was built. This palace became David's home. He danced in the streets of Jerusalem when the Ark of the Covenant came into the city. David had many wives and many other women who all produced many children. (Many people were killed in battle, so many children were needed keep the population strong. The wives of men killed in battle needed a man to support them, so they became the wives of other men.)

God told David through the prophet Nathan, "I will make your name great. I will provide a place for my people so they have a home of their own and will no longer be disturbed. When your days are over, I will raise up your offspring to succeed you, and I will establish his kingdom. When he does wrong, I will punish him, but my love will never leave him. Your house and kingdom will endure forever."

David's armies defeated the Philistines several times and the enemies in the southeast. He pressed far northward past Damascus and eastward to occupy more territory. The Lord gave David victories wherever he went, and he always gave God the credit for the military victories and material prosperity as the empire expanded.

David and Bathsheba

One evening, David saw a beautiful young woman bathing. He wanted to know who she was, and he learned that her name was Bathsheba. She was married to Uriah, a soldier who was far away at a battle. David called to his palace, and they had sex. Soon afterward, she told David that she was pregnant. David arranged to have Uriah killed at the battlefront. David then married Bathsheba and she had his baby.

David thought he had committed the perfect crime. Nobody knew the full story of all the events leading to Uriah's death. But God knew. The prophet Nathan told David a story about a rich man who stole from a poor man. David was angry with the rich man and said he must die. Then Nathan said to David:

> You are the rich man! The God of Israel says to you, "I anointed you the king of Israel and saved you from Saul. I gave you his house and wives. I gave you all of Israel and Judah. Why did you despise the Lord by doing evil? You had Uriah killed and took his wife. Now, the sword will never leave your house. Your family will be affected by evil, and you will watch when I take your wives and give them to somebody close to you. You sinned in secret but this will all happen in broad daylight."

After hearing this prophecy, David said to Nathan, "I have sinned against the Lord."

Nathan replied, "The Lord has forgiven your sin — you aren't going to die. But your child will die because of your sin." Soon after Bathsheba's baby was born, it became sick and died a week later. The couple soon had another baby boy and named him Solomon.

David was a lenient father and for many years, there was strife within his family and throughout the empire. As Nathan had predicted, immorality and rebellion grew, and there was much bloodshed within Israel and within his family.

David eventually made plans to build an elaborate Temple, and at the end of his reign, he held a public meeting to recognize Solomon as his successor (Solomon was not yet 30 years old). When David died, he was buried in Jerusalem, the City of David. He is still known as Israel's greatest leader, even though he and many others suffered because of his many sins.

King Solomon and the Temple

Solomon was king during a time of peace and prosperity. His most important accomplishment was the construction and dedication of a permanent Temple that became the central point for religious worship of Israel. Up until then, the tabernacle used tents for worship. Israel had a peace treaty with the Phoenicians, and they provided skilled architects and technicians to design the Temple that conformed to the plans for the tabernacle laid out by Moses. The Temple was gigantic in scale and took up twice the amount of land that the set of tents for the tabernacle required. For example, the Temple entrance had huge pillars made of bronze, 24 feet high and 18 feet around. Its huge doors had inlaid gold and elaborate decorations that opened into the sanctuary, which had well-decorated floors and walls from Lebanon — no stone could be seen on the inside. All the stones for the Temple were cut at the quarry so no tools made a sound where the Temple was being built.

It took seven years to complete the Temple, and when it was finished, the people were so happy that they sacrificed thousands of animals at its dedication to show their gratefulness to God. Solomon prayed publicly to God at the dedication.

Solomon's Wisdom and Wealth

Solomon was also known for being a wise king who knew how to deal with complex and unusual cases. He prayed to God for wisdom, and he got it. In one case, two women came to him, both claiming to be the mother of a child. Solomon said since both of them said they were the mother, he would cut the child in half and give each woman part of the child. Hearing that, one mother said she would give up the child to the other, thereby showing that she was the true mother.

People from all over the world came to Solomon to learn from his wisdom. When the Arabian queen of Sheba visited him with many riddles, he answered them all. She left astonished and said he was much wiser than everybody said. Solomon also wrote extensively about wisdom.

Solomon's wisdom and excellent organizational skills kept Israel at peace with its neighbors and helped make the nation wealthy as its trade with others grew strong. Israel was in the crossroads between Europe, Asia, and Africa, which allowed it to trade with others. The growing wealth of the people trickled upward as they paid heavy taxes, and with the gifts from many visitors, Solomon became the wealthiest king in the world.

During his reign, Solomon took many wives, including women from other nations. Despite Moses's warning not to marry foreigners, he married the daughter of the Egyptian pharaoh and women from five of the nations on Israel's borders. He pushed Israel's empire further than David had and met women with different value systems and beliefs, which Solomon tolerated in the spirit of being flexible. His harem had 700 wives and princesses and another 300 women that produced more children for him. Success and prosperity tainted his judgment, and he gradually compromised his values and acquired idols of worship and built altars to worship gods associated with his many wives. This disobeyed God's first command. Because of his disobedience, the kingdom was to be divided after Solomon died.

Near the end of Solomon's reign, adversaries rose up around the kingdom and challenged his rule. Threats also came from within. Jeroboam was one of Solomon's officials and met a prophet who told him that Israel would be divided into two parts after Solomon died and that Jeroboam would be the leader of one part of the kingdom. Solomon then tried to kill Jeroboam, but Jeroboam fled to Egypt.

Solomon reigned for 40 years. He was replaced by his son Rehoboam. His reputation as a wise ruler endures to this day, but many of his accomplishments depended on the slave-like labor of the Israelites, who were taxed heavily to make Israel great. It had been nearly 500 years since Moses led the Israelites out of Egypt and set up the tabernacle in the wilderness. Now Israel was a nation like others, with a king and a permanent place to worship. Like David, Solomon's legacy was a mix of greatness and personal failures.

CHAPTER 10

THE DIVIDED KINGDOM

Evil Kings in the North and South
Resist Prophets' Warnings

When Solomon died, two men thought they should be king. As Solomon's successor, Rehoboam was crowned king by the tribes of Israel. However, some leaders complained that they wanted relief from the low wages and heavy taxes Solomon put on them. Jeroboam returned from his exile in Egypt and was with them. When Rehoboam decided not to relieve these burdens and would demand even more from the people, those from all the tribes except Judah walked out and made Jeroboam their king.

The nation was on the brink of a civil war. But war was averted when a prophet said God wanted the tribes to split into two kingdoms. Those in the tribes of Judah and Benjamin were in the south, and they called themselves *Judah*. It was known as the *Southern Kingdom* and included the capital in Jerusalem. Those from the 10 other tribes in the north called themselves *Israel*, and their "nation" was known as the *Northern Kingdom*.

The two nations were rivals and often battled in the many years that followed. The border between the kingdoms was about 10 miles north of Jerusalem. Both nations had 20 kings, and their division reduced each kingdom's power. As a result, they were often attacked by foreign invaders. Various prophets spoke and wrote to both nations when their people strayed from God's ways.

The Northern Kingdom and Its Prophets

Jeroboam changed the ways religion was practiced in the north. He set up golden calves as their god and appointed priests who had no experience carrying out their duties.

Anybody could be a priest, and it was an easy job with many benefits. Jeroboam's reign as king lasted 22 years. He resisted prophets who condemned his decisions that were evil.

Of the 20 kings that served in the North, a few had very long reigns (one king ruled for 41 years), and some were very short (one king lasted only seven days). Nearly all the kings were evil. Many prophets spoke God's truth to these power men about the need to turn from wicked ways, but these prophets were usually ignored or killed. Here are the stories of some of these prophets.

Amos

During the latter part of Jeroboam's reign, the farmer Amos wrote a message from God to the people of God. The region was experiencing easy living during a time of prosperity. But wealth was not distributed evenly, and many social injustices existed. Through selfish luxury and the oppression of the poor, the wealthy lived well while many others struggled. Moral corruption and pride were present throughout Israel's culture.

Amos wrote that religious rituals are meaningless when a lack of fairness exists. He first criticized social injustice in other nations, and said divine judgment would come to them. The Israelites were happy to hear that their hated neighbors, godless foreigners, would be punished! Then he mentioned the wickedness of the Israelites in the Southern Kingdom who were proud about how religious they were, but they disobeyed God. He knew his northern audience would agree with everything he had written thus far.

But then he described all the things that were happening in the Northern Kingdom. Social evils, injustice, immorality, profanity — they all existed, just as they did in the places he had just named. If others deserved punishment, so did Israel. In fact, it was even worse because the Israelites were God's chosen people and should know better. The wealthy people of Israel hated accountability, resisted the truth, accepted bribes, neglected the poor, and harassed the righteous. Their punishment would be inevitable. Amos predicted an exile, and nothing was going to stop it. This punishment would apply to all of God's people, not just those in the Northern Kingdom. God could not be bribed with offerings and sacrifices as long as the people's sinfulness prevailed.

The chief priest wanted Amos killed, but Amos knew he spoke the truth of God, so he kept condemning the leaders and people. Amos ended by predicting the Israelites would return from exile and experience a time of peace and that David's dynasty would continue through a remnant of people who stayed faithful.

Elijah

Elijah was the main prophet who spoke God's truth in the Northern Kingdom. He lived during the reign of Ahab and his evil wife Jezebel. After Elijah predicted a drought that would end only when he said it would, he hid in the desert, and then he lived with a very poor widow north of Canaan. Jezebel sent men to kill him, and they killed other prophets along the way, but they couldn't find Elijah.

God told Elijah to tell King Ahab that the drought occurred because Israel didn't follow God. Elijah told Ahab to call 850 prophets of Baal and other gods to Mount Carmel for a test of power. Elijah would be God's only prophet. Each side had a bull that was to be consumed by fire caused by their god. The king's prophets went first. They put a bull on an alter and called on Baal to light the bull.

Nothing happened. The prophets danced and prayed from morning until noon, but no fire started. Elijah taunted them: "Shout louder. Surely Baal is a god! Maybe he's deep in thought, or busy, or traveling. Maybe he's sleeping." The prophets shouted louder and cut themselves. They tore down Elijah's alter and kept praying frantically until it was time for the evening sacrifice. There was no response from Baal.

Then Elijah rebuilt his altar and dug a trench around his altar. He told the king's prophets to pour water on the bull so it was totally soaked and water filled the trench. Then Elijah prayed, "God of Abraham, Isaac, and Israel, let everybody know today that you are God in Israel and I am your servant." Fire fell from the sky and burned the bull, the alter, the soil, and consumed all the water in the trench.

Then everybody who were watching fell down and cried, "Your Lord is God!" Elijah told them to kill all the prophets of Baal, and he told King Ahab to return home before the rains came. Heavy rains started and the 40-month drought ended.

When Jezebel heard what happened, she wanted to kill Elijah. He fled to the southern wilderness, about 200 miles away. When he was there, God told him in a quiet whisper to Damascus, far in the north. God assured him that there were still 7,000 people who still honored God and had not worshipped Baal.

When Elijah traveled north, he found Elisha and anointed him as the next prophet. Elijah had several more encounters with King Ahab over the coming years, and he worked alongside Elisha to speak truth to the Northern Kingdom until Elijah was taken into the sky in a tornado right before Elisha's eyes. A large search party spent three days looking for Elijah's body, but no body was found.

Elisha

Elisha then became the main prophet in the Northern Kingdom, and he performed many miracles among the people. In one case, a Syrian working for Israel's army named Naaman had a noticeable skin disease. He had married an Israelite woman who told him about Elisha's miracles of healing. He met Elisha who told him to wash in the Jordan River seven times. Naaman got upset at this demand, but his servants told him that if Elisha had asked him to do some great act that used his strength in order to be healed, he would surely do it. Was he too proud to wash in the river? So Naaman humbled himself and washed in the river, and he was healed.

Israel and Syria battled occasionally and the Northern Kingdom gradually shrank as it lost land. By using his God-given insight, Elisha often advised Israelite leaders of the

Syrian plans, so Israel was always prepared for their attacks. The Syrian king thought there was a traitor in their midst, but he was informed that Elisha could predict the future and knew about the attacks in advance.

The Syrian king then wanted Elisha dead. When the king heard where Elisha was staying, he sent his army to surround the city. In the morning, Elisha's servant saw the Syrian chariots and asked Elisha what they should do. Elisha said, "Don't be afraid. We have far more chariots than they have. Open your eyes and see them."

The servant saw a multitude of horses and chariots burning with fire in the hills. When the Syrians approached the city, God blinded them. Elisha then told their leaders that they were going to attack the wrong city and he would lead them to where they would find who they were looking for. Elisha then led the blind army to Samaria, which was where Israel's king and army were located. When God opened their eyes, they were surrounded by their enemies!

Israel's king asked Elisha what he should do. Elisha said the Syrian army should be given food and drink and then be sent home. The king followed Elisha's command, and after the Syrians returned home, they stopped their raids into Israel for many years.

When the Syrian attacks started again, they surrounded Samaria and stopped food from entering the city. This caused a famine in the city. Elisha told the people that God would provide food the next day. Four homeless lepers living near the city were so desperate for food that they asked the Syrians for food. When they came to the enemy camp, they found no soldiers. Instead, they found lots of food and all the Syrians' animals. In the middle of the night, God had created thunder-like sounds that resembled a charging army with chariots, and the Syrian army fled for their lives, well beyond the Jordan River. Then the people of Samaria went to get all the food and animals that were left behind.

Hosea

Hosea was one of the last prophets to warn Israel of its coming doom. Writing in poetry, he told his audience that God asked him to take a prostitute as his wife and produce children with her. That way he would understand how God feels when dealing with an unfaithful partner. The names of his children indicated that Israel was like somebody who had been unfaithful in a marriage by falling in love with other gods. Therefore, God would leave them because they had committed adultery.

Hosea was warning Israel that they would be cut off from God's protection, and their palaces and fortified cities would be destroyed. God desires mercy and recognition, not sacrifices and burnt offerings. "Israel must return to God, maintain love and justice, and always wait for God." Hosea ended his message like Amos, who previously predicted God would still love them the way parents love their children. God forgives and heals the faithful, and some would return and live in the land God had given them.

The Southern Kingdom and Its Prophets

Like the kings in the north, many of the kings of Judah were unfaithful to God. There were longer periods of peace and prosperity in the Southern Kingdom than in the north and longer periods when these descendants of David and Solomon listened to God's prophets and stopped worshiping other gods. Some of the faithful who lived in the north defected and moved into the Southern Kingdom — Jerusalem was still respected and was close to the border. Of the 20 kings of Judah, Manasseh was king the longest (55 years), while several others were king for only three months.

Like those who lived in the North, those living in Judah did evil in the sight of the Lord. Under Rehoboam, the first king, people set up many altars to other gods and misbehaved in the same awful ways of those who originally lived in Canaan. Egypt attacked Jerusalem and took away all the gold items that Solomon had put in the Temple and royal palace.

Just as prophets spoke and wrote to the leaders and people in the north and made predictions about events to come, various prophets spoke and wrote in the same ways to those in the Southern Kingdom. Here are the stories of some of these prophets.

Jehoshaphat

Jehoshaphat was a king who had a 25-year reign. He made reforms that returned the people to the religious practices used under David and Solomon. He had altars to foreign gods removed, and his good policies brought peace between Judah and the Philistines and Arab nations. He also had good relations with the Northern Kingdom, so Judah didn't have any enemies on its borders. These religious and political policies led to peace and economic prosperity in the Southern Kingdom. When he was rebuked by a prophet, he listened and made reforms. For example, he installed judges who emphasized fairness and did not take bribes.

Yet Jehoshaphat didn't listen to every prophet when he was confronted, and some of his ways were passed on to his son Jehoram when they ruled together. When Jehoram took full control of the throne, Judah fell back into idol worship and experienced wars again. Jehoram murdered six of his brothers and built altars to idols. His only son Ahaziah continued the horrible rule of his father.

Isaiah and Predictions of a Coming King

Isaiah wrote the most of all the prophets. He was born during prosperous times, and his extensive poetry and other writings harshly condemned Israel's steady moral decline due to its corruption and unrighteousness. But he also provided great hope in things to come in the future. Judgment and hope are woven throughout Isaiah's words, which were written over many years.

He first wrote that God condemns those in Judah and Jerusalem because they are corrupt and full of evil ways. Their sacrifices and religious gatherings are meaningless because the people don't obey God. Through Isaiah, God said,

> Do you think I want all these sacrifices and offerings? I'm disgusted by the smell of your incense. When you raise your hands in prayer, I don't look at you; when you say many prayers to me, I'm not listening. Stop doing evil! There is blood on your hands, for you have not been fair to others, you have not helped those who suffer because of your unfairness, and you have not supported orphans and widows.

Israel was like God's vineyard, and if it didn't produce fruit despite the owner's many efforts, the vineyard would be destroyed. In real life, the godless nations of the Assyrians and Babylonians would be the destroyers, used by God to punish the Israelites.

Isaiah also provided hope for restoration. Although the Israelites would be defeated and destroyed, correct living would lead to peace for those who trusted God. Eventually the conquering evil nations would be overthrown, and out of what remained of the Israelites that survives, a descendant of David would come to power and lead a worldwide kingdom that would last forever. Evil would be destroyed and God's vineyard would be fruitful once again.

Isaiah wrote about the righteous leader to come as Immanuel ("God with us"), who will be "Mighty God" in human form and prevail throughout the entire world. God says: "I lay a precious cornerstone for a solid foundation. Those who rely on it never need to panic. People will be judged based on their justice, fairness, and correct living." However, judgment and destruction will come first. Those who have faith don't need to worry because the "grains of wheat will be separated from their chaff." Their hope is in what comes after their struggles, and those who wait will be blessed, for God gives strength to those who are tired and weak. "Those who have hope in the Lord will renew their strength. They will soar high like eagles, they will run and won't be weary, they will walk and won't faint."

The one to come is described as a "servant." Abraham was God's first servant because he obeyed the call to move to Canaan. Israel was a nation chosen by God to be an obedient servant and a witness to the world of God's power and compassion. The coming servant will have God's spirit so his kingdom will establish justice that extends to other nations (the non-Israelites, also called "Gentiles"). He will be innocent and live correctly. He will be like a shepherd who tenderly cares for his young sheep. He will look like any normal human being, but he will be very special in other ways — the only one of his kind to walk the earth. Yet he will be misunderstood and rejected by many people, and he will be killed in a gruesome manner. Yet through the sacrifice of his own blood, this servant will save all people from their sins, bringing all people to God, even those who are not part of the nation of Israel. He will later be raised and praised.

These unusual messages are intertwined. A person of great power and goodness will be rejected by those he comes to serve. He will not use his power or reason to defend or save himself, and his death brings life to others. He goes into hell, conquers death, and comes back more powerful than ever, and he gives others some of his great powers. The servant is the greatest of all!

Isaiah wrote extensively about the coming king to the tribes of Israel and Judah who had become blind, deaf, and disobedient. He wrote that God says:

> Can't you see I am doing something new? I'm making a road through the wilderness. I will lead the blind in ways they haven't known and guide them along new paths. I will turn darkness into light and make rough places smooth. Don't be afraid — I have saved you! I've called you by name and you are mine. When you pass through the waters, I will be with you; the strong rivers will not sweep you away. When you walk through the fires of life, you won't be burned.

The coming king will be despised and rejected, he will suffer much pain and will not be respected. He will be considered punished by God, but he will take on our pain and be killed for our sins. His punishment will bring us peace — through his wounds we will be healed. Even though he has committed no violence and never lied, he won't protest. He will be led to death like an innocent lamb going to be slaughtered. But he will know what is coming and why. It's God's will for him to be crushed, for his life is an offering for our sin, and he will intervene for everybody who sins.

Isaiah continued writing about judgment. He knows what God requires and doesn't see it among the people. He appeals to the people and leaders to turn away from violence, idol worship, and being unfair to those who lack power. He calls people to return to the Lord. God says:

You have your religious rituals and practice fasting and praying, but you don't treat others fairly. Do you expect me to listen to your prayers, be impressed, and bless you? Your rituals occur once a week. What I want is for you to have a humble spirit and to offer encouragement and support to those with broken hearts. I'm pleased when I see my people breaking the chains of injustice, releasing people from the heavy yokes that are on them, feeding the hungry, giving shelter to the homeless, clothing the naked, and supporting those who lack power — these are signs of true religion. When I see these things happening, I will hear you and heal you, and light will come to your darkness. But there will be no peace for the wicked.

Isaiah says that God sees nobody who meets the definition of holiness, and he concludes with a description of the signs that indicate the coming king, the Redeemer, has arrived. The Redeemer will say:

The Spirit of the Lord is on me and has anointed me to proclaim good news to the poor. God has sent me to comfort the brokenhearted, to free captives and release prisoners from their darkness, to proclaim the Year of the Jubilee, to comfort all who mourn and grieve, to give them a crown of beauty instead of ashes, oil of joy instead of sorrow, and a garment of praise instead of a spirit of despair.

Isaiah said the peace-creating ruler of this revived kingdom would be a descendant of David. The ruler's kingdom would grow and dominate the world, bring peace, influence other nations, and triumph over the godless. Isaiah writes:

> In the last days, nations will go to the Lord together and learn how to work with each other in the right way. God will be the judge between people and will settle the disputes nations have with each other. Nations won't fight with each other, and their people won't train to wage war anymore. They will change their swords into plows and their spears into pruning hooks.

Micah's Messages of Judgment and Hope

The prophet Micah wrote at the same time as Isaiah and Hosea and in the same poetic style. He saw the political and religious corruption in the region, and his strong criticism was similar to what Isaiah and Hosea said. He said both Jerusalem and Samaria (the main cities in the south and north) were evil because of their idolatry, their corruption that oppressed the poor and ignored justice in the courts, and their general lack of interest in solving society's problems. King Solomon had written wise proverbs about how laziness caused people's poverty, but Micah writes that people may also be poor because those with power ignore the problems of the poor and use all their privileges to maintain their extravagant lifestyle.

But unlike Amos, Isaiah, and Hosea, Micah doesn't tell the Israelites to repent. Instead, he calls them to "court" to make their case before God, who is both the witness and the judge. What does God require for people to escape possible punishment? People are to "act fairly, love kindness, and walk humbly with God." Moses said people should love God and their neighbor as themselves, and the people had not done that. Therefore, the people will lose in God's court because they didn't have the right relationship with God and others. The penalty for their misbehavior was the destruction of their nations and cities, and they would be hauled away in exile to Assyria and Babylon.

After predicting judgment and exile, Micah provided hope for the future. A small number of weak and exiled Israelites would return and build the cities again. "God does not stay angry forever but delights when people show mercy." Micah also predicted that Israel's future leader would come from the town of Bethlehem.

* * * * *

The Israelites in the north and south didn't listen to the prophets' warnings and predictions of the coming invasions by their enemies. Injustice, violence, and religious sinfulness continued in both Israel and Judah, and their leaders didn't realize how soon the prophets' predictions would come true.

CHAPTER 11

BOTH KINGDOMS FALL

Assyrians and Babylonians Conquer Israelites

The Assyrians often attacked areas occupied by the Israelites, Syrians, and Phoenicians. One Assyrian king was particularly brutal as he expanded towards the Mediterranean Sea, and he started taking captives back to Assyria instead of letting conquered peoples stay in their land. Outsiders were brought into areas where the local people had lived, and Assyrian officials supervised the land. This reduced the chances that people would rebel.

The Northern Kingdom Falls

When the Assyrians first attacked areas in the Northern Kingdom, Israel's kings would give them money, food, and other things to buy peace. But Israel's kings also worked with the Syrians to stand up against the Assyrians. When Assyria attacked and won battles against the Syrians, the Northern Kingdom had no chance to survive. Eventually, the Assyrian army conquered all areas in the region except for the hills in central Canaan. When the Assyrian king died, Israel's king stopped paying the Assyrians and got Egypt's help to resist Assyrian aggression. But the new Assyrian king was just as aggressive and attacked the rest of Israel's territory. His forces captured the capital in Samaria after a three-year siege and forced Israel's king to surrender.

The Assyrians captured more than 27,000 of Israel's political and military leaders and took them back to Persia and Mesopotamia. The Assyrians replaced them with their own people. Most of the Israelites stayed behind and continued working on the land. The mix of people from many areas and cultures outside Israel resulted in many different types of religious practices. None of the people followed the Lord, and all the cultures intermarried with each other. Collectively, they were known as Samaritans because the capital city had been Samaria.

The Northern Kingdom ceased to exist in 722 BC. The kingdom had lasted about 210 years after splitting off from those living in Judah. In the final 30 years, Israel had six kings and was in rapid decline. Their collapse was predicted by the prophets, but their leaders never appealed to God for help. They had forgotten how obedience to God had made them great.

The South Survives

In the south, Judah's strategy to deal with Assyria was different. It was further away from the invaders from the north and east. Judah was happy to see the Assyrian army defeat the Philistines as its army moved along the coastline to reach the more prized Egyptian empire. Judah didn't join the north's alliance with Syria against the Assyrians, and the Southern Kingdom no longer had to fight against the Northern Kingdom.

During this time, the Southern Kingdom continued their evil religious practices. Many prophets spoke against the north and predicted its fall from power, and their predictions had come true. Instead of listening to their warnings to the Southern Kingdom, Judah's leaders depended on political strategies to maintain their prosperity and peace. When one prophet warned the people of Judah that they wouldn't prosper if they continued to disobey God's commands, he was killed in the Temple courtyard.

Hezekiah

Some of the southern leaders were faithful to God. For example, when King Hezekiah came to power after the north collapsed, he started many religious reforms. He abolished idol worship and smashed altars to false gods. He cleansed the Temple and started celebrating Passover again. He invited the Israelites in the north to take part in these activities. Twenty years after the Northern Kingdom fell, he gave the king of Assyria 11 tons of gold from the Temple as payment for peace and the withdrawal from cities in Judah that had been captured.

When an Assyrian military commander planned to attack Jerusalem and rebuked God, Hezekiah asked Isaiah for advice from God. Isaiah told Hezekiah not to worry: the Assyrians would die and not attack — the Lord had a reputation to defend. That night 185,000 Assyrian soldiers died mysteriously, and their army retreated all the way back to their capital in Nineveh about 600 miles away.

But when Hezekiah died, his son Manasseh took over as king and led Judah into its worst period of wickedness. Altars to Baal were rebuilt and practices associated with strong evil powers were commonplace, including human sacrifices, awful sexual practices, and demon worship. The prophets who condemned these practices were killed (Isaiah was probably one of them). Hezekiah had led Judah to its highest point of morality, but his son led Judah to its lowest point. Late in his rule, Manasseh was captured and taken to Nineveh, where he repented and returned to Jerusalem as a king who served the Assyrians. But he didn't have time to make any reforms, and when he died, his son continued the worship of false gods and evil powers.

Josiah

Hezekiah's grandson Josiah became king when he was only eight years old. Judah had kept the peace by making treaties with other nations, paying the Assyrians, and sometimes benefiting from God's powers. Judah gained more independence when the Assyrians started pulling out of the region to deal with problems back in Mesopotamia. This gave Judah an opportunity to have more influence in the areas where the northern tribes. This renewed a sense of nation pride among all the Israelites.

By the time King Josiah was 16 years old, he had stopped worshipping false gods and was honoring the true God. A few years later, he started another round of religious reforms. The Temple was repaired, the people celebrated Passover, and the religious practices associated with the Assyrians stopped. After a thorough evaluation of the region's religious practices, Josiah abolished evil religious practices in Judah and among the northern tribes, and he removed the priests who led idol worship. The Levites took over the Temple.

The original book of the Law written by Moses was found in the Temple's rubble, and when Josiah read it, he was disgusted with how far the Israelites had fallen away from God and the Law. A female prophet in Jerusalem told Josiah that God's judgment was unavoidable — the chosen people had not obeyed the laws and commands that God had given Moses. Even though the book of the Law had been lost for decades, ignorance of the Law was not an excuse to avoid punishment. Oral instruction and the words of the prophets should have been enough for the kings to know what should be done.

Jeremiah and Other Prophets

During this period, the prophet Jeremiah spoke to the people and leaders of Judah and said that Jerusalem's fate would be the same as that of Samaria a century earlier — destruction and exile. Josiah and Jeremiah were born at about the same time and knew each other. God called Jeremiah to be a prophet, and he knew people would not like what he would say. But he also knew God would support and protect him through difficult times and keep him out of trouble. God told him, "I chose you before I formed you in the womb; I set you apart before you were born. I appointed you to be a prophet to the nations." Jeremiah told God that he didn't speak well and was too young to be a prophet. But the Lord told him, "Don't say you are too young. You must go everywhere I send you and say what I tell you to say. Don't be afraid — I will be with you and will rescue you."

Jeremiah supported Josiah's religious reforms and was very sad when Josiah died. When Judah's next set of kings returned to idol worship, Jeremiah often warned them about the coming disasters of defeat and exile. The people and leaders persecuted him — he was arrested, beaten, imprisoned, and threatened with death many times. At one point, Jeremiah was thrown into a waterless well to starve slowly in the mud, but he was pulled out by a team of men who used a long rope made of rags. False prophets said Jeremiah's predictions wouldn't come true and that people should ignore his messages of judgment and the need to repent.

Jeremiah's messages also contained hope. A small number of God's people would return from foreign lands, and God would create a new agreement with them that replaced the original agreement made with Moses and the Israelites. In this new agreement, God's laws would be written on the hearts of all people, and all their sins would be forgiven. A descendant of David would emerge and install justice and right living on earth, and their land would never again be overthrown.

The writings of other prophets to Judah were similar to Jeremiah's messages: God will judge the people for their disobedience, they should repent because God is merciful and forgiving, those who don't repent and obey will be destroyed and taken away, but there is hope for those who love God and survive.

- The prophet **Joel** wrote to the people of Judah and Jerusalem. His message used the locust that had just invaded their land as a symbol of how God would punish them. He also wrote that God has a Spirit who is available to all people without regard to their age, gender, or social status. As the only universal God who has authority over all creatures on earth, God would eventually judge all nations. Those opposing God will be defeated, but the faithful will be victorious.
- The prophet **Zephaniah** shocked the proud and satisfied people of Judah by writing that God's judgment would come soon. He predicted that Jerusalem would be destroyed and its people would be captured and moved to Mesopotamia as their punishment. He said

the people should accept this punishment and submit to the foreign invaders. People were to be humble, repent, and live the right way. If God punished other nations for their godless behavior, surely God would punish the Israelites for doing the same thing.

- The prophet **Obadiah** condemned the Edomites, the descendants of Esau who lived near the Salt Sea and who had many conflicts with the Israelites over the centuries. In the shortest book of the Old Testament (one page of poetry), Obadiah says Edom would fall from power because of its pride in their ability to support themselves. The Edomites took advantage of the misfortune of others, especially migrants and refugees. But they would be destroyed and their land would be taken over by the Israelites who return from exile.

- The prophet **Nahum** wrote poetry that condemned the Assyrians for their oppression, cruelty, and wickedness. The leaders of cities they conquered were badly tortured before being executed. While those in Nineveh repented after being condemned by **Jonah** (see chapter 13), they soon resumed their violence and sinfulness. While God is "slow to anger and a refuge for those who trust the Lord, God will not leave the guilty unpunished." Any nation built on sinful living and cruelty will eventually fall. God's kingdom, which is based on fairness for all and correct living, will triumph. God is the Lord of all nations and controls their future.

- The prophet **Habakkuk** wrote about a conversation he had with God rather than address the people of Judah directly. The faithful wondered why those who were unfair to others were not punished. God replied that something highly unusual would happen — the evil Babylonians would be used by God to punish Judah. Habakkuk then asked why God would use evil to punish evil. God replied that eventually the Babylonians would be conquered themselves and God's people would rise again. Meanwhile, "the righteous will live by their faithfulness" and must trust the Lord patiently until the Babylonians are overthrown. Being faithful means trusting and being dependent on God, not simply following laws and rules in an unthinking manner.

The Southern Kingdom Falls

The Assyrians eventually lost their power to the Babylonians, which used their power against Judah as they pushed south to conquer Egypt. At one point 10,000 leaders of Jerusalem were captured and sent back to Babylon. Any hope of a revived Israel crumbled as Judah was gradually torn apart and its kings did what foreign nations wanted them to do. Jeremiah continually told Judah's King Zedekiah to surrender to the Babylonians in order to avoid bloodshed, but he didn't surrender.

Jerusalem was captured by the Babylonians in 586 BC after being surrounded for two and a half years. Jerusalem was burned to the ground and its walls were torn apart. The poorest of the survivors stayed behind and tried hard to stay alive. Jeremiah was treated kindly — he had served as God's prophet for 40 years, and the Babylonians knew he told the Israelites to surrender. They gave him a choice: he could either go to Babylon and be treated fairly, or he could stay in Canaan. He chose to stay.

The survivors were then attacked by nomads in the east and they lost their homes. When they asked Jeremiah what to do, he said they should stay in Palestine and be part of God's people, along with others who would eventually return from Babylon. But they decided to go to Egypt, thinking they would be safe there. Jeremiah probably went with them and died in Egypt.

Jeremiah had wept for many years about the stubborn Israelites and how they ignored his messages of God's judgment and need to repent. He was often very depressed and even cursed the day he was born when he was being persecuted. He is probably the author of the book of poetry known as **Lamentations**. The book carefully describes what happened when the Babylonians destroyed Judah and the people's incredible sadness when Jerusalem and the Temple were destroyed. The Israelites would no longer live in the land God promised to give them. The only reasonable response to judgment from a loving God is accepting responsibility for their sin and rebellion. But he wrote that there is still hope because "the Lord's compassions never fail. They are new every morning — great is your faithfulness. The Lord is good to those whose hope is in God and who seek God."

The Southern Kingdom lasted 136 years longer than the Northern Kingdom, and Zedekiah was the last of the 40 kings. The descendants of Abraham and Sarah who moved to Canaan were known as Jews, a term derived from the tribe and nation of Judah. The term was later expanded to apply to all Israelites, regardless of their tribe or nation. Their religion became known as Judaism, and it created a unique Jewish culture. Jewish people have a shared sense of nationhood and an identity as God's chosen people. The area known as Canaan, from the Mediterranean Sea to the Jordan River, is also called Palestine and the Holy Land.

CHAPTER 12

LIFE IN EXILE, THEN RESTORATION

Israelites Thrive in Distant Lands and
a Remnant Returns to Canaan

The Israelites kept good records of historical events and important people who lived in Canaan, migrated to Egypt, wandered in the wilderness, conquered Canaan, and lived in Palestine. But when Jerusalem was raided and most of the Jews were taken to Babylonia, good record-keeping stopped. As a result, we don't know much about the lives of those living in foreign lands.

The land the Israelites left behind was controlled by the Edomites and Babylonians. The Jews had left slavery in Egypt, defeated local powers in Canaan, and withstood stronger nations of Syria, Assyria, and Babylonia. But due to their disobedience to God, in about 500 years the Jews went from having their first king to having no king at all. By the time Jerusalem was conquered, it had been more than 1,250 years since Abraham moved to Canaan, and now most of the Jews were in Mesopotamia, hundreds of miles from the home of their ancestors in Canaan. Palestine mainly became a battleground between the Egyptians and Babylonians.

Eventually the Babylonians suffered from bad leadership and the strains of war as its empire grew. Corruption and cruel treatment of the people who were conquered caused rebellions in the empire. In 539 BC, people of northern Persia led by Cyrus the Great captured Babylon. As the prophets had predicted, both the Assyrians and Babylonians had been defeated.

The Persian religion was Zoroastrianism, and their priests were called Magi. The region that had been controlled by the Assyrians and Babylonians came under Persian control. Jews had been exiled to Babylonia several times, and they were joined by those leaving the Southern Kingdom.

The Jews were usually treated kindly, and they learned the language of Aramaic, which was used in business, trade, and diplomacy.

Most of the Jew became active in local economy. Some worked on construction projects; they had experience building large structures in Palestine, and the Babylonians took advantage of their skills. Some pursued worked in agriculture in the fertile Mesopotamian plains, and others became involved in business and trade. A few got involved in government affairs. They tried to live together in cities scattered across the region where they could maintain their customs and religion.

The Jews who lived in Babylonia wondered when they would return. False prophets predicted they would return soon, and this led to rebellions against the Babylonians because they thought God would free them. But the rebel leaders were executed. Meanwhile, Jeremiah wrote letters from Palestine to those who were in exile to say they should settle down and accept their punishment from God. He told them to "build and live in houses, plant gardens, take wives and have children, seek the welfare of the city where God sent you, and pray to God for the city, for in its welfare you will find your welfare." His predictions that they would return one day gave them hope — they just had to be patient for the right time to go. That confused those living in exile: were they going home soon or not?

Ezekiel's Messages to the Exiled

The prophet Ezekiel was a well-educated and religious Jew who lived in Babylon. When he was 30, God called him to speak to the Jews who lived in Babylonia about when they would return to Palestine. He had a very unusual vision from God, and he used symbolic riddles, stories, and actions to dash the hopes of the Jews who wanted to return to Jerusalem. He said God would punish the Jews in Jerusalem because of their sexual immorality and unfairness. Jerusalem would be destroyed, so those in exile would not return home in the near future — there would be no place to go.

Ezekiel's methods of communicating were unusual. For example, he laid only on his left side for 390 days straight, then only on his right side for 40 consecutive days, to symbolize the fall of the Northern and Southern Kingdoms. He didn't talk to anybody unless God told him he should. He acted so strangely that the Jews in Babylon visited him to see his weird behavior. His visions also contain the message that the Jews would return to their homeland, and his messages were consistent with those of Jeremiah.

When Jerusalem was destroyed and those from the Southern Kingdom arrived in Babylonia, the Jews were more willing to listen to him—his predictions had come true. He also had message of hope. He said God's reputation throughout the world would be restored and Israel would be one nation again. Ezekiel had a vision of dry bones lying in a field that came back to life and were joined together and then covered with skin to be alive again. He explained what God wanted them to know:

> It is not for your sake that I'm doing these things, but for the sake of my holy name, which you have harmed among the nations. I will show that my name is holy. The nations will know I am the Lord. I will gather you from all the nations and bring you back to your own land. I will cleanse you from your filth. I will give you a new heart and put my spirit in you. There will be one king over all of you, one shepherd.

Daniel and His Faithful Companions

Daniel was both a religious leader and a political leader who lived among those exiled to Babylonia before Jerusalem was destroyed. He was well trained in religious activities when he lived in Judah, and he was very bright and wise. He became fluent in Aramaic because he and three other Jews (Shadrach, Meshach, and Abednego) were invited by King Nebuchadnezzar to learn Aramaic when they arrived in Babylon. Daniel wrote messages in both Hebrew and Aramaic, which made his messages available to non-Jews in other nations.

When he and his three friends were given unclean food during their training, they refused to eat it. They asked to receive just vegetables and water, and in 10 days they were healthier than those who ate from the royal menu. After that, they ate only vegetables. After three years of training, the four men were brought to the king, who found them all to be far superior to any others who served him.

When the king had a disturbing dream, he asked his magicians and astrologers to tell him what he had dreamt and what it meant. The wise men said this was an impossible task — no one could read the mind of another person except a god! The king was so upset with their answer that he had all the wise men in Babylon killed.

When the king's men came to take Daniel away, he asked why he was being killed. When he heard about the king's order, he asked to talk to the king. He then asked the king for more time so he could determine what the dream was and what it meant. The king agreed and Daniel went to his three companions and explained the situation. They all prayed hard to God for mercy and insight into the dream, for they didn't want to die.

That night, Daniel had a dream that revealed the answers to the king's questions. In the morning, he told the king, "Nobody on earth can answer these questions, but there is a God in heaven who knows the meaning of your dreams. This God has revealed to me that it describes what will happen in the future." Daniel then explained to the king what the dream was and what it meant. The end of the dream revealed that God would establish a kingdom that would never be destroyed.

Daniel had answered correctly. King Nebuchadnezzar honored Daniel and his God, saying, "Surely your God is the God of gods and the Lord of kings and a revealer of mysteries, for you have revealed this mystery." The king then made Daniel the ruler over the entire province of Babylon and put him in charge of all its wise men. Daniel arranged to have the king appoint his three friends to supervise all the government's work of Babylon.

Later during his reign, King Nebuchadnezzar made a 90-foot golden statue of himself in a field near Babylon. At its dedication, everybody was ordered to bow down and worship it; those who didn't would be thrown into a furnace of fire. Daniel's three friends were at the dedication but didn't bow down, and it was obvious to everybody there that they disobeyed this order. The three men were arrested and taken to the enraged king. The men told the king, "We don't need to defend ourselves to you. If you throw us in the fire, our God can deliver us from it. But even if our God doesn't save us, we want you to know that we won't worship another god or bow to the golden image you set up."

The king was furious and ordered them tied up and thrown into the furnace. Its heat was so hot that the soldiers who took the men to the furnace were killed by the flames. But the three men did not burn in the furnace, and those watching saw four figures walking around in the fire — God was with them. The king ordered them to come out of the furnace, and when the three men emerged, they had not suffered any burns. Even their hair and clothing were unburned, and there was no smell of smoke on them. The king was so amazed that he issued an order that nobody should say anything bad about the God of the Jews, and anybody who did would be killed. The king then promoted the three men.

Many years later, Daniel had a number of visions that predicted the future and were full of vague symbolism where animals and strange beasts represented kings and nations. He didn't understand these visions, so he kept them to himself. But his ability to interpret other mysterious messages was reconfirmed when he revealed the fall of Babylon at a large banquet of dignitaries. Babylon fell to the Persians the next day.

The Persians did not destroy Babylon, and Daniel continued working as a leader in the Persian government. Others were jealous of his power and plotted against him, but Daniel's reputation as a wise and fair government official was flawless. Two officials plotted to have Daniel punished because of his religion. They got the king to issue an edict that anybody found worshiping a god other than the king during the next 30 days would be thrown into a pit with lions. When the officials found Daniel praying toward Jerusalem in his usual way, they told the king.

Since Daniel was such a highly respected person, the king was dismayed. But the officials reminded the king that he had issued an edict that couldn't be changed, so Daniel was thrown to the lions. The king told Daniel, "May your God, whom you always serve, rescue you!"

The den was sealed with a large stone and the king couldn't sleep that night. In the morning, the king went to the pit and called Daniel's name. Daniel replied, "My God sent an angel who shut the mouths of the lions. They have not hurt me because God found me innocent."

The king then gave orders to lift Daniel out of the pit, and he came out without a scratch. The king then had the men who plotted against Daniel thrown into the pit, along with their wives and children. They all were quickly killed and eaten by the hungry lions.

Daniel continued serving as a leader in the Persian government. When he was very old, Daniel had more strange dreams and visions about what would happen in the future. He wrote that many evil kingdoms would rise, and many holy people would fall into their hands. But these earthly kingdoms would someday be destroyed forever by a final kingdom, set up by God, that will not end. Although he didn't understand the meaning of these visions, he wrote them down so others could read them later when their meaning could be determined. Daniel died soon after Cyrus the Great came to power in Babylon.

A New Policy Prompts Their Return and Restoration

Persia's King Cyrus reversed the policy of moving people from areas he conquered back to Mesopotamia. He encouraged people who had been captured to return home and worship their own gods, and he allowed Jews to return home. But by that time, many of them had settled into well-paying jobs and were living comfortably, and they ignored the opportunity to move to Palestine.

King Cyrus believed in the Jewish God and wanted to rebuild the Temple in Jerusalem. He encouraged Jews in Babylonia to give gold, animals, and supplies to those who wanted to return home and rebuild the city and Temple. (The prophet Isaiah predicted this would happen.) About 50,000 Jews soon made the 900-mile journey back to Palestine, and Cyrus sent articles that had been taken from the Temple. When they arrived, it had been about 70 years since the first set of exiles from Judah arrived in Babylonia. (Jeremiah predicted there would be 70 years of exile.)

Jerusalem had been deserted for 50 years and was in ruins. It took the Jews seven months to get organized and start practicing their religious activities again. They made burnt offering and celebrated their festivals. Construction of a new Temple began using materials purchased from the Phoenicians, and the Levites supervised the work. While many celebrated their return and praised God, the elderly who remembered what Jerusalem had looked like cried openly and bitterly at the shape it was in.

Those living in nearby Samaria wanted to help build the Temple. The Samaritans occupied land in what had been the Northern Kingdom and had intermarried with the foreigners who were brought to the region. When they were not allowed to help, they were mad at the returned Jews and worked against their efforts to rebuild the area. Work on the Temple stopped for 16 years because of their opposition.

Haggai and Zechariah

Work on the Temple resumed when King Cyrus was replaced by a new king in Persia who was interested in the religion of his empire. The prophet Haggai reminded the people that building the Temple was a higher priority than making their own nice houses even better. Construction on the Temple soon started again, but their enthusiasm for the project weakened when they realized the new structure would not come close to what had been built under King Solomon.

Although they lacked the workers and money to do the job right, Haggai encouraged the people by predicting the new Temple would be greater than the previous one. God spoke through Haggai.

> Be strong, for I am with you. My Spirit remains among you. In a little while, I will shake all nations, and what is desired by all nations will come, and the house will be full of glory. The glory will be more than in the previous house. In this place, I will grant you peace.

At the same time, the prophet Zechariah had a similar but longer message for the Jews. In a series of symbolic dreams, visions, and messages, he sees that God's people have returned and their nation is gradually restored. When the Temple is built, the people are promised a glorious future. Although Judah had fallen, Jerusalem will rise again while all the other nations will fall. The Lord said "Jerusalem won't have walls because so many people and animals will live in it. My fire will be the wall around it, and I will be the glory in it." God would rebuke evil (Satan) and a servant leader called the Branch would lead the restoration. This leader will be a priest before God and remove the sins of all people in a single day. Justice and peace will replace wickedness, and God's spirit will spread out all across the world. All these things will happen if the people obey God — it is not enough for them to fast and pray. The Lord spoke through Zechariah:

> Provide true justice. Show mercy and compassion to one another. Don't be mean to the widow, the homeless, the foreigner, or the poor. Don't plot evil against each other. Those who came before you didn't listen, and they were scattered and became strangers in other nations. So speak the truth to each other and make fair judgments in your courts.

Zechariah also made predictions about the future. A humble and good king will enter Jerusalem riding on a young donkey. Weapons of war will be removed, and peace will come to earth. Many types of people and powerful nations will tell each other about this king. "They will grab you and ask to go with you because they know God is with you." But Zechariah ended with a warning: Jerusalem will be destroyed again and many people will leave the region because the Jews reject the shepherd who came to save them. But after a massive crisis, God will return and rule the entire world.

Encouraged by these two prophets and a hope for a glorious future, the people completed the Temple five years after construction restarted. It was built on the same site as the previous Temple, but it was not nearly as nice. Nevertheless, the Jews began their religious activities using the same instructions provided by Moses, and the Israelites who had stayed in Palestine joined them in their religious ceremonies and festivals.

Esther and Mordecai in Persia

Many Jews decided to stay in areas controlled by the Persians. When the queen of the Persian King Xerxes disobeyed a direct order in Susa, the king decided she should be replaced. If he let her get away with such disrespect, word would spread and women would stop obeying their husbands. So young women from all across the empire were brought to the king so he could select a new queen. Each woman went through a year of beauty treatment before seeing Xerxes.

Esther was among those brought to prepare to see the king. She was a young and faithful Jew who also lived in Susa. She had been adopted by her older cousin Mordecai when she was orphaned because her parents died. When it was her turn to meet the king, she impressed him so much that she was chosen to be the next queen. But Mordecai told her not to say she was adopted or a Jew.

When Mordecai overheard a conversation about a plot to kill the king, he reported it to Esther, who then told the king, saying she heard it from a man named Mordecai. When the king learned the plot was true, he executed the conspirators.

A man named Haman was the prime minister and ordered everybody to bow to him when they saw him. But Mordecai refused to do it. Haman found out that Mordecai was a Jew, so he devised a plan to get rid of all the Jews in the kingdom (about two million people). He told King Xerxes, "There is a certain group of people scattered across your kingdom who keep themselves separate from others. Their customs are different and they don't obey your laws. It's not good for you to have them live this way. If you want, you can issue an order that they all be killed."

The king agreed, and an order that was sealed with the king's ring was sent to every province. It said that all Jews, including women and children, should be killed on a specific day 11 months later.

Jews throughout the Persian empire wept and fasted when they heard this order. When Esther found out about the order, she decided to talk to the king. But nobody was allowed to see the king in his private room of the palace unless he invited them in — those who entered without an invitation were killed by his guards.

Mordecai told Esther that it was her duty as a Jewish leader to do something — she might be killed because she was a Jew. Esther told him to have all the Jews in Susa pray for her for three days, and then she would go into the king's private room. She told Mordecai, "If I die, I die."

After three days, Esther went into the king's private room and stood at his door. He invited her into his room, and she was relieved she wasn't arrested and killed. She asked him if she could host a dinner with just him and Haman. He agreed, and as they ate and drank that night, the king asked Esther what she wanted — he would do almost anything for her. She said she would give him her answer the next day when the three of them could eat dinner together again.

That evening, Haman went home and bragged to his wife that he had a private dinner with the king and queen and was going to do it again the next night. But he said he still had a bad day because Mordecai didn't bow down to him. His wife said Mordecai should be killed and hung on a tall pole the next morning before he had dinner. That way, he could enjoy his meal with the king and queen. Haman liked the idea and ordered the pole to be set up.

The king couldn't sleep that night. In the morning, he found out Mordecai, the man who reported the assassination plot, was a Jew, but nothing had been done to honor him. When Haman entered the room to talk to the king about killing Mordecai, the king first asked him what should be done for somebody who honors the king. Haman thought the king was going to honor him, so he said the person should put on royal clothes and be featured in a grand parade. The king then told Haman to go and do what he suggested to Mordecai. The humbled Haman did it, and then he returned to have dinner with the king and queen.

As they ate, Esther said her request was for the king to spare the Jews, her people. The king had forgotten who thought of the idea, so he asked who was responsible for the order. She said it was Haman, the man sitting with them!

The king left in a rage, but Haman stayed behind and begged Esther for his life. When the king returned, he saw Haman kneeling at Esther's feet and thought he was trying to assault her. The king ordered his guards to haul Haman away. The guards said there was a tall pole outside of Haman's house that was going to be used to hang Mordecai. The king ordered Haman to be killed and hung on the pole, and the king gave Haman's estate to Esther. When the king found out that Esther and Mordecai were related, he made Mordecai his new prime minister.

But the order to kill all the Jews was still in place. Esther begged the king to issue another order that removed the order to have all Jews killed. The king told Mordecai to write the new order. It was quickly written, translated into every language spoken in the empire, sealed with the king's ring, and sent to every province using the king's fastest horses. The order granted Jews in every city the right to assemble and protect themselves and to kill any man who attacked a Jew. The text of the order was made known to the everybody in the empire so the Jews could protect themselves on the day they were to be killed.

When the news arrived, the Jews in every province were overjoyed. Their courageous queen and new prime minister had spared them. They celebrated by feasting. Many people of other nationalities became Jews and started following their religious activities because they were afraid of what the Jews might do to them.

Mordecai then sent letters to all the Jews in the empire, telling them to celebrate the two days of the month when they got relief from their enemies. Their sorrow had turned into joy, and their mourning turned into a day of celebration. During the two days, Jews were to have feasts, give presents of food to one another, and give gifts to the poor. The occasion became known as the days of Purim and is still celebrated among the Jews.

Ezra Returns to Jerusalem

After King Xerxes died, his son Artaxerxes took his place as king. A highly educated Jew named Ezra lived in exile in Babylon at the time. He was a Levite and a descendant of Aaron, and he understood all the religious writings that had been handed down through the centuries. He also kept track of all the events that had occurred among the Jews over the centuries and wrote them down as historical records. He was eager to return to Jerusalem, and he approached King Artaxerxes to get permission to leave.

The king supported the idea of having more Jews return to Palestine, so he gave Ezra permission to set up a government in Palestine. The king gave Ezra all the financial help he needed to reestablish religious systems and buildings, including whatever he needed for the Temple. The king also said that everybody who worked at Temple did not have to pay any taxes.

Ezra alerted the Jews about the planned trip back to Palestine, but not many people wanted to walk nearly 1,000 miles to a land they didn't know and start a new life. Many were also worried about their safety during the trek. Very few Jews decided to return to Palestine, and even after a special appeal to the tribe, only 20 Levites agreed to go.

Ezra did not want to ask the king for any guards for their trip because the Jews were known to rely on God for their protection. So they all prayed for God's protection during the trip, and after a journey lasting three and a half months, they all arrived safely in Jerusalem.

Ezra soon determined that the Israelites in the region, including the priests, had intermarried with people from other cultures and religions. Ezra was disgusted and angry that the Jews had adopted non-Jewish practices. He prayed loudly in the Temple and confessed the sins of the Jews. He then ordered all Jews to come to the Temple for a meeting. He addressed the crowd and talked about the danger of intermarrying with non-Jews.

The people were willing to change their ways, and leaders were selected to represent all the people at future meetings so only a few people would have to travel to Jerusalem. Ezra led an investigation to determine which priests and Levites had intermarried, and every priest was guilty. All of them agreed to cancel their marriage promises.

Nehemiah

More than 13 years after Ezra returned to Jerusalem, the city was still being rebuilt. The Temple had been completed, but the walls of the city were still broken down and the gates were burned. The city was not a safe place to live.

Nehemiah was a highly loyal Jew who worked for the Persian king in Susa. When his brother visited him from Palestine, he learned that life among the few exiles who returned to Palestine was not good. He wept after hearing this and prayed for several months to determine what God wanted him to do.

His face was sad when he served drinks to King Artaxerxes and his queen, and the king asked him why he was sad. Nehemiah told the king about conditions in his homeland and asked for permission to go back and rebuild Jerusalem. He got the king's permission and got many supplies to take to Jerusalem. He also got letters from the king to make sure his caravan was treated well and to get free lumber.

When Nehemiah arrived in Jerusalem, he and a few others went out privately at night to inspect the city's defenses. In the morning, he told the local officials what they already knew — the city was not safe and needed to have its walls and gates rebuilt. They all agreed to start working immediately on the repairs. He set up a system to guard the gates and gaps in the walls while repairs were made by groups of men from Israel's different tribes.

All this activity got the attention of officials in the surrounding area. They felt threatened by a stronger city controlled by the Jews, and they claimed the Jews were rebelling against the king. They plotted to attack the city, and Nehemiah increased the security around the city. Everybody contributed what they could. Some worked while others stood guard armed with weapons and trumpets to blow in case of an attack. The poor in the city worked as well, and they did not have to pay any taxes or interest on their debts because they weren't making money doing their normal jobs. Nehemiah made sure everybody treated the poor fairly. His enemies kept trying new ways to trick him into doing something wrong, but Nehemiah wisely managed each situation and avoided getting in trouble.

The wall and gates were completed in 52 days. All the people in the region were impressed with the strength of the Jews and their God, and it restored respect and prestige to the Jewish nation among those living in the region.

When the city walls and gates were secure, Nehemiah set up a system for people to guard the walls near their homes. Jews from the countryside filled open areas of the city, and within the safer city, people felt more secure.

Nehemiah also worked with Ezra to strengthen the religious activities of the Jews. The people got back into the habit of confessing their sins, making sacrifices and offerings, supporting the work of the Levites, and celebrating their festivals just as the Israelites did during the days of Moses. The people also pledged not to let their children marry anybody who was not a Jew.

After dedicating the walls in a big celebration, Nehemiah went back home to Susa. When he returned to Jerusalem years later, he found the Jews had stopped practicing their religion properly. They worked and sold goods on the Sabbath. Levites had left to take jobs somewhere else because tithes were not given to support them and other Temple workers. Foreigners had offices in the Temple courtyard. All this made Nehemiah very angry. He threw out the furniture owned by the foreigners, closed Jerusalem's gates on the Sabbath, and reminded the people that those who ignored God's commands were punished by being captured.

Malachi

The prophet Malachi reinforced Nehemiah's warnings because the Jews were not relying on God. These were their sins: offering imperfect animals in sacrifices, marrying non-Jews, being unfaithful in marriage, neglecting the tithe, not taking care of widows and orphans, and mistreating the poor and foreigners. Malachi also offered insight into things to come in the future. Blessings and judgment would come, sometimes through a painful process. Through him, God said to the Jews:

> I won't change the way I deal with you: I will bless you if you honor me and obey my commands; I will punish you if you are arrogant and disobey. I will be compassionate if you return to me. I will send my messenger to prepare the way before me. Suddenly, the one you seek will come to the Temple — the messenger of the agreement will come. He will be like a refiner's fire or a soap. He will purify the Levites the way gold and silver are refined. Then the Lord will have people who will bring offerings in righteousness, and their offerings will be acceptable to the Lord as they were previously. I will also strike the land with total destruction.

(The story continues in chapter 14.)

CHAPTER 13

UNIQUE BOOKS IN THE OLD TESTAMENT

Several books of the Bible provide lessons about living correctly, such as dealing with problems and loving others, rather than discussing historical events.

- The books of Proverbs and Ecclesiastes are about wisdom. Proverbs provides short sayings and stories about how humans should live correctly. In Ecclesiastes, Solomon points out that real life is much more complicated than giving simple truths about the consequences of human behavior.
- Jōb is a story about why a person who has faith in God and leads a good life still experiences pain and suffering. The story ends with an unexpected twist.
- Jonah is a short biography of a man called by God to speak truth to a dangerous enemy. When he fails to do so, he suffers unusual consequences.
- The Song of Solomon is a dialogue between a young woman and her lover.
- Psalms is a collection of poems that reflect strong emotions and thoughts about events that took place among the Israelites.

Proverbs

Most of Proverbs was written by King Solomon. A proverb is a statement of a general truth and often deals with the right and wrong way to do things. In general, the proverbs indicate that those who follow these truths will avoid evil and be rewarded; those who don't follow their advice will suffer negative consequences.

Positive and negative statements are often coupled to provide a contrast between good and evil. Sometimes these are just one sentence long. For example, the last verse of chapter 3 states, "The wise inherit honor but fools inherit dishonor" (Proverbs 3:35). In other cases, there are clusters of proverbs that discuss the same idea. Many of the sayings and short stories deal with money, justice, and sexual morality (many verses talk about avoiding the temptations of sex-related sins and making money the wrong way). The book has many reminders to its readers that they must constantly pursue wisdom and avoid doing evil things.

The book starts by saying that wisdom comes from God. So, a wise person behaves in an upright, righteous, and godly manner. The last chapter focuses on the qualities of a good wife at that time. Many of the verses in the 31 chapters make the same point. Here are examples of some of the proverbs — they come from the chapters and verses that are noted.

Chapter 1:7, 20–23, 33

> Respect for the Lord is the beginning of wisdom; fools despise wisdom and instruction. Wisdom shouts in the street, she lifts her voice in the square. At the entrance of the gates in the city she says, "How long will you naive ones love being simple-minded? How long will you scoffers delight yourselves in mocking others and you fools hate knowledge? If you had responded to my rebuke, I would have poured out my spirit on you and made my words known to you. Those who listen to me will live securely and not be afraid of the dread of evil."

Chapter 4:23–27

> Guard your heart because everything you do flows from it. Keep your speech clean and honest. Let your eyes look straight ahead, and think carefully about the paths of your feet. Don't turn to the right or the left — keep your foot from evil.

Chapter 6:6–11

> Lazy one, look at the ant and see its ways. It has no chief, officer, or ruler, yet it prepares its food in the summer and gathers food in the harvest. How long will you lie

down and do nothing? When will you rise from your sleep? With a little sleep, a little slumber, and a little folding of the hands to rest, your poverty will come in like a beggar and your need like an armed intruder.

Chapter 10:1–5, 8–9, 12–13

A wise son makes a father glad, but a foolish son brings grief to his mother.
Money earned the wrong way does not produce a profit.
The Lord won't allow the righteous to hunger but rejects the craving of the wicked.
Those who don't work become poor, but those who work become rich.
Those who gather in summer act wisely; those who sleep in harvest are disgraceful.
The wise will receive commands, but a talking fool will be ruined.
Those who walk in integrity walk securely, but those who do evil things will be discovered.
Hatred stirs up strife, but love covers every transgression.
Wisdom is found on the lips of those who think carefully, but a rod is used on the back of those who lack understanding.

Chapter 15:1–4

A gentle answer turns away wrath, but a harsh word stirs up anger.
Wise people provide useful knowledge, but the mouths of fools spout folly.
The eyes of the Lord are in every place, watching the evil and the good.
A soothing tongue is a tree of life, but perverse words crush the spirit.

Chapter 22 (excerpts)

A good name is more desirable than great wealth. Being respected is better than gold or silver.
The rich and the poor have this in common: the Lord made all of them.
Train children how they should go; when they are old, they won't depart from it.

Those who are generous will be blessed, for they give food to the poor.

Those who oppress the poor to make more for themselves or give to the rich will end up in poverty.

Chapter 25:21–22

If your enemy is hungry, feed them; if they are thirsty, give them water to drink. This will heap burning coals on their heads,3 and the Lord will reward you.

* * * * *

Ecclesiastes

The book of Ecclesiastes contains the reflections of a wise king, probably King Solomon later in his reign. In contrast to Proverbs, wisdom is viewed more realistically — there is neither blind optimism for doing right nor skeptical pessimism for doing wrong. Instead, life is seen with its complexities and frustrations. Like life itself, the structure and content of the book's 12 chapters are disjointed, rambling in different directions and often repetitious. This may be due to the likelihood that the book had several authors.

The book begins with the Teacher exclaiming, "Everything is meaningless!" The endless cycles of life and nature never seem to change anything on earth. Gaining wisdom and knowledge brings sorrow and grief. Both have their limitations, and creating change to improve life is like "chasing after the wind — nothing is gained under the sun."

---

3 This phrase has several meanings. It can be taken literally within the context of that culture, in which a person provides a large amount of charcoal to rescue a neighbor's dwindling fire. In ancient times, some people carried things on their heads. The phrase also has a deeper meaning, in which a person's extravagant generosity toward an enemy makes the enemy think about how to treat others. The result is to increase the chances of a more peaceful relationship between the two people. The phrase does *not* mean hurting your enemy by burning their head in some way.

The Teacher tried to find happiness in different ways. He first pursued earthly pleasures — drinking, having sex, working hard, acquiring materials and wealth, and obtaining power. But when he reflected on his actions, none of these made him happy. Next, he thought about the pursuit of wisdom and the consequences of sinfulness, but he realized that both the wise and fools die the same death. The possessions acquired during life are passed on when a person dies to others who may be either wise or foolish, so the fruits of a life's labors may be squandered. Why pursue what you cannot keep?

The Teacher concluded that the best people can do to find true happiness is to honor God, enjoy their food and drinks, do good, and find meaningful work. He also concluded that instead of following fixed rules in every situation, the right behavior depends on the specific circumstances of each context — there is a right time for every human experience.

> A time to be born and a time to die, a time to plant and a time to reap,
> a time to kill and a time to heal, a time to tear down and a time to build up,
> a time to cry and a time to laugh, a time to mourn and a time to dance,
> a time to throw stones and a time to gather them,
> a time to embrace and a time to stay apart,
> a time to search and a time to give up, a time to keep and a time to throw away,
> a time to tear and a time to sew, a time to be silent and a time to speak,
> a time to love and a time to hate, a time for war and a time for peace.

The Teacher admits good can come from negative experiences, but he still prefers the attributes of wisdom, even though life can be unfair. He concludes by encouraging people to enjoy life to the fullest, work hard, and embrace the unexpected events of life as opportunities given by God to learn and grow.

* * * * *

Jōb

Job is a long story that includes many conversations about faith, obedience, rewards, punishments, good and evil, and why bad things happen to faithful people. God's loving and fair nature is questioned through a dialogue among the main characters: God and Satan, Job and his friends, and God and Job. The book is not a true story (there are no clear authors, dates, or locations).

The book begins by describing Job as a wealthy man living with his large family and 11,000 animals. He is "the greatest man in the east and is blameless, upright, faithful to God, and always careful to avoid doing evil." He makes sacrifices to God just in case members of his family have sinned.

Satan tells God that Job is only good and faithful because God blessed him in every way. Satan challenges God to take away all of Job's blessings to see if Job will still love God, saying that Job will curse God when the blessings are removed. God agrees to let Satan torment Job but God forbids Satan from killing him.

Job and his family soon start suffering disasters. Job gets a message that an enemy has stolen his animals and killed the servants tending the herd. Then fire from heaven kills his sheep and the servants tending the flocks. Then a different enemy steals all his camels and killed all the servants except for the messenger. Finally, he hears that the house where his children were eating collapsed from a strong wind, killing everybody.

After hearing what happened, Job tears off his clothes and worships God by saying, "I came naked from my mother's womb, and I will leave the world with nothing. The Lord gives and the Lord takes away. Blessed be the name of the Lord." Job did not sin or blame God for these events.

God reminds Satan about how Job stayed faithful even after losing everything. Satan makes a new accusation, saying that Job will curse God if his own body suffers. God agrees to let Satan bring pain and sickness to Job, and Job's body develops painful sores from his head to his toes. Job's wife asks him, "Why do you still live the right way? Curse God and die!" Job replies, "Should we just accept good from God and not trouble?" And Job does not sin or curse God.

When three of Job's friends hear what has happened, they visit him to comfort him. They barely recognize him, and they weep loudly and then sit silently with Job for a week.

Job breaks the silence and the four men have a long conversation. Job talked about all his problems and that he wishes he had never been born. But his friends say that Job's afflictions are due to sins Job has committed and urge him to repent and obey. That way, he will gain back God's favor. The three friends say that God does not punish good people for nothing.

Job disagrees and says he has done nothing wrong. The friends mock Job's attitude and claims of innocence, but Job insists he has not done anything to deserve any of the afflictions. As the friends blame the victim, Job gets very irritated at their false accusations of his sinfulness and their self-righteous confidence in their simple answers to address his situation. He tells them to shut up!

Nevertheless, Job is confused about how his life changed so quickly without committing any sin. He wonders how people can please a God who can be both just and forgiving to those who deserve punishment. God's ways are beyond human understanding. Job is sad about his life but believes God will eventually say he is innocent. His experience proves that suffering is not automatically linked to sinfulness and evil. And even if he dies, he says he will live again. "I know my redeemer lives and that in the end, God will still be standing. After my body is destroyed, I will still see God." Job does not know why certain things happen — sometimes the wicked prosper, life can be unfair. But his faith brings him hope that God's love and judgment will result in a "not guilty" verdict for him in the next life.

One the friends then says Job suffers because he neglected the poor. But Job insists these accusations are untrue. He has obeyed God's commands, comforted the hopeless, and helped the powerless and those in need. Job is frustrated at not being treated fairly — he has not committed any offense. God has the power to change things but is silent. Job maintains his innocence and mocks the younger men who think they know everything. "My tongue will not speak lies, and I will never admit you are right. I will live the right way and maintain my innocence and not admit to doing something I have not done." Job is a broken man and suffers as he listens to his false accusers.

Another friend arrives and criticizes the three friends for accusing Job without providing any evidence of wrongdoing. But he also says God will not reward those who don't repent and will not answer when wicked people cry out.

All this time God has been listening to Job and his friends as they justify their views to each other. God then enters the conversation and asks Job many questions that expose Job's ignorance about how the world works and God's power. For example, God says, "Where were you when I laid the earth's foundation? Who marked off its dimensions? You're so smart, surely you know! Where do light and darkness live? What about the rain and wind — where do they come from?" Job is overwhelmed and cannot answer God's questions.

God then turns to Job's friends in anger for incorrectly saying that suffering only occurs due to sin and that justice only occurs during one's lifetime. Easy answers may ease the conscience of the messenger, but they don't apply to complex situations. Ironically, Job's friends ignored his pain and had no empathy as they tried to help him.

The story ends very quickly without giving important details. God honors Job's humility and faithfulness and blesses him again with more than he originally had. But the story does not include anything about the deal between God and Satan. In the end, good prevails against evil because Job does not waver. Defeated again, Satan does not appear to God with another wager. Also, the story never explains why faithful followers suffer or why the wicked prosper, so readers are left to think about the answers for themselves. Life is unpredictable when good and evil forces coexist. God's ways are not our ways, God's timing is not our timing. Faithfulness to God and our response to the events in our lives matter the most. The crises of life can be used for good—people are humans developed and shaped in difficult times.

* * * * *

Jonah

In this brief story, God calls the prophet Jonah to speak truth and judgment to the people of Nineveh, the capital of the Assyrian empire. The story has few details, and its two pages can be read very quickly, yet it has many universal lessons. The story relates to human disobedience, the consequences of not following God's call, how nature is sometimes used to show God's power, bigotry toward foreigners, God's grace and forgiveness for all people, and how we are disappointed when God shows love to those who we think don't deserve it.

We first find that Jonah was afraid to go preach judgment to Nineveh. Instead of traveling east and risking death, he takes a boat to Spain (2,000 miles in the other direction). A strong storm threatens to sink the ship, and the crew call to their gods to save the ship. The captain tells Jonah to pray to his god.

The storm is so unusual that the crew knows somebody on the ship is cursed. They discover it is Jonah, and he explains that he is an Israelite who is disobeying God. He says the storm will stop if they throw him overboard, and when the crew does this, the storm immediately stops. This which makes everybody on board worship the Israelite God.

Jonah gets caught in seaweed and is swallowed by a large whale. He spends three days inside the whale and nearly dies. Jonah promises God that he will go to Nineveh if he survives. The whale gets sick and vomits Jonah onto land.

Eventually Jonah goes to Nineveh. He tells the people that the city will be destroyed because of their evil ways. The people believe his message and change their ways. The king orders everybody in the city to pray and stop their wickedness.

When seeing how the people of Nineveh respond, God shows compassion and does not destroy the city. This makes Jonah very angry — he wants the enemy to suffer. He tells God, "I know You are gracious and compassionate, slow to anger and generous in Your love, a God who does not like sending calamity. Lord, take away my life, for I'd rather die than live."

Jonah goes up a hill near the city to watch what will happen. A worm eats the plant he used for shade and he gets very sunburned. He feels sorry for himself and says, "I'm so angry I'd rather be dead than alive." God tells Jonah, "You are worried about not having shade? Shouldn't I be concerned about a city with more than 120,000 children who are innocent and ignorant?" Jonah lacks love and forgiveness, even though the God he follows is loving and forgiving.

* * * * *

Song of Solomon

The author of the Song of Solomon is unknown. The writer uses a dialogue written in poetry to describe a perfect love story between a young woman and her boyfriend. The romance has no conflict, and the author uses vivid images of plants and animals to describe the couple's attraction to each other. The story affirms that physical love is a blessing within a marriage.

The short story describes the couple. The young maiden is tan from working in a vineyard, and the man is well-respected. He falls in love with her at first sight and thinks about his wedding day with her. They long to be with each other and think about the features of the other's beautiful body and movements. Although there are many eligible women around him, she is unique in having both external and internal beauty — this humble and sincere worker is the only one for him. She dreams about him and is sad when she wakes up and finds that he is not there.

When they get married and leave town together, they show their love for one another. Later she says to him:

> Place me as a necklace hanging next to your heart,
> Like a bracelet on your arm, exposed for all to see,
> For love is as strong as death; its jealousy as unyielding
> as the grave.
> Love burns like a blazing fire, like a divine flame.

* * * * *

Psalms

Poetry was used in some books of the Bible, and some books were written totally in poetry form. The book of Psalms has 150 poems written by David and other authors about 3,000 years ago. They reflect strong emotions and thoughts related to what took place among the Israelites. Most relate in some way to the concepts of good and evil. About half of the psalms deal with prayers during times of trouble, and some simply praise God. Some psalms were meant to be accompanied with music. Rather than using words that rhyme, the psalms often contain repeating ideas.

Three complete psalms appear below. The authors usually used male pronouns and nouns (he, his, him, man) to describe God and all people.

Psalm 1 *(The Righteous and Wicked Contrasted)*

Blessed is the man who does not walk in the counsel of
the wicked,
Nor stands in the path with sinners, nor sits in seats with
scoffers!
But his delight is in the law of the Lord,
And he meditates on His laws day and night.
He will be like a tree firmly planted by streams of water,
Which yields its fruit in its season
And whose leaf does not wither.
Whatever he does prospers.
Not so with the wicked! They are like chaff the wind
blows away.
Therefore the wicked will not stand in the judgment,
Nor will sinners assemble with the righteous.
For the Lord knows the way of the righteous,
But the way of the wicked will perish.

Psalm 23 *(A Psalm of David)*

The Lord is my shepherd, I have everything I need.
He makes me lie down in green pastures;
He leads me beside quiet waters.
He restores my soul;
He leads me in the paths of righteousness for His
name's sake.
Even though I walk through the valley of the shadow
of death,
I will not fear any evil, for You are with me;
Your rod and staff comfort me.
You prepare a table before me in the presence of my
enemies.
You have anointed my head with oil;
My cup overflows.
Surely goodness and mercy will follow me all the days
of my life,
And I will dwell in the house of the Lord forever.

Psalm 100 *(A Psalm of Thanksgiving)*

Make a joyful noise to the Lord, all you lands!
Serve the Lord with gladness, come before His presence
with singing.

Know that the Lord is God; He has made us, not we
ourselves;
We are His people and the sheep of His pasture.
Enter into His gates with thanksgiving, and into His
courts with praise.
Be thankful to Him, and bless His name.
For the Lord is good and His mercy is everlasting,
And His truth endures to all generations.

PART TWO

THE NEW TESTAMENT

CHAPTER 14

THE MESSIAH ARRIVES

Two Babies Grow Up and Announce a New Era

Background

Malachi's prophecies were written in 420 BC and are the last record of the prophets in the Old Testament. Many Jews lived outside of Palestine, mainly in Babylonia and Egypt, and their communities became quite large. To maintain their faith in God, these communities set up places of worship (synagogues) that were led by a religious scholar (rabbi) who read and explained the scriptures to the Israelites.

During the 400 years that followed Malachi's prophecies, important events took place that influenced the Jews.

- The Greeks, led by Alexander the Great, conquered many parts of the world, including Palestine. The Greeks brought new ways of thinking about the world through their religious and political ideas, and the Greek language became widely spoken and written (Hebrew and Aramaic were also used by the Jews). Jewish communities enjoyed peace during Alexander's reign.

- After Alexander died, Judaism was banned. A few Jews rebelled because they were required to make sacrifices to other gods. A revolt spread throughout Palestine, and the Greeks were eventually expelled in 142 BC. (Hanukkah celebrates this victory.)

- The Romans conquered Palestine and took control of Jerusalem in 63 BC. They did not tolerate rebellion and they executed many priests and Jewish leaders. In 37 BC Herod the Great was declared the king of the Jews and started constructing many buildings, including a larger Temple in Jerusalem. When he died in 4 BC, Rome put other leaders in his place.

The People of Palestine

During this 400-year period, Greek ways of thinking became attractive to many of the Jews, and differences emerged among the Jews about how they should live in a world dominated by Greek ideas while preserving their faith.

- The *Pharisees* were a small but influential group who focused on strict obedience to God's commands. They also wanted to be separate from the world rather than "mingle" with nonbelievers. They stressed being very religious and held a rigid view of right and wrong. Staying away from foreign influence was very important to them, and they followed additional rules to make sure they did not come close to breaking any of God's essential commands. They were proud and expressed their religious beliefs to others in very visible ways.
- The *Sadducees* were another small but influential group, but they focused on morality and did not believe in supernatural powers. They accepted foreign ideas, especially those of the Greeks. The Sadducees were typically wealthy and well-educated and did not follow the additional rules the Pharisees followed.
- The *Essenes* focused on self-control and withdrawing from the world. This small group retreated to remote parts of the region, mainly into the desert near the Salt (Dead) Sea.
- *Zealots* wanted to use physical force to ensure no foreign power controlled the lives of God's people. They were willing to die for their cause.

Other types of people lived in Palestine. Some were labeled based on where they lived, such as the impure Samaritans and Galileans who were hated because they had often intermarried with non-Jews or were not Jewish at all. (Galilee was the northern part of Palestine, Samaria was the central part, and Judea was the southern part that was previously known as Judah.) Galileans were also known for being rebellious against foreign authority. Some groups were distinct based on their profession, such as the scribes, who wrote important documents (often religious in nature), and members of the Sanhedrin, a large and diverse group of leaders who watched over the religious life of the Jews and had the power to punish Jews. Some were known for their allegiance: Herodians were Jews who followed Roman traditions and beliefs, Hellenists were Jews who followed Greek traditions and beliefs, and Nazarites still existed (those taking a vow to dedicate themselves to God).

Because of the immigration of non-Jews into Palestine and the emigration of Jews out of Palestine, most of the people living in Palestine 2,000 years ago were not Jews, and more than 80% of the Jews lived elsewhere. Palestine did not have a good system of road, and it was not easy to travel in the area. People usually walked or used a donkey or mule. A few primitive inns existed along the roads, so many travelers relied on their network of friends and family for lodging as they traveled.

Many of the prophets had written about a Servant-King who would come and bring the nation back to glory. The Jews wondered when God would send this leader and why it was taking so long. Events in the region made the Jews think that somebody would deliver them from oppression. Roman brutality reminded them of when their ancestors were mistreated in Egypt and when they were conquered by the Assyrians and Babylonians. It had been 400 years since they last heard from a prophet about somebody who would suddenly appear. They watched closely for the coming Messiah (*Christ* in Greek), the Anointed One who would come and save them as Rome crushed Jewish rebel leaders and executed them slowly by nailing them alive to crosses that dotted the region.

The Life of Jesus

The rest of this chapter and chapters 15–18 describe the important events that took place in the life of Jesus and his main teachings as they were recorded by four men. Two authors were eyewitnesses who followed Jesus closely and were among the first disciples (John was a fisherman and

Matthew was a tax collector). The other two authors were Mark, a close friend of Peter, and Luke, a Gentile doctor who investigated the stories about Jesus told by others. Mark's account was the first one written, and John's account was written last and includes many stories and details that the others did not include. Each author had a different audience and their own style and perspectives, so the accounts are somewhat different. Collectively, they are known as the "gospels" (good news about Jesus).

A Baby Is Born

In 5 BC when Herod was the Roman king in charge of Judah, a priest named Zechariah and his wife Elizabeth had grown old without having any children, even though they often prayed for a son. When Zechariah was burning incense in the Temple, he was startled by an angel and became afraid. But the angel told him, "Don't be afraid. God has heard your prayer. Your wife will have a son, and you will call him John. He will never drink wine, and the Holy Spirit will fill him. He will bring many disobedient people of Israel to the Lord, and he will prepare the people for the Lord."

Zechariah asked, "How will happen? I'm an old man, and my wife is also old." The angel replied, "I am Gabriel. I was sent to tell you this good news. But you won't be able to speak until the child is born because you doubted me."

When Zechariah came out of the Temple, he couldn't speak. He used hand motions to described to others near the Temple what happened and that he could not speak. He told Elizabeth about it the same way.

When Elizabeth was six months pregnant, the same angel appeared to a young teenager named Mary who lived in Nazareth, a town in Galilee (about 70 miles north of Jerusalem). She was engaged to Joseph, a descendant of King David. The angel said to Mary, "Greetings, you are highly favored! The Lord is with you!"

Mary was confused and afraid when she heard this from a complete stranger who had suddenly appeared. But the angel said, "Don't be afraid. You will give birth to a son and are to call him Jesus. He will be great and be called the Son of the Most High. God will give him the throne of King David, his ancestor. He will reign over Jacob's descendants forever."

Mary asked the angel how it could happen — she was still a virgin and not yet married. The angel replied, "God's spirit will be the father, and your relative Elizabeth is pregnant, even though she is very old."

Mary was amazed that such an impossible thing would happen to Elizabeth. She immediately went to see Elizabeth. When Mary greeted Elizabeth, the baby inside her jumped and God gave Elizabeth insight into what had happened to Mary. She said to Mary, "Blessed are you among women and the child of your womb! I am so blessed that the mother of the Lord has come to me." Mary stayed with Elizabeth for three months until her baby boy was born.

When it came time to circumcise the child, everybody thought he would be named Zechariah after his father (that was the tradition). But Elizabeth said his name would be John. Her neighbors and relatives were puzzled – nobody in their families was named John. They turned to Zechariah and asked him to write the child's name on a tablet. He wrote John and was immediately able to talk, and he explained what had happened to him. He also made predictions about the boy's life.

> God has come to save us, one from the house of David that the prophets told us about long ago to remember the covenant made with our father Abraham. He will rescue us from the hand of our enemies and enable us to serve God without fear. My child will be called a prophet of the Most High because he will go on before the Lord to prepare the way for God, to give people the knowledge of being saved through the forgiveness of their sins.

Another Baby Is Born

When Mary returned home, her fiancé Joseph found out she was pregnant. He was a faithful man and he considered divorcing her quietly (they were legally bound to be married). But as he thought about it, an angel appeared to him in a dream and said, "Don't be afraid to take Mary as your wife. The Holy Spirit of God is the father. She will have a son, and you are to name him Jesus, for he will save people from their sins."

This had been predicted by the prophet Isaiah: "The virgin will conceive and bear a son, and he will be called Immanuel" (meaning "God with us"). When Joseph woke up, he did what the angel said — he took Mary home as his wife.

When Mary was about to give birth, the Roman emperor Caesar Augustus ordered that a census be taken. Everybody had to go to their hometown where they would be counted. Mary and Joseph traveled south from Nazareth to Bethlehem, a town close to Jerusalem. The town was full of people returning to be counted, and there was no place for Mary and Joseph to stay. There was space to sleep in a barn, and that is where Mary gave birth to her son. She wrapped him up using long strips of cloth, and she used a manger (a feeding trough for animals) as a crib.

That night, an angel appeared to shepherds who were watching their flocks nearby. They were very frightened, but the angel said to them, "Don't be afraid. I bring you good news that will make everyone happy! A Savior was born today in Bethlehem. He is the Messiah, the Lord. Go and see him. He is the one wrapped in cloth and lying in a manger." Then suddenly, many other angels appeared and boldly shouted, "Glory to God in the highest heaven and on earth. He will bring peace to those he favors."

Then the angels disappeared. The shepherds all agreed they should go find the baby. They hurried into town and found Mary and Joseph and the baby. After they saw him, they told others what had happened, and everybody was amazed when they heard their story.

When the child was eight days old, Mary and Joseph had him circumcised and named him Jesus. They took him to the Temple in Jerusalem and presented him to the Lord with the required sacrifices. An old and faithful man named Simeon was in the Temple. God had told him that he would not die until he saw the Messiah. When Jesus appeared in the Temple with his parents, Simeon was overcome with emotion. He took Jesus in his arms and said, "Lord, you can take me now in peace. As you have promised, I have seen your salvation that you have prepared for all nations: a light for the Gentiles and the glory of your people Israel."

Simeon blessed them and told Mary, "This child will cause many people of Israel to fall and rise and will be spoken against so their thoughts are revealed."

Three Wise Men

Before Jesus was born, priests from Persia (Magi) who studied the stars saw a bright light in the sky that convinced them that a new king was born in Judah. They traveled hundreds of miles and went to Jerusalem to ask King Herod where the Jews' king was born. The thought of another king worried Herod and other leaders in Jerusalem. Herod found out from the Jewish leaders that the Messiah was to be born in Bethlehem, and he told the Magi to find the boy and report back to him about where he was. Herod told the Magi that he wanted to worship the boy himself.

The bright star hovered over Bethlehem a few miles away. The Magi went and found Jesus with his parents, and they fell down and worshipped the baby. They also gave the baby gifts of gold, frankincense, and myrrh. Before they left, they were warned in a dream to use a different route to return home and not tell Herod where Jesus was staying.

After the Magi left, Joseph had a dream. He was to take Mary and Jesus to Egypt and stay there. Herod was looking for Jesus and wanted to kill him. Joseph woke up in the night and immediately left for Egypt.

When Herod realized the Magi had left without telling him where Jesus was, he was furious. He gave orders to kill all the boys in Bethlehem and its vicinity who were two years old or younger. (Jeremiah had predicted this would happen.)

The family stayed in Egypt until Herod died. This fulfilled what the prophet Hosea said: "I called my son out of Egypt." Joseph and Mary then returned to their home in Nazareth.

Jesus grew up strong and was filled with wisdom. His ancestors went back many generations and included Abraham, Isaac, Jacob, Judah, Boaz, Jesse, David, Solomon, Rehoboam, Hezekiah, Amos, and Josiah. Four women, including Rahab and Ruth (both foreigners), were also among his ancestors.

The Family Visits Jerusalem

Every year the family went to Jerusalem for the Festival of the Passover. When Jesus was 12 years old, Mary and Joseph accidentally left him behind after going to the festival. They traveled for a day with their friends and relatives before they realized Jesus was missing. They couldn't find him in their caravan, so they went back to Jerusalem to look for him. They found him three days later in the Temple as he sat among the teachers, listening to them and asking questions. Everyone who heard him was amazed at his understanding, insights, and answers, even though he was still a young boy.

Mary was both relieved and frustrated when she found him. She said to Jesus, "Why have you done this to us? Your father and I have been very worried."

Jesus replied, "Why did you spend so much time looking for me? Didn't you know I had to be in my Father's house?" But Mary and Joseph didn't know what he meant. They all went home to Nazareth, and Jesus was an obedient child. He grew in wisdom and size, and he pleased God and everybody who knew him.

John Emerges from the Wilderness

When John became an adult, he lived in the wilderness. When he was 30 years old, he came out of the desert. He wore strange clothes and ate strange food. He went into the countryside along the Jordan River and told people to change their ways and ask for their sins to be forgiven. John told the people, "Repent, for the kingdom of heaven is coming." His arrival had been predicted by the prophet Isaiah, who wrote: "A voice calls in the wilderness, 'Prepare the way for the Lord, make his paths straight and the rough places smooth. Everybody will see God's saving work.'"[4]

Thousands of people came to see John. After they confessed their sins, John baptized them in the river. He baptized thousands of people and became known as John the Baptist. When he saw Pharisees and Sadducees coming to the river to see what was happening, John talked to these religious leaders harshly.

> You poisonous snakes! Who warned you to flee from the wrath to come? Produce fruit that shows you have repented. Don't think you can say to yourselves, "We have Abraham as our father." I tell you, God can raise children of Abraham from these stones. The ax is ready to cut the root of the trees. Every tree that doesn't produce good fruit will be cut down and burned.

Scribes and Levites from Jerusalem came and asked him if he was the Messiah. John said no, then he quoted Isaiah, saying he was "the voice crying in the wilderness, 'Make straight the way for the Lord.'" He was saying to them that the Messiah was coming soon.

When the crowds asked him what they should do next, John said, "Anyone who has two shirts should share one with a person who has none. Anyone who has food should share in the same way." When the despised tax collectors who worked for the Romans came to be baptized and asked what they should do, John told them not to collect any more than they were required to collect. Soldiers asked him what they should do. He replied, "Don't force people to give you money or accuse people falsely — be content with what you are paid."

---

[4] Whenever a king traveled at that time, he would send workers ahead to ensure the route was direct and smooth, thus making the king's trip faster and more comfortable.

The people were all wondering if John was the Messiah. John responded:

> I baptize you with water, but another will come soon who is more powerful than I am. I'm not good enough to carry his sandals. He will baptize you with the Holy Spirit and fire. He will gather the wheat into his barn, but he will burn up all the chaff.

Jesus was also 30 years old and went to the Jordan River to be baptized by John. As relatives who were born at about the same time, the two men knew each other well. When John saw Jesus coming, he said aloud, "Look, it's the Lamb of God who takes away the sins of the world!" Turning to Jesus, John said, "Why are you coming to me? You should be baptizing me!"

Jesus replied, "This needs to happen in order for me to fulfill all the signs of righteousness."

So John baptized Jesus, and when Jesus came out of the water, the sky opened, and God's Spirit came down in the form of a dove and landed on him. A voice from above said, "This is my Son. I love him and am pleased with him." The people who were there thought an angel had spoken.

Jesus Is Tested and Starts to Preach

Many people fasted and prayed after being baptized, and Jesus was no different. He left the river full of the Holy Spirit and was led by the Spirit into the wilderness. After eating nothing for 40 days, he was very hungry, weak, and vulnerable.

Then Satan came as an evil spirit and tempted him. "If you really are the Son of God, tell this stone to become bread."

Jesus answered, "It is written: 'We are not to live on bread alone, but on the words of God.'"

Satan led Jesus to the highest point of the Temple in Jerusalem and said, "If you are the Son of God, throw yourself down. For it is written: 'God will command your angels to guard you carefully. They will lift you up so you won't strike your foot against a stone.'"

Jesus answered, "It is also written, 'Do not put the Lord your God to a test.'"

Satan then led Jesus to a high place and showed him all the kingdoms of the world, saying, "I will give you power to control all of this. It's all mine, and I can give it to anybody. If you bow down and worship me, it will all be yours."

Jesus answered, "I order you to leave, for it is written: 'Worship and serve only the Lord your God.'" After these three temptations failed, Satan withdrew and waited for another chance to tempt or trap Jesus.

While Jesus was in the wilderness fasting, John rebuked Herod Antipas (the son of Herod the Great) because of all the evil things he had done. Herod had John arrested and thrown into prison. When Jesus found out what happened to John, he started preaching John's message, "Repent, for the kingdom of heaven is about to come." Preaching in that area was another prediction by Isaiah about the coming of the Messiah.

Later, Jesus went back to Nazareth where he had been raised as a child and worked as an adult. One Sabbath day, he went to the synagogue as he usually did. Everybody knew him, and he stood up in front of the congregation and unrolled the scroll. He found the place that contained Isaiah's prophecies and read this to the assembly: "The Spirit of the Lord is on me, because God has anointed me to proclaim good news to the poor. God has sent me to proclaim freedom for the prisoners and recovery of sight for the blind, to set the oppressed free and proclaim the year of the Jubilee." This well-recognized part of Isaiah's writings was about the Messiah. He rolled up the scroll, gave it to the attendant, and sat down. Everybody watched him closely to see what would happen next. He said, "Today this scripture is fulfilled."

Everybody was saying nice things about him and all were amazed at his wise words. They wondered if this well-spoken man was the same Jesus they knew who was a carpenter and the son of Joseph and Mary. But their happiness quickly changed to anger when Jesus scorned them and other Jews.

> You ask me to do here in my hometown what you heard I have done in Capernaum. But no prophet is welcomed in his hometown. Elijah didn't help any of the Israelites but instead helped a widow in another country. And there were many in Israel with leprosy when Elisha was the prophet, but only Naaman, the Syrian, was cleansed.

Everybody in the synagogue was furious. How could a person who implied he was the Messiah show a preference for foreigners! They followed him as he walked out and to the top of the town's highest hill, a place where people were taken to be stoned. But when Jesus got to the top of the hill, he turned around and walked right back through the crowd and down the hill. Nobody touched him, and he never performed any miracles in Nazareth.

Jesus then went to Capernaum and taught in the synagogue on the Sabbath. Everybody was amazed at his teaching and how he understood the scriptures. A man in the synagogue who was possessed by a demon yelled to him in a loud voice, "Go away! What do you want from us? Have you come to destroy us? I know you are the Holy One of God!"

Jesus said firmly to the man, "Be quiet and come out of him!" The demon threw the man to the ground and came out without injuring him. All the people were amazed! His orders had authority and power over evil spirits, and the demons he confronted came out of people! News about Jesus and his powers spread quickly throughout the region.

Jesus Calls His First Followers

Jesus was now attracting large crowds who wanted to hear his views and see his amazing powers. When he was preaching on the banks of the Sea of Galilee, the crowd got so large that he was pressed up against the water. He saw two empty boats on the shoreline and pushed one of them into the water. He got in the boat and spoke to the crowd as he sat in the boat floating close to shore.

The boat belonged to brothers named Simon and Andrew. When Jesus finished talking, he got out of the boat and told them to take the boat into the deep water and put down their nets. Simon replied, "Master, we worked all night and caught nothing. But we will do it." When they did, they caught so many fish that their nets started to rip. They called to their two partners on shore (brothers named James and John) and had them bring their boat to help haul in all the fish. These fishermen caught so many fish that both boats started to sink.

Everybody was amazed at the size of the catch. They wondered how a carpenter would know so much about fishing and also understand the scriptures so well. When Simon came on shore with all the fish, he fell at the feet of Jesus and said, "Depart from me, Lord. I'm a sinful man." Jesus told Simon not to be afraid. He gave Simon the name Peter (meaning "rock") and told him he would soon be catching men, not fish. In fact, Jesus told Peter that he would be the rock on which a new kingdom was to be founded, and the powers of death would not overcome it. All four men left their boats and nets in the hands of their parents and followed Jesus.

The next day, Jesus told Philip, a friend of Peter and Andrew, to follow him. Philip told his friend Bartholomew about Jesus, who wondered if anything good could come out of Nazareth. Philip said, "Come and see!"

Jesus saw the two men approaching and said about Bartholomew, "Here is a man who is honest and does not deceive others." Bartholomew was impressed that Jesus knew him well even though they had never met. Jesus now had six men who would follow him closely. Such people were known as "disciples" — they dedicated themselves to learning from a wise teacher, the way an apprentice is guided by a master. (It was common for wise teachers to have people follow and learn from them.)

Jesus went to the home of Simon Peter whose mother-in-law had a high fever. Peter asked Jesus to help her. Jesus commanded the fever to leave her. She got up at once and began serving all of them. Word spread that Jesus could heal the sick, and that evening, people started bringing him those who were sick in some way. He laid his hands on each one and healed them.

The next morning, Jesus went out to be alone. People found him and tried to keep him from leaving. But Jesus said he had come to preach good news of the kingdom of God in many areas.

CHAPTER 15

ACTS OF JESUS

Unusual Encounters and Miracles
Attract Large Crowds

Jesus kept on preaching in synagogues and performing miracles. He had unusual charisma and acted with authority. News about him quickly spread, and people brought to him people who were ill or had physical ailments. Large crowds of people from all over Palestine and large cities east of the Jordan (most were Gentiles) started following him. He often associated with non-Jews and people considered by religious Jews to be immoral. Many of his actions helped non-Jews and those living on the margins of society (women, those with a disability, those possessed by an evil spirit).

Jesus performed many miracles. Sometimes he did it to make a point, and sometimes it was simply an act of kindness. He healed people's bodies, emotions, and spirits. He intentionally performed miracles on the Sabbath in order to teach about God's priorities — the Pharisees believed these miracles were a type of work, which was prohibited on the day of rest. This chapter describes some of the important acts of Jesus after he became a public figure in Galilee at the age of 30.

Meaningful Encounters

The Samaritan Woman

Jesus once took a trip with his disciples from Jerusalem to Galilee. Instead of taking the usual road that avoided Samaria, he took a more direct route through Samaria. He arrived at a well at noon and he was tired from the journey and heat. The disciples went into town to get food while Jesus sat by himself at the well.

When a Samaritan woman came to draw water from the well, Jesus asked her for a drink. The woman said, "You are a Jew and I'm a Samaritan woman. How can you ask me for a drink?" (Jews didn't associate with Samaritans.)

Jesus answered, "If you knew who I am, you would ask me for a drink, and I would give you living water" (a term referring to fresh water in a well).

She replied, "But sir, you don't have anything to draw with, and the well is deep. Where can you get this living water? Are you greater than Jacob, who gave us the well?"

Jesus answered, "Everyone who drinks water from this well will be thirsty again, but those who drink the water I give them will never be thirsty. The water I give becomes a spring of water in your soul and brings eternal life."

The woman said, "Sir, give me this water so that I won't get thirsty and don't have to come here to get water in the middle of the day."

He told her, "Go call your husband and come back."

She replied, "I have no husband."

Jesus then said, "You're right to say you have no husband. That's because you have had five husbands, and the man you live with now is not your husband."

Being embarrassed, the woman changed the subject. "Sir, I see you are a prophet. Our ancestors worshipped on this mountain, but you Jews claim that we must worship in Jerusalem."

Jesus replied, "A time is coming when you won't worship God on this mountain or in Jerusalem. True worshippers will soon worship God in the Spirit."

The woman said, "I know the Messiah is coming. When he comes, he will explain everything to us."

Jesus said to her, "I am that man."

Just when Jesus said this, his disciples returned with food and were surprised to see him talking with a woman. But nobody asked him about it. The woman left her water jar at the well and went into town and told everybody, "Come see a man who told me everything I ever did. Could this be the Messiah?"

Many people came to see him, and many believed in him. The people invited him to stay, and Jesus stayed there for two days. As a result, even more Samaritans started following Jesus because of his teachings—they believed he was the Messiah.

Oddly, the powerless and immoral Samaritan woman was despised among even her own people, yet she was the first of only a few people Jesus told that he was the Messiah. He was vague about who he was to everybody else and usually referred to himself indirectly as the Son of Man. Daniel used that term when he predicted the coming of the Messiah.

A Secret Meeting in the Night

A member of the Jewish ruling council named Nicodemus came to Jesus secretly in the night. He was curious to learn more about Jesus and said to him, "Rabbi, we know God sent you, for nobody could do what you do if God were not with him."

Jesus replied, "Nobody can see the kingdom of God unless they are born again."

Nicodemus was puzzled and asked, "How can anybody be born when they are already old? Surely they can't be born a second time!" Jesus responded and described a new covenant.

> Nobody can enter the kingdom of God unless they are born of water and the Spirit. The flesh gives birth to the body, but the Spirit gives birth to one's spirit. You are a teacher but don't understand these things? Just as Moses lifted up the snake in the wilderness in order to live, so the Son of Man must be lifted up so everyone who believes may have eternal life. For God loved the world so much that God sent the Son into the world so that whoever believes in him will not die but will live forever. The Son existed before the creation of the world, and God didn't send him into the world to condemn the world. He has come to this world to save it. Those who believe and follow him are not condemned; those who

don't will stand condemned. Light has come into the world, but people love darkness because their deeds are evil. Everyone who does evil hates the light because they are afraid their actions will be exposed. But those who live by the truth come into the light so what they do can be seen.

Zacchaeus the Tax Collector

As Jesus traveled through Jericho, a man named Zacchaeus wanted to see him. Zacchaeus was wealthy because he was the chief tax collector in the city, but he couldn't see Jesus in the crowd because he was very short. So Zacchaeus ran ahead and climbed a tree so he could see Jesus walk by.

When Jesus reached the tree, he looked up and told Zacchaeus to climb down so they could go to his house that evening. Zacchaeus came down and warmly welcomed Jesus.

Everybody knew who Zacchaeus was, and they started gossiping that Jesus was going to be a guest of a sinner! But Zacchaeus was a changed man and said to Jesus, "Look Lord! I will now give half of my possessions to the poor, and if I have cheated anybody out of anything, I will pay back four times the amount."

Jesus said to him, "Today you and those in your house have been saved. This man is also a son of Abraham. The Son of Man came to save the lost."

A Rich Young Ruler

A young ruler came to Jesus and asked him what must be done to inherit eternal life. Jesus replied the man must obey the 10 commandments.

The man said he had obeyed all of them since he was a boy. When Jesus heard this, he said to him, "You still lack one thing. Sell everything you have and give to the poor, and you will have treasure in heaven. Then follow me."

When the man heard this, he became very sad because he was very rich. Jesus looked at him and said to those who were there, "It's very hard for the rich to enter the kingdom of God! In fact, it's easier for a camel to go through the eye of a needle than for someone who is rich to enter the kingdom of God." Those who heard this asked Jesus who could be saved. Jesus replied, "What is impossible for people is possible with God."[5]

A Sinful Woman Anoints Jesus

A Pharisee named Simon invited Jesus and others to his house for dinner, and they sat on the floor as they ate. A well-known sinful woman named Mary Magdalene found out that Jesus was eating there, and she went to the house with an expensive jar of fragrant ointment. She came up behind Jesus as he laid on the ground with his feet and legs behind him. She started crying and wet his feet with her tears. She wiped his feet with her hair and kissed them. Then she broke the jar and put oil on his head and feet.

Some disciples who were there were disgusted that she had wasted the jar and oil. They said the jar and oil could have been sold for more than a year's wages and the money could have been given to the poor.

The host thought that if Jesus was a prophet, he would know a sinner was touching him. Jesus knew what the host was thinking, so he told Simon a story. He described two people who owed money to a moneylender. One owed 500 denarii (nearly two years' wages for an average worker), and the other owed 50 denarii. Neither had money to pay him back, so the moneylender forgave the debts of both.

Jesus asked Simon which person would love him more? Simon replied, "I suppose the one who had the bigger debt forgiven."

---

[5] The "eye of a needle" was a very small opening in Jerusalem's wall. A camel would need to be completely unloaded and lying flat on a board, then dragged through on a wooden plank in order to get through the gate. The message implies that a person cannot inherit eternal life simply by becoming very humble and poor—God's help is needed. Also, a person's possessions may be a stumbling block to living an obedient life.

Jesus said that was correct and looked at the woman when he spoke to Simon:

> Look at this woman. I came to your house, but you didn't give me any water for my feet, yet she wet my feet with her tears and wiped them with her hair. You didn't give me a kiss, but this woman hasn't stopped kissing my feet. You didn't put oil on my head, but she poured the oil on my feet. Therefore, her many sins are forgiven because she has shown great love. But whoever has been forgiven little loves little. She has done a wonderful thing. The poor will always be with you, but I am only here for a little while.

Then Jesus said to her, "Your sins are forgiven. Your faith has saved you; go in peace." Some guests said quietly to each other, "Who is this who forgives sins?"

Miracles Performed by Jesus

A Wedding Miracle

Soon after Jesus spoke from the boat in the Sea of Galilee, he went to a wedding in Cana with his mother and a few of his disciples. On the third day of the celebration, his mother told Jesus that there was no more wine. Jesus said, "Why are you telling me this? It's not my time." But Mary told the servants to do whatever Jesus said.

Six large stone water jars stood nearby that were used by Jews to wash their hands before a meal. Each held at least 20 gallons of water. Jesus told the servants to fill the jars with water. After the jars were full, he told the servants to take some of it to the master of the banquet.

The master tasted it, not knowing where it came from. Then he called the bridegroom aside and said, "Everyone brings out the best wine first and then the cheaper wine after the guests have had too much to drink. But you have saved the best until now!" The water had turned into wine — more than 100 gallons of it after many of those who were there already had too much to drink!

Jesus Heals Many Types of People

Jesus was teaching in a house and people from every part of Palestine were there. Pharisees and scribes sat in the front row of a crowded room. Jesus had been healing many people, and some men came to the house carrying a paralyzed man on a mat. They tried to get in the door and take him to Jesus, but they couldn't get in. So they went on the roof, took off the tiles, and slowly lowered the man on his mat, with ropes tied at each corner, down to where Jesus was talking. Everybody was watching as the man came down from the roof.

When Jesus saw their faith, he told the man on the mat that his sins were forgiven. The Pharisees and scribes wondered what kind of man would speak such blasphemy, for only God can forgive sins.

Jesus knew what they were thinking and asked, "Which is easier, to say, 'Your sins are forgiven,' or to say, 'Get up and walk'? But I want you to know that the Son of Man has authority on earth to forgive sins." Jesus then turned to the paralyzed man and said, "Get up and take your mat home." Immediately the man stood up and took what he had been lying on and went home, praising God as he went. Everyone was amazed and also praised God.

* * * * * *

A Roman centurion once came to him and asked for help. He had a paralyzed servant at home who was in great pain. Jesus offered to go to his home to help, but the soldier said, "Lord, I don't deserve to have you in my house. Just say the word, and my servant will be healed. I understand authority — I have soldiers under me, and if I tell one of them, 'Go,' he goes. If I say to my servant, 'Do this,' he does it."

When Jesus heard this, he was amazed and said to the centurion, "Truly, I haven't found anyone in Israel with such great faith! Go, it has been done, just as you believed it would." The servant at his home was healed at that moment.

* * * * * *

Some people brought a blind man to Jesus so he could be healed. Jesus put his own saliva on the man's eyes and put his hands on him. Then he asked the man if he saw anything. The man looked up and said, "I see people who look like trees walking around." Jesus put his hands on the man's eyes again, and the man's eyes opened, and he saw everything clearly.

* * * * * *

When Jesus was in Jerusalem for a Jewish festival, he went to a pool that had healing powers. Many people with disabilities would lie near the pool, and one man had been lying there for 38 years. When Jesus saw him there and learned how long he had been there, he asked the man if he wanted to get well.

The crippled man told Jesus that he didn't have anybody to help him into the pool when the water stirred. Someone else always got to the water first and got healed. Jesus said to him, "Get up! Pick up your mat and walk." At once the man was cured. He picked up his mat and walked out of the pool area.

Since this took place on the Sabbath, Jewish leaders reminded the man that it was forbidden to carry a mat on the Sabbath. But he told them that the man who made him well told him to pick up his mat and walk. They asked him who it was that told him to do this. The man had no idea because Jesus had quietly left the crowd at the pool. Later Jesus found him at the Temple and told him, "You are well again! Don't sin anymore so something worse doesn't happen to you." The man then went and told the Jewish leaders that it was Jesus who healed him.

* * * * * *

A synagogue leader named Jairus met Jesus and pleaded with him to come to his house. His only daughter was dying and was just 12 years old. As Jesus was going to his house, many people were crowded around him. A woman who had bled continuously for 12 years had not been able to find anybody who could heal her. She thought she would be healed if she could touch Jesus's clothes. She came behind him and touched the edge of his robe, and immediately her bleeding stopped.

Jesus stopped suddenly and asked who had touched him. When nobody said anything, Simon Peter said, "Master, the entire crowd is pressing on you."

But Jesus said, "Someone touched me and power has gone out from me." The bleeding woman came to him very afraid and fell at his feet. Everybody was listening as she told him why she touched him and that she had been healed. He told her, "Take heart, daughter, your faith has healed you. Go in peace."

While Jesus was still speaking, someone came and told Jairus that his daughter was dead and that Jesus wasn't needed anymore. Jesus heard this and told Jairus to believe and she would be healed. When Jesus arrived at the house, he didn't let anyone in with him except for three disciples and the child's parents. Everybody else stayed outside and cried loudly about the dead child.

Jesus told those outside to stop crying because she was asleep, not dead. The people laughed at him, knowing she was dead. But he went to her bed, took her hand, and told her to get up. Her spirit returned and she stood up. Jesus told the parents to give her something to eat to show she wasn't a ghost. She ate and everybody was amazed.

Jesus Heals Those with Evil Spirits

Among those Jesus encountered were people who had evil spirits living in them. When he met them, they recognized him as the Son of God because evil spirits know who he is. But when the spirits revealed what they knew about him, Jesus would stop them and not let them speak because he didn't want people to know he was the Messiah until the time was right.

Some Pharisees brought Jesus a demon-possessed man who was blind and couldn't talk. Jesus healed the man so he could both see and talk. While all the people there were amazed and thought Jesus was the Messiah, the Pharisees told those watching that it was the power of Beelzebul, the prince of demons, that drove the evil spirits out of the man. Jesus knew their thoughts and said,

> No kingdom, city, or family can survive if it is divided. If Satan drives out Satan, he is divided against himself and his kingdom cannot stand. If I drive out demons by Beelzebul, by whom do you drive them out? Let people decide. If I drive out demons using the Spirit of God, then the kingdom of God has come upon you. Every kind of sin can be forgiven, but telling lies about God's Spirit will not be forgiven.

* * * * * *

At one point in his ministry, Jesus needed time away from the crowds and went to the coast of Phoenicia with only his disciples. A Greek woman living in the area came and begged Jesus to have mercy on her daughter who was demon-possessed and suffering terribly. Jesus ignored her and told his disciples, "I was sent only to the lost sheep of Israel." But she kept bothering them and become a nuisance. She knelt in front of Jesus and asked for help.

Jesus replied, "It's not right to take the children's bread and toss it to the dogs."

She responded in an unusual way: "But Lord, even the dogs eat the crumbs that fall from their master's table."

Jesus said to her, "Woman, you have great faith! The demon is gone." She went home and found her child lying on the bed without the demon.

* * * * * *

Jesus once took an unusual trip to a Gentile region east of the Sea of Galilee to help two men who had many demons. They lived in tombs, cut their bodies with sharp objects, didn't wear any clothes, and were so violent that nobody could be close to them.

When Jesus approached them, they shouted, "Why have you come to use your power over us now?" Jesus asked them what they were called. They said "Legion" because there were so many demons in the men. (The term *legion* refers to a group of several thousand Roman soldiers.) The demons saw a large herd of pigs in the distance, and they asked Jesus to cast them into the pigs instead of sending them to the Abyss. Jesus pointed at the pigs and said "Go" to the demons. The demons left the men and entered the pigs, and the entire herd ran down a hill and off a cliff into the sea.

Those tending the pigs went into town and through the countryside to tell everybody what happened. Many people came to see Jesus and the men who had the demons, who were sitting at Jesus's feet, dressed in normal clothes, and in their right minds. But the people asked Jesus to leave — they were afraid of him, and he had just destroyed their pigs, a very valuable source of income. As Jesus was returning to his boat, one of the men begged to go with him, but Jesus told him to go home and tell everybody about how much God had done for him. Jesus returned to Galilee in his boat and the man did what he was told to do.

The Dead Come to Life

Jesus raised people from the dead, and news of his power traveled fast. For example, he was in the town of Nain with his disciples, and a large crowd approached the town gate. A dead man was being carried out, the only son of his mother, a widow. When Jesus saw her, he had compassion for her and told her not to cry. Jesus touched the structure the dead man was on. Those carrying him stood still. Jesus told the dead man to get up, and the dead man sat up and began talking.

* * * * * *

One of Jesus's best friends was a man named Lazarus. His sister was Mary Magdalene who had been delivered from demons. Lazarus was very sick, and Mary and her sister Martha sent word to Jesus to come as fast as he could to heal his good friend.

Jesus was in another town far away and said the sickness would not cause him to die. Rather, it was an opportunity for him to glorify God. So he stayed where he was for two more days, and then he told his disciples it was time to go see Lazarus because he was dead. It took them two days to get there.

When they arrived, Lazarus had been in a tomb for four days. Many Jews were there to comfort Martha and Mary. When Martha heard Jesus was close, she ran to meet him and said, "Lord, if you had been here, my brother would not have died. But I know God will give you whatever you ask."

Jesus told her that Lazarus would rise from the dead. Martha said she knew he would rise again in the resurrection at the last day. Jesus said to her, "I am the resurrection and the life — those who believe in me will always live, even though they die. Do you believe this?" She replied, "Yes, Lord, I believe you are the Messiah, the Son of God, who has come into the world."

After saying this, she went and told her sister Mary that Jesus had arrived. Mary quickly ran to meet him. The Jews who had come to comfort the sisters thought Mary was going to the tomb to cry, so they followed her. But she went to Jesus and complained that that if he had come sooner, Lazarus would not be dead.

When Jesus saw her crying and the Jews who had come along with her were also crying, he was very sad. He asked Mary to show him where Lazarus was buried, and she took him to the tomb.

When Jesus arrived at the tomb, he knelt and wept as he was overcome with emotion. Lazarus was young but was now buried in a cave, and a large stone blocked the entrance.

Jesus told others to move the stone out of the way. Martha said, "Lord! He's been in there four days. He won't smell good!" (Martha was constantly trying to do things right in order to make a good impression.) Jesus told her it was to show people the power of belief in God.

After the stone was removed, Jesus looked up and said, "Father, I thank you for hearing me. I know you always hear me, but I say this for the benefit of the people standing here, that they may believe that you sent me."

After saying this, Jesus said in a loud voice into the cave, "Lazarus, come out!" The dead man came out with his hands and feet wrapped with strips of linen. A cloth was around his face. Jesus told those who were there to take off his graveclothes and let him go.

Jesus Behaves in Unusual Ways

Jesus Associates with Sinners

Jesus saw a tax collector named Levi sitting at his tax booth. He told Levi to follow him. Levi got up, left everything behind, and followed Jesus. Later, Levi (also called Matthew) held a large banquet for Jesus at his house, and many tax collectors and others were there. But the Pharisees and scribes complained about Jesus's disciples and asked him why he ate and drank with tax collectors and sinners.

Jesus answered, "Healthy people don't need a doctor, but the sick do. I have come to call sinners to repent, not the righteous."

The religious leaders continued questioning Jesus. They noted that the disciples of John and the Pharisees often fasted and prayed, but those who followed Jesus were happy with their eating and drinking.

Jesus answered, "Can you make the friends of the bridegroom fast while he is with them? But the time will come when the bridegroom will be taken from them; in those days they will fast." Then Jesus told them this parable:

> No one tears a piece out of a new garment to patch an old one. Otherwise, they will have torn the new garment,

and the patch from the new will not match the old. And no one pours new wine into old wineskins. Otherwise, the new wine will expand and burst the skins — the wine will run out and the wineskins will be ruined. New wine must be poured into new wineskins, and nobody who drinks old wine wants the new, for they say, "The old is better."

(Jesus was saying that people are more comfortable with the usual ways of thinking and doing things — people tend to resist doing new things and thinking in new ways. We find it hard to change the way we normally think and act.)

Jesus Disrupts the Temple

When it was time to celebrate the Passover, Jesus went to Jerusalem. In the Temple courts he found people selling animals for sacrifices and others sitting at tables exchanging money. This made him very mad. He made a whip and drove all the animals out of the Temple courts. He turned over the tables, scattering the money across the ground. He told the men selling doves, "Get these birds out of here! Stop turning my Father's house into a market! It is written, 'My house shall be a house of prayer,' but you have made it a den of thieves!"

The Jews asked Jesus what sign he could give to prove his authority and justify his actions. Jesus said, "Destroy this Temple, and I will raise it in three days."

They replied, "It took many years to build this Temple. You are going to raise it in three days?" The Temple Jesus was talking about was his body.

The chief priests and elders then asked Jesus who gave him the authority to ruin the Temple stalls. Jesus answered, "I'll ask you a question, and if you answer it, I will give you my answer. Was the baptism of John from heaven or from man?" The priests and elders talked among themselves and realized no matter what they said, they would look bad to the people. So they said they didn't know. Jesus said that since they didn't answer his question, he wouldn't answer theirs.

Jesus and the Sea of Galilee

One evening, some of the disciples set sail in a boat to go from one side of the Sea of Galilee to the other. Jesus was not with them. Late in the night, a strong wind started blowing and the waters became very rough. After rowing four miles toward Capernaum, they were very tired. Jesus saw from a distance that the boat was struggling against the waves and wind, so he walked out to them on the water.

When the disciples saw him coming and was walking on the lake, they were afraid — they thought he was a ghost. But Jesus identified himself and told them not to be afraid. Peter said, "Lord, if it's really you, tell me to come to you." Jesus told him to come, and Peter got out of the boat and started walking on the water toward Jesus. But when Peter saw the wind, he was afraid and started to sink. He cried out to be saved, and Jesus immediately reached out and caught him. He told Peter as he held him, "You have little faith. Why did you doubt?"

When they climbed into the boat, the wind died down. The people in the boat worshipped him and said he was truly the Son of God. The next day, some people who knew that Jesus had not set sail with the disciples in the boat were surprised to see Jesus with them.

On another occasion, Jesus and his disciples were in a boat on the lake. A furious storm suddenly caused large waves to crash over the sides of the boat, and it began to sink. Jesus was sleeping, even when the boat was filling with water. The disciples woke him up because they thought they were all about to drown. Jesus said to them, "Men of little faith, why are you so afraid?" He got up and told the winds and waves to stop, and everything became totally calm. The men in the boat were amazed that even the winds and waves obeyed him!

The Twelve Disciples

While Jesus attracted huge crowds as he moved around Palestine, there were 12 men who remained his closest disciples. Jesus called these dedicated disciples "apostles." The 12 were:

- Peter (Simon) and his brother Andrew (fishermen and small business owners)
- James and John (fishing partners of Peter and Andrew)
- Philip (the fishermen's friend) and his friend Bartholomew (also known as Nathaniel)
- Matthew (a tax collector, also known as Levi)
- Thomas (also known as Didymus)
- James (son of Alphaeus)
- Simon the Zealot
- Judas (son of another man named James)
- Judas Iscariot (a man with financial expertise).

Jesus told the 12 disciples and about 60 others to spread word in towns and villages that he was coming to visit. He gave these men power and authority to drive out all demons, heal the sick, and announce the kingdom of God. They took nothing with them: no walking stick, no bag, no bread, no money, no extra shirt. When they entered a house, they first said, "Peace be to this house." If someone there was promoting peace, they stayed there. But if people in the town didn't welcome or listen to them, they left the town and shook the dust off their feet as a sign against them. They went in pairs proclaiming the good news and healed people everywhere.

Many women followed Jesus as well. These included Mary Magdalene, Joanna (the manager of Herod's household), and Susanna. These women supported Jesus and the disciples with their own money.

John the Baptist

John the Baptist was in prison as Jesus's ministry grew. John's followers told him what Jesus was doing and saying, and John was confused. He sent two men to ask Jesus, "Are you the one we are expecting to come, or should we expect someone else?"

Jesus told the messengers, "Tell John what you have seen and heard: The blind receive sight, the crippled walk, those with leprosy are cleansed, the deaf hear, the dead are raised, and good news is proclaimed to the poor."

After the men left, Jesus spoke about John to the crowd and the religious leaders who were there. "John is the one the prophets wrote about when they wrote: 'I will send my messenger ahead of you, who will prepare your way before you.' John the Baptist came eating no bread and drinking no wine, and you said he has a demon. The Son of Man came eating and drinking, and you say, 'He is a glutton and a drunk, a friend of tax collectors and sinners.'"

John was soon killed while in prison because he had told King Herod that he should not have married his brother's wife. The king's wife ordered the execution, and the king reluctantly agreed.

CHAPTER 16

TEACHINGS OF JESUS

Unorthodox Views Challenge Religious Traditions

Jesus was the most interesting person to speak to the Jews in centuries, but his messages and actions confused many people. He mainly taught by telling stories that the people would understand. He could quote any scripture at any time, even though he hadn't been trained as a rabbi. He provided new ideas about the commands Moses had written, and he didn't follow strict religious rules.

The number of people who started following Jesus threatened the usual religious activities. Many who looked for the coming Messiah assumed the person would bring military victories and overthrow the Romans, but Jesus had a different message. He spoke about the kingdom of God and kingdom of heaven as if they were near, present, and coming.

Jesus had very different views about the scriptures from what the religious leaders believed. At times, his teaching directly conflicted what had been written. He would say, "You have heard it said ... but I say to you ...." Sometimes his messages were hard to understand and were not meant to be taken literally. Sometimes his messages related to things that would happen in the future that people did not know about yet. He only condemned those who were very religious and those who used religion to benefit themselves. He focused on spiritual growth rather than changing the government — he never criticized the cruel Romans. Jesus said the problem was the inappropriate religious beliefs and expectations held by very religious Jews.

What Defiles a Person

Religious Jews did not eat until they washed their hands in a certain way, and they followed other traditions related to cleanliness, such as washing their dishes. Some Pharisees and scribes went to see Jesus and saw his disciples eating food without washing their hands. The religious leaders asked Jesus why his disciples didn't follow the normal practices but instead ate food with dirty hands. Jesus said that food was clean.

> Isaiah was right when he talked about you hypocrites. He wrote, "You honor me with your lips but your hearts are far from me. Your worship is worthless to me, your teachings are just human rules." You have let go of the commands of God and you only follow human traditions. You're good at putting aside God's commands in order to observe your own traditions! Eating with unclean hands does not make a person bad. It's what comes out of a person's heart that shows their sin. Evil comes from a person's heart: sexual sins, stealing, being unfaithful, killing, being selfish and mean, plotting evil, jealousy, telling lies, being proud and foolish. All these evils come from inside a person.

Jesus then went to have dinner with a Pharisee. When Jesus sat down to eat, the Pharisee was surprised that Jesus had not first washed. Jesus said to him, "You Pharisees clean the outside of the cup and dish, but inside you are full of greed and wickedness. A sign that you are clean inside is that you are generous to the poor."

The Sabbath

When Jesus was walking through fields of grain during the Sabbath, he and his disciples picked some heads of grain and ate the kernels. Some Pharisees asked Jesus why he was doing what was unlawful on the Sabbath. Jesus answered them:

> Haven't you read what David did when he and his friends were hungry? They entered the house of God and ate

the blessed bread that was lawful only for priests to eat. People were not made for the Sabbath; the Sabbath was made for people. If you knew what it means when God said, "I desire mercy, not sacrifice," you wouldn't condemn the innocent. If your sheep falls in a pit on the Sabbath, won't you lift it out? How much more valuable is a person than a sheep!

When Jesus was teaching in the synagogue on the Sabbath, a man with a shriveled hand was there. The Pharisees and scribes were looking for a reason to accuse Jesus, so they watched him closely to see if he would heal somebody on the Sabbath (they considered healing a type of work). Jesus knew what they were thinking and told the man to stand up in front of everyone. When he stood up, Jesus asked the religious leaders, "Which is lawful on the Sabbath: to do good or evil, to save life or destroy it?" When nobody responded, Jesus told the man to stretch out his hand. When he did, his hand was completely healed. The Pharisees and scribes were furious that Jesus healed the man that day.

The Good Samaritan

A religious leader wanted to test Jesus and asked him what must be done for a person to live forever. Jesus responded that people should do what was written in the Law. The leader quoted the Law: "Love the Lord your God with all your heart and with all your soul and with all your strength and with all your mind" and "Love your neighbor as yourself." Jesus replied, "You are correct. Do this and you will live."

But the leader wanted to look smart and asked Jesus, "Who is my neighbor?" Jesus replied with a story.

A man walked down the dangerous road from Jerusalem to Jericho and was attacked by robbers. They stripped him of his clothes, then beat him and left him half dead. A priest traveling on the road saw the man and passed on the other side of the road. A Levite also saw the man and passed him on the other side of the road. But a

Samaritan came along and saw the half-dead man and felt sorry for him. He first cleaned and covered his wounds, then he put the man on his donkey and took him to the nearest inn where he told the innkeeper to take care of him. He gave two days' wages to the innkeeper and said, "When I return, I will pay for any extra expenses you have for taking care of him."

Jesus asked the leader which of the three men was a neighbor to the man who was attacked. The leader replied, "The man who showed him mercy."

Jesus told the leader, "Go and show mercy to those who need it."

Joy in Finding What Is Lost

Tax collectors and sinners often gathered around Jesus to hear him speak. One day some Pharisees and scribes were in the crowd and talked quietly in disgust that Jesus welcomed and ate with sinners. Jesus knew what these religious leaders were saying and gave them two hypothetical scenarios.

If a woman has 10 silver coins and loses one, doesn't she light a lamp, sweep the floor, and search carefully until she finds it? If you have 100 sheep and lose one of them, won't you leave the 99 and look for the one that is lost until you find it? When you find it, won't you be so happy and put it on your shoulders and take it home? In both cases, people rejoice when they find what they are looking for. God does not want to lose anybody. There is more joy in heaven when one sinner repents than for 99 righteous people who don't need to repent.

The Prodigal Son

Jesus also told a long parable about a man with two sons. The younger son asked his father for his inheritance. After the father sold enough of his estate to give the son his half share, the son took his money and went on a long trip. He wasted his money by living recklessly. After he spent all his money, a severe famine occurred and he became so poor that he took a job feeding pigs (Jews don't touch pigs or eat pork). He was so hungry that he wanted to eat what the pigs were eating.

The son soon came to his senses. He thought about his father's servants who had lots of food, but he was starving! He decided to go back to his father and ask to be one of his servants.

The father watched for him every day after he left, hoping he would return. Many months later, the son appeared in the distance and the father recognized his walk. Filled with joy and love and not worrying how he looked to others, he ran to his son, threw his arms around him, and kissed him. (In that culture, older men did not run.) The son started to apologize, but the father interrupted him and said to his servants, "Go quickly and bring the best robe and put it on him. Put a ring on his finger and sandals on his feet. Kill the largest calf so we can have a feast and celebrate. For my son was dead but is alive; he was lost and has been found." Then they started to celebrate.

Jesus continued with the story. The older son was in the field, and as he was coming home, he heard music and saw people dancing. He asked a servant what was happening and was told that his brother was alive and had come home. His father had killed the largest calf to celebrate his brother's return.

The older brother became angry and refused to join in the celebration. The father begged him to come in, but the older son said, "Look! I've slaved for you all these years and never disobeyed you. But you never gave me even a young goat so I could celebrate with my friends. But when this son of yours comes home after squandering your money in wild living, you kill the largest calf for him!"

The father said with deep love, "My son, you are always with me, and everything I have is yours. But we have to celebrate because your brother was dead and is alive again — he was lost but now he has been found."

(The term *prodigal* means spending resources freely and recklessly or being wastefully extravagant. The usual understanding of this story applies the term to the son, but in the context of Jesus's other teachings about God's concern for those who are lost, a better understanding of the story is to apply the term to the extravagant love the father had for his lost son, even when he embarrassed the family. Hence, "The Prodigal Father" is a better title for the story.)

More Examples of Unexpected Generosity

Jesus was invited to dinner by a highly respected Pharisee who had also invited many of his religious friends. Jesus noticed that the men tried to pick seats of honor at the table. Jesus saw this happening and told a parable.

> A man prepared a lavish dinner for many invited guests. When dinner was ready, he sent his servant to tell all who had been invited to come. But they all made excuses for not coming. The first said he just bought a field and must look at it. Another said he just bought five oxen and needed to take care of them. A third man said he just got married and couldn't come. The servant came back and said nobody was coming. The host was angry and told his servant, "Go into the streets and alleys of the town and bring in the poor, the crippled, the blind, and the lame." The servant did it, but there was still space for more guests. The host then had the servant go into the entire region to get more people, and his house became full. None of those who were initially invited got a taste of his dinner.

At a different gathering, Jesus told a parable about how God would be generous to those who don't appear to deserve it. The coming kingdom would be like a landowner who went out early in the morning and hired workers for his vineyard, saying he would pay them one day's wage for one day of work. But a few hours later, the landowner saw others waiting to be hired, and he hired them, telling them he would pay them a fair wage. He did the same thing several more times, including hiring men late in the afternoon.

At the end of the day, everybody came to be paid. The owner started with the last ones hired, and those who came last received a day's wage. Those who were hired early in the morning saw this and expected to receive much more than one day's wage. But each man received the same amount, a day's wage, regardless of how many hours they worked.

Those who were hired first began grumbling. They told the owner, "Those hired last worked only one hour, but you made them equal to us—we did most of the work!"

But the owner said he wasn't being unfair. He paid them a day's wage, just as he had promised. He said they should accept it and then said, "Don't I have a right to be generous with my own money? You are jealous of my generosity!"

Jesus ended by saying, "The last will be first, and the first will be last."

Forgiveness

Peter once asked Jesus how often people should forgive others. The Jewish tradition was to forgive somebody three times, and Peter suggested that the right number might be up to seven times, more than double the what had been taught in the past. But Jesus replied said the right number was 77 times, and then told this story.

> A king was owed a very large sum of money by one of his servants. When the king came to collect, the man could not pay it. The king then ordered him, his family, and all their possessions sold to repay the debt. But the servant fell to his knees and begged for mercy, saying he would pay everything back. The king felt sorry for the man and cancelled the debt and let the servant and his family go.
>
> But the servant then went to a man who owed him a tiny debt. When the man said he couldn't pay it back, the servant choked the man and demanded the money. When the man begged for patience and said he would pay it all back, the servant had him thrown into prison until he could pay the debt.

When the other servants saw him do this, they told the king, and he called the servant and said, "I cancelled your large debt, so you should have shown mercy to the man who owed you a small debt." The king then threw the servant who had been forgiven into jail where he was tortured until he could pay back what he owed.

There was no way either servant could ever pay the king what was owed. Jesus concluded by saying God would not forgive those who did not forgive others. By saying that people should forgive others 77 times, he was really saying that people should always forgive those who ask for it.

Parables about Seeds

As Jesus traveled to towns and villages, he spoke good news about the kingdom of God. His disciples were with him when he told this parable.

A farmer went out to scatter his seeds. Some fell on the path where they were walked on and eaten by birds. Some seeds fell on rocky ground, and when they sprouted, the plants withered because they had no moisture. Other seeds fell among thorns, which grew up and choked the plants. Other seeds fell on good soil, and they grew up and produced a huge crop, a hundred times more than what was sown.

When his disciples asked him what this parable meant, he explained it to them.

The seeds are the word of God. The seeds on the path are those who hear, but the devil comes and takes away the word from their hearts, so that they do not believe anymore. The seeds on the rocky ground are those who receive the word with joy, but they have no roots. They believe for a while, but when things get hard, they fall away. The seeds that fell among the thorns are those who hear, but as they live their lives, they are choked by life's worries, riches, and pleasures — they don't mature in their faith. But the seeds on good soil are those with good hearts, who hear the word and keep it, and produce a good crop because of their perseverance.

Jesus told another story about the kingdom of God. It was like the seeds scattered on the ground. Over time, the seeds somehow grow. All by itself, the soil gradually produces grain, which is harvested when it is ready.

He gave other illustrations about what the kingdom of God is like. The kingdom is like a very small mustard seed. When it is planted, it grows and becomes so large that its branches can support birds. The kingdom is also like invisible yeast that mysteriously makes bread rise.

The Sermon on the Mountain

Jesus sometimes spoke to thousands of people at a time. Once he spoke for a very long time on a mountain to several thousand people. Some of what he preached was hard to understand and was different from what had been taught previously.

> Blessed are the poor in spirit, for theirs is the kingdom of heaven.
> Blessed are those who are sad, for they will be comforted.
> Blessed are the humble, for they will inherit the earth.
> Blessed are those who hunger and thirst to live correctly, for they will be filled.
> Blessed are those who are kind, for they will be shown kindness.
> Blessed are those who have good thoughts and desires, for they will see God.
> Blessed are the peacemakers, for they will be called children of God.
> Blessed are those who are persecuted because they live the right way, for theirs is the kingdom of heaven.
> Blessed are you when people are mean to you and say all kinds of false and evil things against you because of me. Rejoice and be glad, for your reward will be great in heaven, for they persecuted the prophets who came before you.
> You are the salt of the earth, but if salt loses its flavor, it is thrown out. You are the light of the world. A town built on a hill can't be hidden. People don't light a lamp and hide it — they put it on its stand where it gives light

to everyone. Let your light shine so others see your good deeds and glorify God.

I haven't come to get rid of the Law or the words of the Prophets — I came to fulfill them. It was written long ago, "You shall not murder, and anyone who murders will be judged." But I say that anyone who is angry with a brother or sister will be judged. So if you are offering a gift at the altar and remember that your brother or sister has something against you, go first and be reconciled to them. Then come back and give your gift.

It was written long ago, "You shall not commit adultery." But I tell you that anyone who looks at a person and wants them for themselves has committed adultery in their heart. If your right eye causes you to stumble, cut it out. It's better for you to lose one part of your body than for all of you to go into hell.

You've heard it said, "Take an eye for an eye and a tooth for a tooth." But I say, if anyone slaps you on the right cheek, turn your other cheek to them. If anyone wants to sue you and take your shirt, give them your coat as well. If anyone forces you to go one mile, go two miles for them. Give to those who ask and don't turn away from those who want to borrow from you.

You've heard it said, "Love your neighbor and hate your enemy." But I say, love your enemies and pray for those who are mean to you. If you love those who love you, that's nothing — even the tax collectors do that! If you only greet the people who are like you, you are doing what everybody else does.

Don't practice your religion for others to see. When you give to the needy, don't announce it with trumpets as religious people do so they get praised by others. When you give, do it in secret. God sees what is done in secret and will reward you.

Don't try to get lots of nice things for yourselves, because they can be destroyed or stolen. Instead, do nice things for others, which can't be destroyed or stolen.

Don't worry about your life or your body and what you will wear. Look at the birds — they don't store food in barns, yet God feeds them. You are far more valuable than birds. Worrying can't make your life a single hour longer. Instead, seek first God's kingdom and do what is right, then everything will be given to you. Don't worry about tomorrow — there's plenty of trouble to deal with each day.

Don't judge others, for you will be judged in the same way you judge others. Why do you look at the tiny bit of dust in another person's eye but ignore the log in your own eye? Don't be a hypocrite! First take the log out of your own eye, and then you will see clearly so you can remove the tiny bit of dust from the other's eye.

Do to others what you would have them do to you — this sums up the Law and the Prophets. This is hard to do. The gate and road that lead to destruction are wide, but the gate and road that lead to life are narrow. Take the narrow road and go through the narrow gate. Few people take that route — most follow false leaders who look peaceful but are like wolves on the inside. You will know them by their fruit. Do people pick grapes or figs from plants with thorns? Every good tree bears good fruit, but a bad tree bears bad fruit. Every tree that doesn't bear good fruit is cut down and thrown into the fire. So not everyone who calls me "Lord" will enter the kingdom of heaven, but only those who do the will of my God in heaven. Many will say to me on that day, "Lord, didn't we teach in your name and drive out demons and perform many miracles?" I'll tell them, "I never knew you. Get away from me, you evildoers!"

Those who put my words into practice are like the wise who built their house on a rock. The rains came, the streams rose, and the winds blew and beat against that house. But it didn't fall because its foundation was on the rock. But those who hear my words and don't put them into practice are like fools who built their house on sand. The rains came, the streams rose, and the winds blew and beat against that house, and it washed away.

Prayer

Jesus taught the people about how to speak to God. Those who pray should not use flowery language so they can impress those who are watching and listening, and they shouldn't say prayers by saying the same things over and over again. Instead, people should pray in private and be honest, telling God about their deepest thoughts and feelings. God knows what people need, even before they ask for it.

Jesus provided a sample prayer that contained certain basic elements. These included (1) a recognition that God is holy, (2) a desire for the kingdom of God to influence this world so it becomes more like what heaven is like, (3) a desire to have God's will be done on earth, (4) asking for the basic necessities we need to survive, (5) asking for forgiveness for our sins and for help to forgive others, and (6) seeking protection and deliverance from evil forces in the world. Prayers can therefore focus on praise, thanksgiving, and requests. Jesus said God loves it when people pray and wants everybody to depend on God to have their needs met.

> Everyone who asks will receive, those who seek will find, and those who knock will have the door opened. Which of you, if your children ask for bread, will give them a stone? Or if they ask for a fish, will you give them a snake? If those who are evil know how to give good gifts to their children, how much more will your God in heaven give good gifts to those who ask!

Jesus often retreated into quiet and private places to eliminate distractions and be alone in order to talk with God. There was not a specific time or place when he prayed; it seemed to be happening all the time. His awareness of God was constant and continual, and listening to God through silence was part of the process.

God Is Revealed in Jesus

When Jesus was teaching in a synagogue, he prayed, "I praise you, Lord of heaven and earth, because you have hidden these things from wise and educated people but made them known to little children. This is what you wanted to do." Then he spoke to the people and referred to God as his Father.

> Everything has been given to me by my Father. Nobody knows the Father except the Son and those the Son chooses. Come to me, all you who are weary and

burdened, and I will give you rest. If you are thirsty, come to me and drink. Let me guide you like a farmer guides his oxen by wearing a yoke. My yoke is easy, my burden is light. If you know me, you know God. I am gentle and humble, and your spirit will find rest. If you know me, you will know the truth, and it will set you free.

The disciples asked Jesus, "What sign will you give that we may believe you? Our ancestors ate the manna in the wilderness and wrote, 'God gave them bread from heaven to eat.'" Jesus replied with this comment about bread.

It wasn't Moses who gave them bread from heaven. It's God who gives you the true bread from heaven. I am the bread of life. Those who come to me will not go hungry, and those who believe in me will never be thirsty. I won't drive away anybody who comes to me. I have not come from heaven to do my will but to do the will of God who sent me. This is the will of the God who sent me, that I will not lose anybody given to me, but that I will raise each one up on the last day. This bread is my body that I will give for the life of the world.

Some of the Jews began grumbling when he said he had come from heaven. They knew him as a child of Joseph and Mary — how could he say he came from heaven? The Jews also started arguing with each other and wondered how Jesus could give them his body to eat.

Jesus interrupted them and said, "Unless you eat the flesh of the Son of Man and drink his blood, you don't have life in you. Those who eat my flesh and drink my blood have eternal life, and I will raise them up on the last day. My flesh is real food, and my blood is real drink. Our ancestors ate manna and died, but those who eat this bread will live forever."

After hearing this, many who were following Jesus stopped listening to him and left. Jesus asked his 12 disciples if they wanted to leave him too. Simon Peter answered, "Lord, who else should we follow? You have the words of

eternal life. We now understand and know you are the Holy
One of God."

The Costs of Discipleship

Large crowds continued traveling with Jesus, and he wanted
them to think carefully about what it meant to follow him.
He told them, "If someone comes to me but loves their
family or their own life more, they can't be my disciple.
Whoever doesn't carry their cross and follow me can't be
my disciple." Then he told several stories to explain what
he meant.

> Suppose you want to build a tower. Won't you first sit
> down and estimate the cost to see if you have enough
> money to complete it? If you lay the foundation and can't
> finish it, everyone will ridicule you. Or suppose a king is
> thinking about going to war. Won't he first think about
> if his 10,000 men can defeat the 20,000 men of another
> king? If he cannot win, he will send people to the other
> king and try to resolve their differences peacefully. In the
> same way, those who don't give up everything cannot be
> my disciples.
>
> I send you out like sheep among wolves, so be on
> your guard. You must be as wise as snakes while also
> being innocent like a dove. You will be handed over to
> local leaders and whipped in synagogues. You will be
> brought before governors, kings, and Gentiles to be my
> witnesses. But when they arrest you, don't worry about
> what to say or how to say it — God's Spirit will speak
> through you. You will be hated by everyone because of
> me, and when you are persecuted, flee to another place.
> Don't be afraid of those who kill the body — they can't
> kill the spirit. But watch out for those who are evil who
> want to destroy both your spirit and body and take you
> with them to hell. I will acknowledge to God in heaven
> those who speak for me to others. But I will disown
> those who disown me to others. Whoever finds their life
> will lose it, and whoever loses their life for my sake will
> find it.

Preparing for Judgment

Jesus told several parables about being ready and prepared for God's return and the judgment of all people.

Parable of the Ten Virgins

He first spoke about 10 virgins who were waiting to meet their bridegroom at an unknown time. Five were foolish — they had lamps to light the night but didn't have oil to refill their lamps. The other five were wise — they had lamps and kept oil to refresh them. After waiting a long time for a bridegroom, they all fell asleep.

The bridegroom arrived in the middle of the night and was ready to meet them. The foolish women couldn't light their lamps and asked to borrow oil from the others. But the wise women wouldn't share their oil; if they did, there wouldn't be enough oil for everybody to light all the lamps. These women told the others to go buy oil for themselves. While the foolish women were away buying oil, the bridegroom came and took the wise women to the wedding banquet. Then the door was closed.

When the foolish women came later with their oil, they said, "Lord, Lord, open the door for us!" But the bridegroom said, "I don't know you." Jesus concluded this parable by saying people should be prepared because the time of judgment is unknown.

Parable of the Gifts of Gold

Jesus also told a story about making wise use of what we have while we are alive. He described three servants who were given various amounts of gold to use while the owner was away on a long journey. The owner gave gold to each based on their ability to use it wisely. One servant got five bags, one servant got two bags, and the third got one bag.

The servant who got five bags of gold used it wisely and earned five more bags of gold. The servant who received two bags also used the gold wisely and doubled the amount of gold. But the servant who had been given one bag dug a hole and hid the gold in the ground.

The owner eventually returned and asked for the gold. The servants who had been given five and two bags presented the owner with double the amount they were given. The owner said to each of them, "Well done, good and faithful servant! You have been faithful with a few things; I will put you in charge of many things. Come and share in my happiness!"

Then the servant who was given one bag of gold told the owner, "I knew you are a hard person, and I was afraid of you and hid your gold in the ground." This servant then gave the owner the one bag of gold he dug up from the ground.

The owner said to this last servant, "You are wicked and lazy! If you knew what I am like, why didn't you deposit my money in the bank? Then I would have at least received the gold plus interest." The owner then gave the one bag of gold to the servant who had 10 bags and said, "Those who use what they have will be given more, but those who don't use what they have will lose what they have." Then the owner had the last servant thrown into the darkness where people will weep.

Parable of the Sheep and the Goats

Jesus told a parable to describe who would go to heaven and who would go to the place of the dead. He said the Son of Man will sit on a throne, and as each person stands before him, he will separate them like a shepherd separates sheep from the goats.

The king will say to some, "Come and take what belongs to you, a kingdom prepared for you since the world was created. For I was hungry and you gave me something to eat, I was thirsty and you gave me a drink, I was a stranger and you welcomed me, I needed clothes and you clothed me, I was sick and you looked after me, I was in prison and you visited me."

But these people will ask, "Lord, when did we see you hungry and feed you or thirsty and give you something to drink? When did we see you a stranger and invite you in or needing clothes and clothe you? When did we see you sick or in prison and visit you?"

The king will say to them, "When you did these things to my brothers and sisters, you did it to me."

Then the king will say to the others, "You are cursed and will go into the eternal fire prepared for the devil and his angels. For I was hungry and you didn't feed me, I was thirsty and you didn't give me a drink, I was a stranger and you didn't invite me in, I needed clothes and you gave me no clothes, I was sick and in prison, and you didn't take care of me."

This group will say in wonder, "Lord, when did we see you hungry or thirsty or a stranger or needing clothes or sick or in prison, and didn't help you?"

The king will tell them, "Whatever you didn't do for those who had these problems, you didn't do it for me." These people will go into eternal punishment, but the righteous will live forever in heaven.

Condemnation of Religious Leaders

Jesus often spoke harshly to religious leaders because they were leading the people astray, not modeling good behavior, and had mixed motives. They were confident in their own religious practices and looked down on everyone else. Jesus told this parable.

> Two men went to the Temple to pray, one a Pharisee and the other a tax collector. The Pharisee prayed loudly saying, "God, I thank you that I'm not like other people — robbers, evildoers, adulterers — or even like this tax collector. I fast twice a week and give a tenth of all I get." But the tax collector stood at a distance, beat his chest and said, "God, have mercy on me, a sinner." I tell you that this man, not the Pharisee, can go home with confidence and stand before God. All those who brag

about themselves will be humbled; those who humble themselves will be praised.

At another gathering, Jesus harshly criticized religious leaders.

Woe to you Pharisees. You give God a tenth of your garden herbs but you neglect being fair, loving kindness, and walking humbly with your God. You should have done these things as well as given your herbs. You love the most important seats in the synagogues and the respect you get in the markets. You love how you look as you wear your fancy robes and say your long prayers. Woe to you scribes—you burden people with loads they can hardly carry, and you won't lift one finger to help them.

You are all hypocrites! You say that you approve of what your ancestors did, but they killed the prophets. God sent them prophets, but some were killed and others were harassed. This generation will be held responsible for the blood of all the prophets that has ever been shed. You are white tombstones that look good on the outside but inside you are dead and unclean.

Jesus told them another parable about a landowner who planted a vineyard and buildings to protect it. Then he rented the vineyard to some farmers and moved away. When the harvest time approached, he sent his servants to the tenants to collect his fruit. The tenants beat one servant and killed two others. The owner sent more servants to collect the fruit, and the tenants treated them the same way. Finally, the owner sent his son, thinking the tenants would surely respect him. But when the tenants saw the son, they said to each other, "This is the heir. Let's kill him and take his inheritance." So they killed him as well.

Jesus asked those who were there, "When the owner of the vineyard comes, what will he do to those tenants?"

The Pharisees said, "He will destroy these evil tenants and will rent the vineyard to other tenants."

Jesus said to them, "You have read in the Scriptures: 'The stone the builders rejected has become the cornerstone.'

Therefore, the kingdom of God will be taken away from you and given to people who will produce fruit." The religious leaders knew he was talking about them.

Jesus then told the religious leaders one last parable with a similar message. In this story, a father had two sons and asked them both to work in the family vineyard. The first son said he wouldn't go, but he later changed his mind and went and worked. The second son said he would go, but he didn't work. Jesus asked the religious leaders which son did what the father wanted, and they all agreed it was the first son. Hearing their answer, Jesus told them, "Truly, people you think are evil will enter the kingdom of God ahead of you. John came and showed you how to live. You didn't respond, but those you think are evil did." Actions, not nice words, reveal a person's true beliefs and desires.

After hearing these rebukes and remembering all the other things Jesus said to them in the past, the Pharisees and scribes were done arguing. They looked for a way to arrest him, but they were afraid of the crowd because most people thought he was a prophet. They watched Jesus closely and sent spies who pretended to be sincere in order to trap him and find something he said so they could turn him in to the Roman governor. These spies questioned him: "Teacher, we know you speak and teach what is right, that you are fair and teach the way of God. Is it right for us to pay taxes to Caesar or not?"

Jesus saw through their clever trap and asked them, "Show me a coin. Whose image and inscription are on it?"

"Caesar's," they replied.

Jesus said to them, "Give to Caesar what is Caesar's, and give to God what is God's." Amazed by his answer, they kept quiet and were not able to trap him in anything he said in public.

Names of Jesus

People had many names for Jesus. For many centuries, people were identified by their family, so people knew him as Jesus, son of Joseph and Mary. In the Old Testament, the Messiah was referred to with many names, and during and after his ministry, people referred to Jesus using other names. Here are some of the names used to refer to Jesus and the Messiah:

Almighty One	King of Kings	Savior
Alpha and Omega	Lamb of God, Lamb	Son of Man, the Son
Advocate	Light of the World	Resurrection and the
Bread of Life	Lion of the Tribe of Judah	Life
Bridegroom	Messiah/Christ	Teacher, Rabbi
Everlasting Father	Mighty God	The Door
God, Lord	Prince of Peace, Prince	The Truth
Good Shepherd	Prophet	The Way
Great High Priest	Redeemer	The Word
Head of the Church	Risen Lord	True Vine
Judge	Rock	Wonderful Counselor

CHAPTER 17

ARREST, TRIAL, AND EXECUTION

Religious Leaders Successfully Eliminate Jesus

In his third year of ministry, Jesus started talking more often about being a servant and his own death. Up to that point, he had been careful when he talked about his role in the world. He often spoke about himself as the Son of Man or as "he" rather than "I" and used symbols when he talked about himself. For example, he said, "I am the bread of life; those who come to me will not go hungry. I am the resurrection and the life — those who believe in me will live, even when they die."

He welcomed being called "teacher" and "prophet" but silenced demons when they said he was the Messiah. He performed miracles in public that fulfilled the predictions about him being the Messiah, the Servant-King referred to by the prophets. However, he told others not to talk about the miracles he did for them that indicated he was the Messiah, and he sometimes took no action because it "wasn't the right time."

Some Jews were getting impatient and wanted to know if he was the Messiah. He referred to God as his Father in heaven and spoke about the kingdom of God that had come. Some were in awe of his power, but the things he said were so radically different that some wanted to stone him — it was a sin to claim to be God. To the religious leaders, Jesus was leading the Jews away from the truth, and the symbolism he used was confusing to his disciples.

Jesus also talked indirectly about his own death and how it would lead to eternal life in heaven. For example, he called himself "the good shepherd."

> I am the good shepherd and the gate for the sheep who know and listen to his voice. He knows the name of each one and leads them out. He goes ahead of them

and they follow him. I am the gate — those who enter through me will be saved and find pasture. I have come that they may have a full and abundant life! The good shepherd lays down his life for the sheep. I have other sheep that aren't here, and I must bring them because they will listen to my voice. There will be one flock and one shepherd. My Father loves me because I lay down my life, only to take it up again. No one takes it from me — I choose to lay it down.

After Jesus raised Lazarus from the dead, some Jews told the Pharisees what Jesus had done. The chief priests and the Pharisees called a meeting of all the religious leaders and debated what they should do. "This man performs many signs, and if we let him continue, everyone will believe in him. Then the Romans will take away both our temple and our nation." The high priest said, "It's better for one man to die for the people than to let the whole nation perish." From that day on, they all plotted to arrest Jesus and kill him.

Jesus Enters Jerusalem

Jesus's time had come. He walked to Jerusalem with his disciples and other followers for the spring Passover Festival. Before entering the city, he sent two disciples to get a donkey and its colt. This fulfilled what the prophet Zechariah wrote about the Messiah: "Your king comes to you, gentle and riding on a colt, the foal of a donkey."

The disciples brought him the donkey and colt and placed their coats on them for Jesus to sit on. A very large crowd spread their coats on the road as he entered the city, and others cut branches from the trees and spread them on the road. The crowds along the road shouted, "Hosanna to the Son of David! Blessed is he who comes in the name of the Lord!"

The entire city was energized and people asked who was causing the excitement. The people said it was Jesus, the prophet from Nazareth. He went to the Temple again and drove out all who were buying and selling there.

The Last Meal with the Disciples

Thursday evening before Passover, Jesus knew it was time for him to leave this world and return to God in heaven. He gathered the 12 disciples together in the upper room of a friend's home for the evening meal.

During the meal, Jesus got up and took off his robe. He wrapped a towel around his waist and poured water into a large bowl. He began washing his disciples' feet and drying them with the towel. Simon Peter asked why Jesus was going to wash his feet and said Jesus should never wash his feet. But Jesus said, "You are not with me if I don't wash you."

After Jesus washed and dried all their feet, he returned to the table. He asked the men, "Do you understand what I have done for you? You call me 'Teacher' and 'Lord,' which are both correct. But I have washed your feet to set an example, that you should do as I have done for you."

While they were still eating, Jesus passed around a loaf of bread so they could each have a piece. After saying a blessing, he took the bread and said, "This is my body, given for you. Eat it and remember me." After they ate their bread together, Jesus passed around a cup of wine and said, "Everybody drink from this cup. It is my blood that is the new covenant which is poured out for many people for the forgiveness of all their sins." (This "meal" became known as the Lord's Supper.)

During the rest of the meal, the disciples started arguing among themselves about who would be in various positions of power under Jesus when he became the king. James and John thought they were the best and asked Jesus to let them sit at each side of his throne. The others got angry when they heard what James and John had asked.

Jesus called them together and said, "The Roman rulers are very proud and like to show their power over all the Jews. But you shouldn't act like this. Instead, whoever wants to become great among you must be your servant, and whoever wants to be first must be a slave of all. For even the Son of Man didn't come to be served but to serve and give his life for many."

Jesus Predicts His Betrayal

Jesus then said that one of them would betray him. His disciples were stunned and stared at each other. John was sitting next to Jesus and asked him quietly who the traitor was. Jesus replied quietly that it was the person to whom he would give a piece of bread after he dipped it in their shared dish. Then he gave a piece of bread to Judas Iscariot. As soon as Judas took the bread, Jesus told him to go do what he was going to do.

None of the other disciples knew what was happening. Judas was in charge of the disciples' money, so some of them thought he was going to buy something for the festival or to give money to the poor. But in reality, Judas had made a deal with the Pharisees to have Jesus arrested that night when the crowds were not around. He offered to identify Jesus in exchange for 30 pieces of silver.

Jesus Gives a New Command and Predicts Peter's Denial

After Judas left, Jesus told the others, "I won't be with you much longer. The Son of Man will be handed over to be killed. You can't come where I'm going. But if you love me, keep my commands. And now I'm giving you a new command: Love one another in the same way I have loved you. It is by your love for each other that people will know you are my disciples. The greatest love is to sacrifice your life to save others."

Peter asked, "Lord, why can't I go with you? I will lay down my life for you."

Jesus replied, "Really? I tell you, tonight you will deny me three times before the rooster crows! You will all leave me as the prophet Zechariah predicted when he wrote, 'I will strike the shepherd, and the sheep of the flock will scatter.' But after I have risen, I will go ahead of you into Galilee."

Jesus Comforts His Disciples

Jesus continued discussing his departure. "Don't worry. I'm going to prepare a place for you in my Father's house. I will come back and take you to be with me."

Thomas said they didn't know where he was going, so they did not know the way. Jesus responded:

I am the way and the truth and the life. Nobody comes to the Father except through me. If you know me, you know my Father as well. Anyone who has seen me has seen the Father. I speak the words of the Father who lives in me and who is doing the work. Those who believe in me will do what I have been doing, and they will do even greater things than these, because I'm going to the Father.

God will give you the Spirit to help you and be with you forever. The world won't understand anything about this invisible Spirit, but it will be in you. Before long, the world will not see me anymore, but I won't leave you as orphans — I will come to you, and you will see me. Because I live, you also will live. The Spirit will teach you all things and will remind you of everything I have said to you.

I am the true vine. You are the branches and God is the gardener who cuts off dead branches and prunes the living branches so they will produce more fruit. No branch can bear fruit by itself; it must stay connected to the vine. You can't bear fruit unless you stay close to me; apart from me you can't do anything. Bear much fruit to show you are my disciples. I have chosen you to produce fruit that will last.

If the world hates you, remember it hated me first. If the world persecuted me, it will persecute you as well. But this is to fulfill what is written in their Law: "They hated me without reason." I leave with you my peace. In this world you will have trouble, but don't be discouraged — I have overcome the world!

Jesus said Satan, the prince of this world, was coming for him. They all left the upper room and walked to the garden of Gethsemane just outside the city walls.

The Garden of Gethsemane

When they got to the garden, Jesus was very sad. He told his disciples to pray for him as he went further into the garden with Peter, James, and John. He told the three men to stay with him and watch for anything that might come their way. Then he went even further into the garden and prayed to God, saying, "If it's possible, take this cup away from me. But do what you must, not what I want."

He returned to his three disciples several times, and each time they were sleeping, not watching. He said to Peter, "Can't you watch for one hour? Watch and pray so you don't get tempted. The spirit is willing, but the flesh is weak."

Each time Jesus retreated into the garden to be alone, he prayed, "Father, if this cup can't be taken from me, I will do it." Finally, he came back to all the disciples and told them, "The hour has come — the Son of Man will now be delivered into the hands of sinners. Get up—here comes my betrayer!"

Judas Iscariot had just shown up with servants of the chief priests and elders of the people and many men armed with swords and clubs because they expected a fight. Judas had arranged to kiss Jesus as a signal to indicate who they were to capture. Judas came to Jesus and kissed him with the traditional greeting for a rabbi.

The armed men then grabbed Jesus. Peter moved quickly to defend him — he pulled out his sword and cut off the ear of a servant of the high priest.

Jesus told Peter, "Put away your sword. Those who use the sword will die by the sword. I could call on my Father and he would send angels to rescue me. But for the Scriptures to be fulfilled, this must happen."

Jesus then healed the servant's ear and turned to those who came to arrest him and said, "Am I leading a rebellion so you have to bring swords and clubs to capture me? I sat in the Temple teaching and you didn't arrest me. But this is happening to fulfill the writings of the prophets." Seeing that Jesus had been captured, all the disciples walked away quickly and quietly.

Jesus Before the Sanhedrin

It was the middle of the night and Jesus was taken to meet all the members of the Sanhedrin. They were looking for solid evidence against Jesus to justify putting him to death, but no evidence was given. Finally, two members said that Jesus claimed he would destroy the Temple of God and rebuild it in three days.

The high priest asked Jesus if this was true, but Jesus was silent. The high priest asked him, "Tell us if you are the Messiah, the Son of God."

Jesus replied, "Yes, you have said it."

When the high priest heard this, he tore his clothes and said, "You have shown disrespect for God! We don't need any more witnesses! What should we do?"

The others answered, "He must die!" They spit in his face and hit him with their fists. Others slapped and mocked him, saying, "Prophesy to us! Who hit you?"

Judas saw what was happening and he realized he had done an evil thing. He brought the 30 pieces of silver to the chief priest and said he had betrayed an innocent man. When the religious leaders said they didn't care, Judas threw the silver coins into the Temple, left the area, and killed himself.

The chief priests picked up the coins and used the money to buy a field as a burial place for foreigners. The prophet Jeremiah had predicted this when he wrote centuries earlier, "They took the 30 pieces of silver and used them to buy a gravesite for poor people."

Peter had followed Jesus from a distance after the arrest in the garden. He went into the courtyard of the high priest and sat down with the guards to see what would happen. A servant girl came to him and said he had been with Jesus.

But Peter denied it and he went out to the gateway of the courtyard. Another servant girl saw him and told others that she had seen him with Jesus. But Peter denied it again and swore he didn't know who Jesus was.

A little while later, those standing there said to Peter, "I'm sure you are one of them; your Galilean accent gives you away." Peter cursed loudly and swore he didn't know the man. Immediately a rooster crowed. Peter then remembered that Jesus said he would deny Jesus three times before the rooster crowed. He left and wept bitterly.

Jesus Faces Pilate

Early Friday morning, the chief priests and all the religious leaders made plans to have the Romans execute Jesus. They tied him up and delivered him to Pontius Pilate, the governor. Pilate asked Jesus, "Are you the king of the Jews?"

"Yes, it's as you say," Jesus replied.

Pilate asked him, "Don't you hear the charges they are bringing against you?" But again, Jesus didn't respond to the charges. Pilate was amazed that Jesus didn't defend himself.

It was the governor's custom at the festival to release a prisoner chosen by the crowd. At that time, a well-known revolutionary named Barabbas was being held as prisoner because he had killed somebody during an uprising against the Romans. When the crowd gathered, Pilate asked them, "Which one do you want me to release to you: Barabbas or Jesus, who is called the Messiah?" The chief priests and the elders persuaded the crowd to ask for Barabbas and to have Jesus executed. (Pilate knew they wanted Jesus dead in order to protect their power.)

The crowd answered, "Barabbas."

Then Pilate asked, "What should I do with Jesus, the one who is called the Messiah?"

The crowd answered, "Crucify him!"

Pilate wondered why the crowd wanted Jesus dead. He told the crowd that they should deal with him themselves, but the religious leaders said they weren't allowed to put a man to death. The Jewish leaders insisted, "According to our Law, he must die because he said he was the Son of God."

When Pilate heard this, he was afraid and went inside the palace and spoke to Jesus. Pilate told Jesus he had the power to either release him or crucify him. Jesus said, "You would not have any power over me unless it was given to you from above."

Pilate asked Jesus why his own people wanted him killed. Jesus said, "My kingdom is not of this world. I was born to be a king and bring truth to the world."

Pilate replied, "What is truth?"

Jesus did not respond, and Pilate wanted to free him because he had done nothing wrong. But the Jewish leaders said that if he let Jesus go, he was no friend of Caesar — there was only one king, and anybody who claimed to be a king was opposing Caesar. The leaders also said Jesus was not following their religion — his teachings were causing the people to believe different things. They would not have turned him over to Pilate if he had not done something wrong.

When Pilate heard Jesus was from Galilee, he sent him to be questioned by Herod, the government leader over Galilee. Herod was in Jerusalem for the Passover and was glad to finally meet Jesus, who was famous all through in Palestine. But Herod could not find anything wrong with Jesus and sent him back to Pilate.

When Jesus returned, Pilate turned again to the crowd and asked, "Why do you want him crucified? What crime has he committed? We find no fault in him."

But the crowd kept shouting, "Crucify him." They wanted Jesus to suffer the death penalty. Pilate said to them, "Here is your king."

The people responded, "We have no king except Caesar."

Pilate was disgusted and washed his hands in front of the crowd, saying, "I'm innocent of this man's death. It is your responsibility!"

The people answered, "We and our children are responsible for his death."

Torture and Execution

Pilate then released Barabbas and the Roman soldiers took Jesus away and tortured him. They surrounded him, took off all his clothes and put a robe on him, and twisted together a crown of long thorns and pushed it on his head. They made fun of him, spit on him, beat him, and hit him on the head again and again so the thorns went deep into his head. They took off the robe, put his own clothes back on him, and led him away to be whipped brutally.

After he was whipped, Jesus had to carry a large cross through the streets. The cross was soon too heavy for him, so a Jewish man from Africa carried it the rest of the way. A large number of people followed them, including women who cried loudly for him.

On a hill outside the city walls called Golgotha (meaning *place of the skull*), Jesus was nailed to the cross. Two common criminals were crucified with him. Huge nails were driven through his hands and feet, and the cross was lifted up high for all to see. The sign above his head said, "JESUS OF NAZARETH, THE KING OF THE JEWS" and it was written in three languages. The Jews wanted the sign to say that he *said* he was the king of the Jews, but Pilate said he wrote what he wanted it to say.

It was around noon when the three crosses were placed in the ground. While he hung on the cross, Jesus was offered a form of wine but he refused to drink it. The Roman soldiers who were there claimed his clothes by casting lots. (This fulfilled another prediction about the Messiah.)

Some of those who passed by insulted him, saying, "You said you would destroy the Temple and build it in three days — save yourself! Come down from the cross if you are the Son of God!" The religious leaders also went up the hill and insulted him. They said to the crowd, "He saved others, but he can't save himself! If he is the king of Israel, let him come down from the cross now, and then we will believe in him. He trusts in God. Let God rescue him now, for he said he was the Son of God."

One of the two men being crucified on a cross next to him also insulted Jesus, saying, "Aren't you the Messiah? Save yourself and us!" But the other criminal said, "We are getting what we deserve. But this man has done nothing wrong." Then he turned to Jesus and said, "Remember me when you enter your kingdom."

Jesus replied, "Truly, you will be with me in paradise today."

Many of his followers watched from a distance. Some expected a miracle to happen. His mother, his aunt, Mary Magdalene, and John were at the foot of the cross, and as Jesus hung there, he told John to take care of his mother. He also said to God, "Forgive all of them, for they don't know what they are doing."

The Death and Burial of Jesus

The skies turned dark for three hours after the crosses were put into the ground. At three in the afternoon, Jesus cried out in a loud voice, "My God, why have you left me?" Shortly after that, he said, "It is finished. God, I give you my spirit."

At that point, the earth shook, the skies stormed, and the thick curtain of the Temple was torn in two from top to bottom. A guard who was watching Jesus was terrified and exclaimed, "Surely he was the Son of God!" Those who were watching cried when they saw what was happening and left the scene very sad.

It was getting late on Friday and the Jewish leaders didn't want bodies left hanging during the Sabbath. They asked Pilate to have their legs broken so the men would die faster and the bodies could be taken down. Soldiers broke the legs of the two men who were crucified with Jesus, but when they came to Jesus and saw he was dead, they didn't break his legs. Instead, a soldier stabbed Jesus's side, and out came a mixture of blood and water (this indicated he was dead). These things fulfilled two predictions about the Messiah: "None of his bones will be broken" and "They will look at the one they pierced."

As evening approached, a rich man named Joseph from Arimathea got permission to take Jesus's body. Nicodemus, the man who visited Jesus at night, went with Joseph to bury the body in a new tomb that had been cut into a wall of rock in a garden. Nicodemus brought a mixture of spices, and the two of them wrapped Jesus's body with the spices in strips of clean linen. This was the normal way Jews buried their dead. Then they rolled a big stone in front of the entrance to the tomb and went away while Mary Magdalene and another Mary sat at the tomb. They had come to see where Jesus was buried so they could come back after the Sabbath and anoint the body.

Less than 24 hours had elapsed from when Jesus met with his disciples for the last meal Thursday night and when Jesus was buried. On the Sabbath, the chief priests and the Pharisees went to see Pilate again. They told him that Jesus had said he would rise from the dead on the third day. In order to make sure the disciples wouldn't steal the body and say he was alive again, they asked for Roman guards to protect the tomb. Pilate ordered guards to make sure nobody disturbed the tomb, and a seal was put on the stone to make sure it stayed closed. Soldiers then guarded the tomb. As this was happening, the Jews were observing the Sabbath while Jesus was dead in the sealed tomb. He was 33 years old when he died, and his ministry had lasted only three years.

CHAPTER 18

LIFE AFTER DEATH

Jesus Returns from the Grave

Before dawn Sunday morning, several women went to the tomb to cover the body of Jesus with spices. It had been about 40 hours since he died Friday afternoon, and they wondered how they would roll away the stone. But when they got to the tomb, the stone had been rolled away. They entered the tomb but didn't find the body. There had been an earthquake earlier in the morning and an angel had rolled back the stone. The guards were so afraid of the angel that they ran away.

As the women wondered what happened, two men in bright clothes came into the tomb. As the frightened women bowed to them, the angels said, "Why do you look for the living among the dead? Jesus isn't here; he has risen! Remember how he told you in Galilee: 'The Son of Man must be delivered into the hands of sinners, be crucified, and on the third day be raised again.'" Then they remembered what he had said.

Mary Magdalene was one of the women who came to the tomb, and she began crying as she wondered where Jesus was. A man came up to her and asked why she was crying. She told the man, "They have taken my Lord away, and I don't know where he is." She thought she was talking the gardener and didn't realize it was Jesus. She said, "Sir, if you have taken him away, tell me where you put him and I will go to him."

Jesus then said, "Mary," and she recognized his voice. She cried out and hugged him passionately, and she knew he was not a ghost. Jesus told her to tell the disciples that he was alive and would see them in Galilee.

The women ran to tell the 11 disciples that Jesus was alive, and Mary said she had seen him. The disciples didn't believe the women — what they said didn't make any sense. Peter and John ran to the tomb and went inside. They saw just the strips of linen lying by themselves but didn't see Jesus, so they didn't know what happened.

Several Roman guards informed the religious leaders what happened. The chief priests and elders gave the soldiers a large bribe and told them to say the disciples had come in the night and stolen the body while they were asleep. Since Roman soldiers would be executed if they were found sleeping on the job or if they left their post, the Jewish leaders promised to bribe the governor if he found out about it. The soldiers took the money and did as they were instructed, and the story about how the disciples stole the body was widely circulated among the Jews.

Sightings of Jesus

The Road to Emmaus

Later that day, two men who had followed Jesus were walking to Emmaus, a village seven miles from Jerusalem. As they were talking about what had happened, Jesus came up and started walking with them. They did not recognize him, and Jesus asked, "What are you talking about?"

They stood still and looked down with sad faces. One of them said, "Are you the only one who doesn't know what happened in Jerusalem the past few days?"

Jesus asked, "What things?"

They replied, "The chief priests and our rulers had Jesus of Nazareth killed by the Romans. He was a powerful prophet for God and the people, and we all hoped he was the one who was going to save Israel. And we just heard that on this third day since he was killed, some women said they went to the tomb but didn't find his body. They said they saw angels who said he was alive. Some of our friends went to the tomb and also found it empty."

Jesus said to them, "Remember what the prophets said, that the Messiah had to suffer these things before entering his glory?" And he began explaining what all the scriptures had to say about himself, all the way back to Moses and all the prophets.

As they entered Emmaus, Jesus stayed on the main road, but the two men urged him to stay with them because it was getting dark. Jesus went with them, and when they started to eat, he took bread, gave thanks, broke it, and gave it to them. They saw his wounded hands and then realized who he was.

But suddenly he was gone. They told each other how inspired they felt as they walked with him while he explained the scriptures to them. They immediately got up and went back to Jerusalem. They found 10 disciples (Thomas was not there) and said they had seen Jesus! They explained what happened on the road and how they recognized him when he broke bread with them.

Jesus Appears to the Disciples

That night, the disciples were hiding together with the doors locked because they were afraid the Jewish leaders would also come after them. Jesus came and stood among them and said, "Peace be with you!" They were surprised and afraid and thought they were seeing a ghost. But Jesus told them, "Don't be afraid or have any doubts in your minds. Look at my hands and my feet. It's me! Touch me — a ghost doesn't have flesh and bones."

He showed them his hands and feet and asked for something to eat. He ate a piece of cooked fish in front of them. He explained the scriptures so they would see how everything made sense now that they knew he was the Messiah, the Christ:

> This is what I told you earlier: Everything must be fulfilled that was written about me in the scriptures. The Messiah had to suffer and die but would rise from the dead on the third day so all the world, beginning in Jerusalem, will know that those who repent will have their sins forgiven. You witnessed these things. I'm going to send you God's spirit.

Thomas was not with the disciples, and the other disciples told him later, "We have seen the Lord!" But Thomas didn't believe them. He said, "I won't believe you until I see the nail marks in his hands, put my finger where the nails were, and put my hand into his side."

A week later all 11 of the disciples were in the house again. The doors were locked, but Jesus came and stood with them and said, "Peace be with you!" He turned to Thomas and said, "Put your finger here; see my hands. Reach out your hand, and put it into my side. Stop doubting and believe."

Thomas exclaimed, "My Lord and my God!"

Jesus replied, "You believe because you have seen me; blessed are those who haven't seen me and still believe."

Jesus Appears in Galilee

Jesus appeared again to some of his disciples near the Sea of Galilee. They had been fishing in Peter's boat at night but caught nothing. Early that morning, Jesus stood on the shore, but the disciples didn't recognize him. He called in a loud voice and asked if they had caught any fish. They said they had not caught anything.

Jesus told them to throw the net on the other side of the boat, and when they did, they caught so many fish that they couldn't haul in the net.

John told Peter that it was Jesus! Hearing this, Peter jumped into the water and went ashore. The other disciples came to shore in the boat, towing the net full of fish from about 300 feet away. When they landed, Jesus told them to come and eat breakfast and bring some of the fish they had just caught. They knew it was Jesus, especially after Jesus gave bread and fish to them. It was the third time Jesus appeared to his disciples after he came back to life.

Jesus Reinstates Peter

When they finished eating, Jesus asked Peter, "Do you love me more than these?" Peter replied, "Yes, you know that I love you." Jesus said, "Feed my lambs."

Jesus asked him a second time, "Peter, do you love me?" Peter answered again, "Yes, Lord, you know I love you." Jesus said, "Take care of my sheep."

Then Jesus said to Peter a third time, "Simon Peter, son of John, do you love me?" Peter was hurt because Jesus asked him a third time. He said, "Lord, you know everything; you know that I love you." Jesus said, "Feed my sheep. Follow me!" Peter had denied Jesus three times, but now he had affirmed his allegiance to Jesus three times.

Final Words and Actions

While the 11 disciples were in Galilee, Jesus said to them, "I have been given all authority in heaven and on earth. I will always be with you, even when you die. Now go and make disciples in all the nations. Baptize them and teach them to obey everything I said to you."

Then all of them went to an area near Jerusalem. The disciples asked Jesus when he was going to restore the kingdom of Israel. He told them, "It's not for you to know the time or day, only God knows. But you will receive power when the Holy Spirit comes on you, and you will be my witnesses in Jerusalem, then in Judea and Samaria, and then throughout the world."

Jesus then lifted his hands and blessed them, and he then went up into the clouds. They watched him closely as he rose, and two men dressed in white clothes suddenly stood next to them. They told the men, "Why are you standing here looking into the sky? Jesus has gone to heaven and will come back the same way." The disciples worshipped him and then returned to Jerusalem filled with joy. It had been 40 days since Jesus had risen from the dead, and more than 500 people had seen him.

After the disciples went back to Jerusalem to the room where they had been staying, they were joined by others, including Jesus's mother and her four other sons (James, Joses, Judas, and Simon) and several women. Since Judas Iscariot was dead, Peter said he should be replaced. One condition that his replacement had to meet was that he must have seen Jesus after he came back to life. Two men were nominated who had been with Jesus the entire time of his ministry, from the time of John the Baptist to when Jesus ascended into the sky. In the end, Matthias was selected to replace Judas Iscariot.

There were about 120 people who had faithfully followed Jesus and believed what he had said. They stayed committed to following his example and to be witnesses to what happened and what Jesus had said.

Jesus hadn't come as a king in the usual way. His entrance in a small town in a barn foreshadowed his humility. He rarely used his unusual powers except to help others. He modeled service as he spoke mainly to the Jews — they were God's people but had misunderstood what God had tried to teach them. Jesus's actions and teachings also showed God's acceptance of all people, not just the Jews. His focus on those who were disadvantaged in some way showed a different set of priorities, and his refusal to conform to the religious rules demonstrated a new way of thinking. Love was the highest priority, not obeying rules. Loving others heals people's bodies, minds, and spirits; sacrificial love brings peace in the human heart and harmony in our relationships with each other.

CHAPTER 19

THE APOSTLES RESPOND AND SCATTER

News About Jesus Spreads as
Believers Are Persecuted

Those following Jesus waited together in Jerusalem for the time when they would receive God's spirit. During the Jewish festival of Shavuot (50 days after Jesus died), they were gathered in a large house. Suddenly a sound like a violent wind filled the house, and something resembling tongues of fire touched each one of them. They were all filled with the Holy Spirit, and each began to speak in another language. (The arrival of the Spirit became known as "Pentecost.") When they went into the city, Jews who had come from Asia, Africa, and Europe were amazed to hear the Galileans speaking their language and talking about the wonders of God. Those who didn't know the other languages made fun of them because they thought they were drunk.

Peter Leads as the Movement Grows

Peter addressed the crowd as the 11 other disciples surrounding him. He told the Jews that those speaking what seemed like babble to them were not drunk. Instead, they were fulfilling the predictions made by the prophet Joel that God would pour out the Spirit on all people, both the young and the old, men and women. Peter told his fellow Israelites:

> Jesus of Nazareth was a man approved by God to perform various miracles and signs. It was God's plan that he was handed over by wicked men to be killed, but God raised him from the dead because it was impossible for death to hold him. God promised King David that one of his descendants would come to the throne who would be the Messiah who died and came back to life. We all witnessed that he came back to life. Be assured of

this: God made Jesus, whom you crucified, both Lord and Messiah.

The people hearing this felt convicted and asked Peter what they should do. Peter replied, "Repent and be baptized in the name of Jesus Christ for the forgiveness of your sins. Then you too will receive the gift of the Holy Spirit. Save yourselves from this corrupt generation." Those who accepted his message were baptized, and about 3,000 people joined the movement that day.

Peter and John later went to the Temple at the time of prayer. A man who was crippled from birth begged every day at the Temple gate for money. Peter said, "I don't have silver or gold, but what I have I give to you. In the name of Jesus Christ of Nazareth, walk." He took the man's hand and helped him stand up. The man's feet and ankles instantly became strong. He started walking and was soon jumping as he praised God.

Those in the Temple courts recognized him as the man who begged at the Temple gate, and they were amazed to see he was walking and jumping. The people ran to the disciples, and Peter said, "Fellow Israelites, it's not our power or godliness that made this man walk. The God of Abraham, Isaac, and Jacob has glorified his servant Jesus. You disowned him, even though Pilate wanted to let him go. You killed Jesus, but God raised him from the dead. We witnessed this. It was this man's faith in the name of Jesus that made him able to walk."

Peter explained how the prophets had predicted the Messiah would suffer and reminded them of what Moses said: "The Lord will raise up a prophet from among your own people, and you must listen to everything he says. Anyone who doesn't listen to him will be completely cut off."

While Peter and John were speaking, the religious leaders arrested them and put them in jail for the night. The leaders were very angry because the two disciples were teaching that Jesus had come back to life after being killed, and many who heard their message believed them. The number of believers had grown to about 5,000 men (not including the women).

The next day all the rulers, elders, scribes, and high priests met in Jerusalem and had Peter and John brought before them. They asked them who gave them the authority to say these things. Peter was filled with the Holy Spirit and told them,

> If we were called here today for an act of kindness shown to a crippled man and are being asked how he was healed, then let the people of Israel know this: It is by the name of Jesus Christ of Nazareth, whom you crucified but God raised from the dead, that this man was healed. Jesus is who the Psalmist said would be "the stone you builders rejected, which has become the cornerstone." Salvation is found in nobody else, for there is no other name in this world that can save a person.

When the religious leaders realized Peter and John were disciples of Jesus, they withdrew and met privately to discuss what to do next. Everybody in Jerusalem had learned about how Peter healed the man at the Temple gate. They decided to order Peter and John to stop teaching about Jesus. But Peter and John said they couldn't stop teaching about what they had seen and heard.

After Peter and John were released, they went and told the other disciples what the chief priests and elders had said and how Peter had been filled by the Spirit when he spoke. They were all amazed and praised God. They realized that the threats against them provided an opportunity for them to speak with boldness because the Spirit would speak for them and miracles could happen by using the name of Jesus.

The apostles performed many signs and wonders among the people. The believers started meeting in public every day in the Temple courtyard. People laid the sick on the streets so Peter's shadow might fall on them as he passed by, and people from nearby towns brought the apostles the sick and those affected by evil spirits. All of them were healed. Those who believed devoted themselves to the apostles' teaching and to fellowship, to the breaking of bread, and to prayer. They gladly ate together with sincere hearts, praising God and earning a good reputation. Every day, more men and women joined their movement.

All the believers shared everything they had, and nobody claimed their possessions as their own—there were no needy people among them. Occasionally, those who owned land or a house sold them, brought the money and put it at the apostles' feet, and it was distributed to anyone who needed it.

A man named Ananias and his wife Sapphira sold a piece of property, but he secretly kept some money for himself and then gave the rest to the apostles. Peter confronted him about lying about the amount of money they got for selling the land. When Ananias heard this, he died on the spot and was taken away. A few hours later, his wife came to the apostles but didn't know what happened to her husband. Peter asked her how much money they got for selling the land. She gave the price, which was the amount Ananias had given the apostles.

Peter said to her, "Why did you plan this lie? The men who just buried your husband are here, and they will carry you out as well." At that moment, she fell and died. Those who had buried her husband carried her out and buried her next to him. Fear spread to everybody who heard what happened.

The Believers Are Persecuted

The religious leaders were threatened by this new religious movement, so they arrested the apostles and put them in jail. But during the night, an angel opened the jail doors. The apostles escaped, and in the morning, they went back to the Temple to continue teaching.

When the religious leaders gathered to have the apostles brought before them, the jail officers found their cells were empty. Someone told them that the apostles were back at the Temple. The captain of the Temple guard brought the apostles to appear before the Sanhedrin to be questioned.

The high priest said, "We gave you strict orders not to teach about Jesus, but you continue with your teaching and say we are responsible for his death."

Peter replied: "We must obey God, not human orders. You killed Jesus by hanging him on a cross, but the God of our ancestors raised him from the dead. God exalted him as Prince and Savior so he might bring Israel to repentance and forgive our sins. We witnessed these things, and God has given the Holy Spirit to those who obey him."

The men in Sanhedrin were furious at Peter and wanted to kill all of them. But a Pharisee named Gamaliel, who had a good reputation, ordered the apostles out of the room. He turned to those who remained and said, "Think carefully about what you want to do to these men. You know two men who had followers and led rebellions, and they were killed. Their followers dispersed and nothing came of it. I advise you to leave these men alone and let them go. If their actions are not from God, they will fail. But if they are from God, you won't be able to stop them because you will be fighting against God."

His speech persuaded the rest of the men. They had the apostles whipped and ordered them not to speak about Jesus. Then they let the apostles go. The apostles left and rejoiced because they had been counted worthy of suffering disgrace in Jesus's name. Day after day, they continued teaching and proclaimed the good news that Jesus was the Messiah.

More Leaders Are Chosen

As the number of disciples increased, the Jews who spoke Greek and followed Jesus complained that the Jews who spoke only Hebrew overlooked their widows in the daily distribution of food. The 12 apostles decided that it wouldn't be right for them to neglect their teaching ministry in order to serve food. They said to the others, "Brothers and sisters, choose seven wise men from among you who are known to be full of God's Spirit. Let them lead the work to help the Greek-speaking Jews who need help. That way, we can focus our attention on praying and teaching."

Everybody liked this idea, and they chose seven "deacons" to oversee the help provided to others. The apostles continued preaching, and the word of God continued to spread. The number of disciples in Jerusalem increased rapidly, and a large number of priests also became followers of Jesus.

Stephen Is Killed

Stephen was one of the deacons and performed great wonders and signs among the people. But opposition arose from leaders in synagogues that served Jews in Africa and Asia Minor (modern day Turkey). They secretly persuaded some men to say that Stephen had spoken disrespectful words against Moses and God. This angered various religious leaders, who had Stephen seized and brought before the Sanhedrin.

The high priest asked Stephen if the charges were true. Stephen gave a long speech about how God had chosen Abraham to leave Mesopotamia and settle in Canaan, and he explained the entire history of the Israelites. This showed the religious leaders that he was an educated and sincere religious man. But he also accused the religious leaders of being just like their ancestors who rejected God and the Spirit. They were responsible for killing Jesus, the Messiah.

When the members of the Sanhedrin heard this, they were furious and yelled at him. Stephen was filled with the Spirit and gazed into the heavens. He said to them, "I can see into heaven, and Jesus is standing right next to God." When the religious leaders heard this, they covered their ears, screamed at him, and dragged him out of the city where they stoned him to death. (This was an illegal act — only Romans could execute a person.[6]) While Stephen was

---

[6] Stoning usually involved dropping a person from a small cliff. If the person survived the fall, a large stone was dropped on them. If the person still survived, others threw stones until the person died.

being stoned, he asked God not to hold it against them. He was the first follower of Jesus to be martyred.

The Believers Scatter

Right after Stephen was stoned, many followers of Jesus in Jerusalem were threatened with death. The believers thought Jesus was coming back very soon to establish the kingdom of God on earth and be a political king who would free them from Roman oppression, so they had all stayed close to Jerusalem. But the danger drove them out of the area, and all but the apostles scattered themselves throughout Judea and Samaria.

Saul

One of the men who watched Stephen get stoned and approved of his execution was a man named Saul. His father was a Pharisee and he was well trained in all the Jewish scriptures. He disrupted meetings of believers by going from house to house and dragging believing men and women to prison.

Saul continued making threats against all of the disciples of "the Way," a term given to this new religious movement because Jesus said he was "the way, the truth, and the life." Saul went to the high priest to get letters he could take to the synagogues of Damascus so that if he found anybody who belonged to the Way there, he could bring them back to Jerusalem as his prisoners.

Saul received the letters and started his trip to Damascus. When he was getting close to the city, a light from the sky suddenly flashed around him. He fell to the ground and heard a voice that said, "Saul, why are you persecuting me?"

He asked, "Who are you?"

The voice said, "I am Jesus, the one you are persecuting. Get up and go to Damascus where you will be told what you must do."

The men traveling with Saul heard the voice but didn't see anyone. Saul got up, but he was now blind. The men traveling with him led him into Damascus, and Saul didn't eat or drink anything.

A disciple in Damascus named Ananias had a vision in which God told him to go to the house on the main road of the city. He was to ask for a man named Saul who was praying. Saul had a vision that Ananias would come to restore his sight.

Ananias was scared. He had heard many reports about Saul and how he was hunting Jesus's followers and arresting them. But God said to Ananias, "Go! I have chosen this man to be my instrument to preach about me to the Gentiles and to the people of Israel."

After three days, Ananias came to the house. He put his hands on Saul and told him, "Jesus told me to come so you will see again and be filled with the Holy Spirit." Immediately, something like scales fell from Saul's eyes, and he could see. He got up and was baptized. His eyes were literally and figuratively opened: he was no longer blind, and he now understood that Jesus was the Messiah.

Saul spent several days with the disciples of the Way in Damascus. He began preaching in the synagogues that Jesus was the Messiah and the Son of God. All those who heard him were amazed and knew his reputation of threatened believers in Jerusalem. Saul grew increasingly powerful and impressed the Jews living in Damascus and proved to them that Jesus was the Messiah.

Eventually, the Jews in Damascus plotted to kill Saul. They watched for him at the city gate so they could catch him, but Saul found out about the plot. He escaped from the city when his followers lowered him in a basket through an opening in the wall during the night. Saul went into the desert and later spent three years working out his understanding of the scriptures with what he learned about Jesus.

Saul eventually returned to Jerusalem and tried to join the disciples, but they were all afraid of him — they thought it was a trick for him to capture all of them at one time. But Barnabas told the apostles what happened to Saul when he went to Damascus and that he was now preaching fearlessly about Jesus. So Saul stayed with them and moved freely in Jerusalem, speaking boldly and debating Hellenistic Jews. These Jews tried to kill him, but he escaped and went to his home in Tarsus in Asia Minor (close to Adana in Turkey).

Philip

The disciples preached about Jesus wherever they went. Philip went to a city in Samaria, and people listened closely and watched him perform miracles. He delivered people from their evil spirits and healed many who were paralyzed or lame. This brought great joy to the people the Jews despised.

The apostles in Jerusalem heard that the Samaritans had accepted the word of God, and they sent Peter and John to the area. When they arrived, they placed their hands on them, and they received the Spirit. After Peter and John taught them more about Jesus, they preached in many other Samaritan villages.

An angel told Philip to take a trip south on the desert road that goes from Jerusalem to Gaza. On his way, he met an official from Ethiopia who was in charge of his queen's money. The man had been to Jerusalem to worship and was going home. As the man sat in his chariot reading the book written by the prophet Isaiah, Philip saw the chariot and found out what the man was reading. Philip asked him if he understood what he was reading. The man said he would only understand it if someone explained it to him. He invited Philip into his chariot to explain the part of Isaiah that said, "He was led like a sheep to the slaughter; as a lamb before its shearer is silent — he did not speak. He was humiliated and deprived of justice, and his life was taken from the earth."

Philip explained the passage was about Jesus and explained who Jesus was and how he had fulfilled Isaiah's predictions. As they traveled along the road, they came to some water. The official stopped his chariot and asked Philip to baptize him. Philip then went and preached the good news in many towns, all the way north to the port city of Caesarea in Phoenicia.

Peter Continues to Lead

Meanwhile, Peter was traveling around the region preaching and performing miracles. He healed a paralyzed man who lived in Lydda who had been in bed for eight years. In Joppa, a disciple named Dorcas who was always doing good and helping the poor became sick and died. Peter found out about it and went to Joppa. When he arrived, he met many people who had been helped by Dorcas. He went into the room where she was dead and prayed. Then he told her to get up, and she opened her eyes and stood up with Peter's help. He then presented her to the people who were grieving her death. Word spread quickly through the town about what happened, and many more people believed in Jesus.

The Encounter with Cornelius

A Roman centurion named Cornelius was living in Caesarea, and all his family were God-fearing people. He prayed to God regularly and gave generously to those in need. One day he encountered an angel who told him to send some men to Joppa and bring back a man known as Peter, who was staying at the home of a man named Simon. Cornelius sent two servants and a devout soldier to Joppa to find Peter.

While the men were traveling to Joppa, Peter was praying at noon and was hungry. While the meal was being prepared, he fell into a trance. He saw a large sheet coming down from heaven by its four corners. It held all kinds of animals, including reptiles and birds, that were considered unclean. A voice told him to kill them and eat.

But Peter had never eaten anything he was taught not to eat. So while he was still in the trance, he said he would not eat it. But the voice spoke again: "Don't call anything unclean that God says is clean." This happened three times, and then the sheet was taken back to heaven, and he came out of his trance.

While Peter was wondering about the meaning of the vision, the men sent by Cornelius arrived. The Spirit told Peter there were men looking for him who had been sent to him by God. Peter met the men and asked why they had come.

The men told Peter about Cornelius, who he was and his reputation, and how an angel had told him to send them to find Peter. The next day, they all returned to Caesarea, and some believers from Joppa went along. When they arrived in Caesarea, Cornelius greeted them at his house, which was full of Gentiles.

Peter said to all of them, "You know that it is against our law for a Jew to associate with or visit a Gentile. But God showed me that I should not call anyone unclean. So when you called for me, I came without raising any objection. Why did you ask me to come?"

Cornelius told him about speaking with the angel and that he should have Peter visit them, but he didn't know why. Peter then realized why he had the vision of the forbidden food. He told the crowd, "Now I understand God doesn't show favoritism but accepts those from every nation who do what is right. God's message was sent first to the Israelites, but Jesus has taught us to tell *everybody* that he is the one God appointed as judge of all people."

While Peter was still speaking these words, the Holy Spirit came on everybody in the room. The Jews who had come with Peter were amazed that the Holy Spirit had come to the Gentiles as well, and that they were also speaking in foreign languages as they praised God. Peter ordered that they all be baptized in the name of Jesus.

The apostles and believers throughout Judea heard that the Gentiles had received the good news about God. When Peter went to Jerusalem, the Jewish believers criticized him for going into a Gentile's house and eating with them. But Peter told them the whole story about what happened in both Joppa and Caesarea and about what he saw while in a trance. He told about how the Holy Spirit came on the Gentiles and reminded them that Jesus said to baptize others with the Holy Spirit. He told the doubters, "If God gave the believing Gentiles the same Spirit we received, who was I to stand in God's way?" After hearing this, they didn't object anymore and praised God when they realized even the Gentiles could be saved by asking for their sins to be forgiven.

The Christians and the Church in Antioch

Those who had been scattered by the persecution traveled as far as Phoenicia, Cyprus, and Antioch, spreading the word only to the Jews. But some of them went to Antioch and began speaking to the Greeks about Jesus. Many people believed, and the number of followers continued to increase.

News of this reached those in Jerusalem, and they sent Barnabas to Antioch. When he saw what was happening, he was glad and encouraged them all to remain true to the Lord. Barnabas went to Tarsus to look for Saul, and when he found him, he brought him back to Antioch. Barnabas and Saul met with the followers in Antioch for one year, and the disciples there were called "Christians" for the first time. Collectively, they were known as the "church," the term Jesus used when telling Peter that he would lead his followers.

CHAPTER 20

PAUL'S TRAVELS

Three Trips Create Churches in Asia Minor, Macedonia, and Greece

The good news about Jesus spread across the region. People were told that Jesus had died as a permanent sacrifice for the sins of the entire world, so anybody could have a relationship with a living God if they wanted it. A sign that they had changed their ways and were Christians was that they were baptized and obeyed the teachings of Jesus, including loving others.

Peter led the teaching of the Jews in Judea and Samaria. A Christian named Mark became close to Peter and wrote a short book about the life of Jesus that was included in the New Testament. At the same time, the church with many Gentiles in Antioch grew under the leadership of Saul, Barnabas, and others. Saul was referred to as Paul, his Greek name.

Paul and Barnabas Travel Together

About 20 years after Jesus had gone to heaven and after spending five years in Antioch, Paul and Barnabas took a trip to preach elsewhere. They first sailed to Cyprus where Paul preached in the synagogues. Then they sailed to Perga (in southern Turkey) and traveled 100 miles north to Pisidian Antioch in the Galatian region of Asia Minor.

They went to the synagogue on the Sabbath, and when it was time for people in the audience to speak, Paul stood up spent several minutes talking about the history of the Israelites, including the prophecies about the Messiah. Then he spoke about Jesus's life, that he was a descendant of David and the Messiah. Although Jesus had been killed, he came back to life and lived for many days and many people saw him. What God promised to their Jewish ancestors had been fulfilled: through Jesus, sins were forgiven, and through him everyone who followed him was set free from every sin, which could not be done under the laws of Moses.

Those in the synagogue invited Paul and Barnabas to come again the next week, and many in the congregation followed Paul and Barnabas out and continued talking to them. The next week, almost the entire city gathered to hear them speak. When the religious leaders saw the crowd, they were jealous and started debating Paul and verbally abused him. Paul and Barnabas responded boldly: "We had to speak to the Jews first. But since you reject what we have said and don't want eternal life, we now turn to the Gentiles. The Lord told us that we are a light to the Gentiles so the entire world can be saved." The Gentiles were glad to hear this and felt honored by God, and many of them believed and became Christians. But the Jewish leaders arranged to have Paul and Barnabas expelled from the area. As they left, the two men shook the dust off their feet to warn them and went to Iconium, a city 75 miles away.

Preaching in Iconium, Lystra, and Derbe

In Iconium, Paul and Barnabas went as usual to the synagogue and spoke so well that many Jews and Greeks believed. But as in the past, many Jewish leaders refused to believe and got others to accuse them of telling lies. Paul and Barnabas spent many days preaching boldly and performing miracles. The people of Iconium were divided — some sided with the Jews while others believed the two apostles. A plot developed to kill the two men, but they found out about it and escaped to Lystra, a city 20 miles away.

Paul and Barnabas preached the gospel in Lystra and the surrounding area. They met a man who had been crippled from birth and had never walked. Paul looked at the man and said his faith had healed him. When he told the man to stand up, the man jumped up and started walking.

When the crowd saw what Paul did, they shouted, "The gods have come to us in human form!" They thought they were the Roman gods, Zeus and Hermes. But the two apostles shouted, "Friends, we are human like you. We have good news — turn from these worthless gods and follow the living God, the one who made the heavens and earth, the sea and everything in them. Until now, God has let everybody go their own way, but God still showed kindness by giving you rain and crops so you would have plenty of food."

Jews who had come from Pisidian Antioch and Iconium turned the crowd against them. They stoned Paul and dragged him outside the city, thinking he was dead. But some disciples took him back into the city. The next day he and Barnabas left for Derbe, where they preached the gospel and many people believed. Then they went back the way they had come, strengthening the believers in each city.

They returned to Perga and sailed back to Antioch and told the believers there what had happened during their trip. They had been gone two years, and the Christians were happy to hear that more Gentiles were now disciples.

The Council at Jerusalem

After Paul and Barnabas had returned, some disciples came from Judea to visit the church in Antioch. They had been teaching that new Gentile believers had to be circumcised in order to be saved, but Paul and Barnabas disagreed. A small group of church leaders in Antioch, including Paul and Barnabas, went to visit the Christian leaders in Jerusalem to discuss the issue. They traveled through Phoenicia and Samaria and told the Christians there how the Gentiles were becoming believers. This news encouraged the new believers there.

When the group arrived in Jerusalem, they reported what God had done through them. Some of the believers who were Pharisees said the Gentiles had to be circumcised as required by the laws of Moses. Everybody discussed the issue, and finally Peter spoke.

Brothers, you know God has allowed Gentiles to become disciples and have the Holy Spirit. God knows our heart and doesn't see a difference between Jews and Gentiles: we can all have faith. Why would we want to add more requirements to the Gentiles that we had a hard time following? No! We believe it is through the free gift from Jesus that we are saved. It doesn't matter how we look; it's the heart that matters.

The entire group was silent as Paul and Barnabas talked about what happened among the Gentiles they met in Asia Minor. When they finished speaking, James rose and spoke:

Peter has described how God first acted to choose a people apart from the Gentiles. Amos wrote, "I will return and rebuild David's fallen tent. All the people of the world will seek the Lord, even the Gentiles." Therefore, we shouldn't make it difficult for Gentiles who turn to God. Instead, we should tell them not to eat foods offered to idols, not to commit sexual immorality, not to eat the meat of strangled animals, and not to drink blood.

Everybody agreed and wrote a letter that listed only these requirements for the Gentile believers in other regions.

Paul Takes Another Trip

A few months later, Paul and Barnabas went back to the cities they had visited in Asia Minor to see how the churches were doing. They decided to split up: Barnabas took a man named Mark who was with them on their first trip, and Paul took Silas, a man he met at the meeting in Jerusalem.

Paul and Silas traveled back to Asia Minor and strengthening the churches as they went. Paul met a disciple named Timothy whose mother was a Jewish believer but whose father was Greek. The believers in the cities respected him, and Paul invited him to join them on the trip. Timothy was circumcised in order to please the Jews in the area, and as they traveled from town to town, they told the church about what the Christian leaders in Jerusalem said about the few things they needed to do. The number of believers grew and their faith deepened.

Traveling to Macedonia

As Paul and Silas traveled, the Holy Spirit had them avoid some areas. They ended up in the port city of Troas and met a Gentile believer named Luke, a doctor, who started traveling with them. (Luke wrote two long accounts about the events of Jesus's life and the trips Paul took. These accounts are included in the New Testament.) While in Troas, Paul had a vision of a man of Macedonia (northern Greece) begging him to come help him. Paul believed this was a call from God to go to Macedonia, so the four men (Paul, Silas, Timothy, and Luke) traveled to Philippi, a Roman colony and a major city in Macedonia.

In Philippi, they found a place where people prayed by a river. They met a woman named Lydia, the owner of a large business. She worshipped God and responded to Paul's message about Jesus. When she and the members of her household were baptized, she spent more time with the men learning about her new faith.

Paul and Silas in a Philippian Prison

Later, the men met a female slave who was a fortune-teller. She earned a lot of money for her owners, and she followed the men for many days, shouting, "These men are servants of the Most High God and are telling people how to be saved."

Paul got so annoyed with her that he said to her spirit, "In the name of Jesus Christ, I order you to come out of her!" An evil spirit immediately left her.

When her owners realized that their source of making money was gone, they dragged Paul and Silas to the local Roman officials. They said the men were Jews and had caused problems in the city. Others joined in the attack, and the officials ordered the two men stripped and beaten.

Afterwards, the two men were put in chains in a cell deep inside the jail.

Paul and Silas were praying and singing hymns to God during the night and other prisoners were listening to them. Suddenly a violent earthquake shook the jail. All the jail doors flew open, and everyone's chains came loose. The jailer woke up, and when he saw the jail doors open, he drew his sword to kill himself because he thought the prisoners had escaped.

But Paul shouted, "Don't hurt yourself! We are all still here!" The jailer rushed in and asked Paul and Silas what he must do to be saved. They told him, "Believe in the Lord Jesus, and you and your household will be saved." The jailer washed the wounds from their beatings, took them to his house, and fed them. He and his entire household were baptized and were filled with joy because they all finally believed in the true God.

In the morning, the officials released Paul and Silas. The jailer told Paul they could go in peace, but Paul told the officials that they had been beaten publicly without a trial, even though they were Roman citizens, and had been put in jail.

When the officials heard Paul and Silas were Roman citizens, they were alarmed and asked them to leave the city. But instead, Paul and Silas went to Lydia's house and were encouraged by other Christians who were there.

In Thessalonica and Berea

Paul, Silas, and Timothy left Philippi and traveled about 95 miles to Thessalonica while Luke stayed in Philippi. They went to the synagogue on three straight Sabbath days to explain the Scriptures and prove Jesus was the Messiah. Some of the Jews and many religious Greeks became Christians, including many prominent women.

But other Jews were jealous. As in other cities, they had evil men from the market form a mob and search for them. The mob went to the house of Jason where the apostles were staying, but they were not there. So the mob dragged

Jason and other believers out of the house and said they denied that Caesar was the king. When the city officials heard this, all the Christians were thrown in jail. (They were soon released after they paid a fine.)

That night, the believers took the three apostles to the nearby city of Berea where there was another synagogue. The Berean Jews were smarter than the people in Thessalonica, and they listened more closely to Paul and carefully examined the Scriptures to see if what Paul said was true. As a result, many of them believed, as did many Greek men and a number of prominent Greek women.

But when the Jews in Thessalonica heard Paul was preaching in Berea, some of them went to Berea and got the crowds to turn against him. The believers quickly sent Paul away, but Silas and Timothy stayed at Berea. Paul was escorted to Athens and told Silas and Timothy to join him as soon as they could.

In Athens

When Paul was in Athens, he was disgusted when he saw that the city was full of idols. He preached first in the synagogue and in the market on other days. A group of Greek philosophers began to debate him and Paul was invited to explain his teachings at a meeting of educated people that gathered to discuss new ideas.

Paul stood before them and said, "People of Athens, I see you are very religious! I've walked around and seen many objects of worship. I even found an altar that said, 'TO AN UNKNOWN GOD.' So you don't know this god. This is what I'm going to talk about."

Paul reasoned with the Greek philosophers but didn't mention any of the Hebrew scriptures. He said that the God who made the world and everything in it didn't need to live in temples built by human hands and didn't look like the gold or silver images made by humans. While God had overlooked this lack of intelligence, God now commanded all people to repent, for someday God would judge everybody. Paul was trying to convince his listeners that there was only one true God, not many gods. When he mentioned the resurrection of the dead, some in them sneered but others wanted to hear more. As a result, some of the people who heard him became believers.

In Corinth

Paul left Athens and went to Corinth, a tough port city 30 miles away that had a reputation for immoral behavior. He met a Jewish man named Aquila who had recently come from Italy with his wife Priscilla because all the Jews in Rome had been ordered to leave. Paul worked and stayed with Aquila and Priscilla, who were tentmakers. (Paul then earned money to pay for his travel expenses by making and selling tents.)

Paul spoke in the synagogue every Sabbath and tried to persuade Jews and Greeks to become Christians. When Silas and Timothy arrived from Macedonia, Paul spent all his time preaching, and several Jewish leaders became believers.

One night, Paul had another vision in which God told him to stay in Corinth and that he would be safe there. So he stayed in Corinth for 18 months while he taught the new believers. The Roman leader in the city allowed Paul to preach, so he stayed safe from the Jews who wanted to silence him.

When it was time to leave Corinth, Paul and the others sailed across the Aegean Sea to Ephesus and took Priscilla and Aquila with them. Paul spent time in the synagogue in Ephesus speaking to the Jews. When they asked him to stay longer, he said he had to leave but would return. He left Aquila and Priscilla in Ephesus and sailed back to Caesarea, then went to Jerusalem to give a report to the Christian leaders.

Paul Takes a Third Trip

Paul later took a third trip through Asia Minor and visited many cities to strengthen the disciples.

Ephesus

Paul was eager to return to Ephesus, a major city on the western coast of Asia Minor. Priscilla and Aquila had been teaching there and were glad to see Paul. They told him about a Jewish scholar named Apollos from Egypt who had been preaching there and teaching about Jesus in a very accurate way. Priscilla and Aquila spent time helping him improve his teaching and support to Christians. Apollos had left to preach and teach in Greece by the time Paul arrived.

When Paul got to Ephesus, he did what he always did: he went to the synagogue to preach first to the Jews. He spoke boldly for three months about the kingdom of God. But some of the Jews did not believe and spoke against the Way. So Paul and some of his disciples left the synagogues and spent two years lecturing in a public hall. Everybody who lived in that region of Asia heard Paul's message about the Lord. God also did extraordinary miracles through Paul. Handkerchiefs and aprons that touched him were taken to the sick, and they were healed and evil spirits left them.

Some Jewish men tried to drive out evil spirits using the name of Jesus, as if the name was a type of magic word. They would say, "In the name of the Jesus whom Paul preaches, I command you to come out." One day an evil spirit responded to their order and said, "I know Jesus and Paul, but who are you?" The man who had the evil spirit jumped on them and beat them all so bad that they ran out of the house naked and bleeding.

When the Jews and Greeks in Ephesus heard about this, they were all afraid. Many of the new believers openly confessed their sins, and some who practiced magic burned their very rare and valuable scrolls together in public. As a result, word about Jesus kept spreading.

Paul's teachings also caused an economic crisis in Ephesus. A silversmith who made silver shrines of Artemis (the local fertility goddess) brought in a lot of business for the craftsmen in the city. He called the workers together and told them that Paul's teachings had driven away much of their business. Paul had influenced the whole province by saying that gods made by human hands were not gods at all. This endangered their trades and discredited Artemis. The craftsmen were furious when they realized this. They started shouting, "Great is Artemis of the Ephesians!"

Soon the whole city was in an uproar and the people rushed into a huge outdoor theater. Paul wanted to speak to the crowd, but the disciples didn't let him. Some government officials who knew Paul begged him not to go into the theater.

The mob in the crowded theater was out of control. Thousands of people were there and everybody was yelling, even though most of people didn't even know why they were there. The Jews in the crowd pushed one of their leaders to the front, who motioned for silence so he could talk to the crowd. But when the crowd realized he was a Jew, they all chanted loudly in unison for almost two hours: "Great is Artemis of the Ephesians!"

Eventually, the city clerk quieted the crowd by reminding them that everybody knew that Ephesus was the guardian of the temple of Artemis and her image had fallen from heaven. (A meteorite that resembled a woman had fallen there.) The people should calm down and not do anything rash. All the craftsmen were entitled to bring their problems to court and could press charges. After the clerk said this, he told everybody to go back to work or go home.

Further Travels

When the uproar ended, Paul left Ephesus and went to Macedonia and Greece with some disciples. He encouraged people along the way and stayed in the region for many months. In some cities, the Jews plotted against him, so he had to change his plans. He was accompanied by believers from many cities where he had preached and taught. He wanted to return to Jerusalem and didn't know what would happen when he returned. But he was convinced that prison and hardship were in his future. He knew he would never see many of his followers again. He warned them that hard times and false teachers were coming, so they needed to be on their guard.

Paul's third missionary trip to the region lasted more than three years. Rather than being a burden to those he visited, he made and sold tents while he taught and debated. He modeled confident humility and service, just as Jesus had done. He reminded the disciples who were in the region what Jesus had said, "It is better to give than to receive." (The routes that Paul took during his trips are found in the maps at the end of this book.)

CHAPTER 21

FROM JERUSALEM TO ROME
Paul Uses His Citizenship to Make Another Trip

When Paul and his traveling companions returned to Palestine, a prophet from Judea said the Spirit revealed to him that Paul would be arrested and handed over to the Gentiles in Jerusalem. Everybody tried to convince Paul that he should not go there, but he said he was ready to be arrested and even die if it advanced the Christian movement.

When Paul and his traveling companions arrived at Jerusalem, they met with the church leaders and discussed everything that happened during their trips, including what God had done among the Gentiles. The church leaders praised God and told Paul that thousands of Jews had become believers in Palestine.

Paul Is Arrested in Jerusalem

When Paul went to the Temple, some Jews from Asia recognized him and accused him of false teaching and letting Greeks into the Temple. This wasn't true, but those in the city were disturbed. People dragged Paul out of the Temple and tried to kill him. News reached the Roman commander that Jerusalem was rioting, and he sent soldiers to calm the crowd. When the rioters saw the soldiers, they stopped beating Paul.

The commander arrested Paul, put him in chains, and asked who he was and what he had done. People in the crowd shouted different accusations, and the commander couldn't determine the truth. Paul was sent to the barracks, and on the way, the mob was so angry that Paul had to carried by the soldiers.

Paul asked the commander if he could speak to the crowd. The commander thought Paul was an Egyptian terrorist and was surprised that he spoke Greek. Paul said he was a Jew from Tarsus and got permission to address the crowd. Speaking in front of the barracks, he motioned for silence and started speaking in Aramaic, which quieted the crowd even more.

Paul explained his background and how he had studied the scriptures while living in Jerusalem. He was as devoted to God as they were and had persecuted the followers of the Way. He told the crowd what happened to him on his trip to Damascus. When he told the crowd about how he had been sent to the Gentiles, the people started shouting at him again and said he should be killed.

Seeing that a riot might start again, the commander ordered Paul to the barracks so he could be whipped and interrogated. As the soldiers got ready to whip him, Paul said to the lead soldier, "Is it legal for you to whip a Roman citizen who has not yet been found guilty?"

The soldier immediately went to the commander and said Paul was a Roman citizen. Paul was taken to the commander and he explained how he was born a Roman citizen. (Some people bought their Roman citizenship.) The commander was alarmed and immediately stopped the interrogation.

Paul Addresses the Sanhedrin

The commander wanted to know why Paul was accused by the Jews. He released Paul and ordered the Sanhedrin to assemble so Paul could stand before them. Paul addressed them and knew some were Sadducees and others were Pharisees. He started by saying, "I am a Pharisee and descended from Pharisees. I stand before you today because of my hope in the resurrection of the dead."

When he said this, a dispute broke out between the Sadducees, who believed there is no resurrection nor angels nor spirits, and the Pharisees who believed in these things. Some Pharisees stood up and argued that Paul had done nothing wrong. The dispute became so violent that the commander was afraid Paul would be killed. He ordered soldiers to take Paul back to the barracks.

The Plot to Kill Paul

That night, the Spirit said to Paul, "Don't worry! As you have spoken about me here in Jerusalem, you must also testify about me in Rome." Meanwhile, more than 40 Jews plotted to killed Paul. In the morning, they asked the chief priests and the elders to ask the commander to have Paul brought before the Sanhedrin again so his case could be heard in more detail. The Jews planned to kill Paul as he traveled to the meeting.

But Paul found out about the plot and informed the commander, who sent Paul to Governor Felix in Caesarea while being protected by 470 soldiers. The Jews would have to go to Caesarea to continue their investigation.

Trials Before Roman Officials

High-ranking Jews went to Caesarea and brought charges against Paul. A Jewish lawyer said Paul was a troublemaker who created riots among Jews all over the world. Others also made accusations against Paul.

After the Jews made their case, it was Paul's turn to speak. He told Felix that he worshipped in Jerusalem but didn't argue with anyone in the Temple or cause any problems in the city. There was no evidence to support the Jews' allegations, but he admitted to being a follower of the Way. Felix was familiar with the Way and ended the proceedings. He wanted Paul to offer him a bribe, but Paul just talked about how to live right. Felix left Paul in prison for two years. Paul was given some freedom and was allowed to have his friends take care of him.

Festus replaced Felix and immediately heard the accusations against Paul. The Jews wanted Paul transferred back to Jerusalem so they could ambush and kill him on the way. But Festus wanted Paul to be tried in Caesarea.

When Festus heard the case, the Jews tried to intimidate Paul, but they couldn't prove any of their accusations. Paul made his defense and said he did not violate any Jewish Law or do anything against Caesar. Festus asked Paul if he wanted to stand trial in Jerusalem, but Paul appealed to have his case tried by Caesar. Festus told Paul that since he appealed to Caesar, his trial would be in Rome.

Festus Consults King Agrippa

When King Agrippa arrived in Caesarea to welcome Festus as the new governor, they discussed Paul's case. The king saw Paul the next day in front of many high-ranking military officers and powerful men of the city. Festus told everybody that the Jews wanted to kill Paul, who was innocent.

Paul explained to everybody that he was a Pharisee and that what God had promised to the Jews had been fulfilled. The reason the Jews were against him was because he believed Jesus was the Messiah and had been raised from the dead. He had previously opposed the movement of the Way and had the disciples of Jesus arrested, but he had come to know that everything that was said about Jesus was true. He described what had happened on the road to Damascus and that God wanted him to preach to the Gentiles, not just the Jews, "to open their eyes and turn them from darkness to light, from the power of Satan to God, so they may receive forgiveness of sins."

The king was well acquainted with the Jewish customs and controversies, so he understood what Paul said. After Paul was finished speaking, the king told Festus and the others that Paul had done nothing wrong. If he hadn't appealed to Caesar, Paul could have been set free.

Paul Sails to Rome

Paul and some other prisoners were handed to a Roman military commander to sail to Italy. Some of Paul's friends went with him, including Luke. They sailed in a path to avoid strong winds. When the northern fall winds grew stronger,

Paul warned the commander that it was dangerous to keep going; the ship could be destroyed. But the commander followed the advice of the ship's captain who owned the ship. There was no good harbor for them to visit at that point, so they kept going, hoping to reach a safe harbor 50 miles away.

But the wind turned very strong and pushed the ship away from shore. The boat was straining from the winds and waves, so ropes were wrapped around the boat to hold it together. Men on the boat threw the cargo overboard to lighten the load while the storm raged. A few days later, the crew threw all the ship's sailing gear overboard. The storm continued for many days and the boat drifted helplessly. Everybody was seasick and couldn't eat, and everybody thought they would all die.

Paul stood up before everybody on the ship and told them not to lose hope. He said an angel of his God told him that he must stand trial before Caesar and that everybody onboard would live, even though the ship would be destroyed when it went aground on an unknown island.

The ship continued drifting west across the Mediterranean Sea. One night, the sailors measured the depth of the sea and it was not as deep in a short time. To keep them from crashing onto the rocks they couldn't yet see, they dropped all the anchors from the back of the ship and prayed for daylight. Some sailors tried to escape in the lifeboat, but Paul told the commander that everybody had to stay on the ship in order for everybody to live. This time the commander listened to him, and the soldiers cut the ropes that held the lifeboat and let it drift away.

Just before dawn, Paul urged them all to eat. The storm had lasted 14 days, and everybody was weak, so they needed their strength to survive. Paul took some bread and gave thanks to God in front of everybody and started to eat. Encouraged by Paul's example, the others started eating. There were 276 people on the ship, and everybody ate as much as they wanted. When they were finished, they threw the rest of the food into the sea to lighten the ship.

Landing on Malta

When daylight came, nobody recognized the land. They saw a bay with a sandy beach and decided to run the ship onto the beach. They cut the anchors loose, hoisted a sail, and drifted toward the beach. But the ship struck a sandbar and ran aground. The bow was stuck and the pounding surf broke the boat into pieces.

The soldiers planned to kill the prisoners to prevent them from swimming away and escaping, but the commander wanted to spare Paul's life, so none of the prisoners were harmed. All those who could swim were ordered to jump overboard and get to land. The rest had to hang on to anything that floated until reaching land.

They all made it safely to shore. They were on the island of Malta, and the islanders helped them with unusual kindness as the cold rain pounded them on the beach. Paul was bitten by a poisonous snake while building a fire on the beach. The islanders saw the snake hanging from his hand and said he was a murderer — they said that although he escaped from the sea, the goddess Justice would not allow him to live. But Paul flicked the snake into the fire and wasn't harmed. The people expected him to swell up or die quickly, but after a long time, nothing happened to Paul. So they changed their minds and said he was a god.

The chief official of Malta lived in a large complex near the beach, and he welcomed the shipwreck victims in his home and showed them generous hospitality for three days. His father was sick, and when Paul placed his hands on him and prayed, the father was healed. Others on the island found out what happened, and the rest of the sick people on the island came and were cured by Paul.

Paul Preaches in Rome Under Guard

Paul and the others stayed on Malta for three months, then resumed their trip to Rome. When they arrived, Paul was allowed to live by himself with a soldier who guarded him. Paul met with the local Jewish leaders and explained why he was there; none of them had heard what had happened in Jerusalem. They wanted to know what he had to say about the Way because everybody was talking against it.

Paul met with a larger number of Jews who lived in Rome. He talked about the kingdom of God, and by connecting it to the Law of Moses and what the prophets had said, he tried to persuade them about Jesus. Some were convinced, but others wouldn't believe. Paul finished by quoting the prophet Isaiah:

> Go to this people and say, "You will keep on hearing and seeing but you will not understand. For the people's hearts have become insensitive: their ears can hardly hear, and they have closed their eyes." Therefore, God's salvation has been sent to the Gentiles; they will listen!

Paul stayed in a rented house for two years and welcomed everybody who visited him. He had written a very long letter to the believers in Rome when he was traveling in Greece, so the believers in Rome knew about him. (This letter is included in the New Testament.) Paul kept teaching boldly about the kingdom of God and about Jesus the Messiah, and nobody stopped him. He sent letters of encouragement to the believers and their leaders in many cities he visited in Asia Minor, Macedonia, and Greece. In those letters, he provided more instructions to the churches, just as he had written to them before he went to Rome.

(Paul was released from house arrest in AD 62 and continued preaching and teaching in various parts of southern Europe and on the island of Crete. He was imprisoned again in Rome and was killed because of his faith during the reign of Nero in about AD 68. His ministry had lasted about 32 years.)

CHAPTER 22

PAUL'S LETTERS TO BELIEVERS
New Churches Receive Encouragement
and Instruction

During his long ministry, Paul wrote letters to the churches in southern Europe and Asia Minor and to a few Christian leaders in the region. He wrote letters to believers in Rome, Corinth, Thessalonica, Philippi, Ephesus, Colossae (a city near Laodicea), and the cities in the region of Galatia (Pisidian Antioch, Iconium, Lystra, and Derbe). He also wrote to Christian leaders in various cities: Timothy in Ephesus, Titus in Crete, and Philemon in Colossae. Paul may also have been the author or coauthor of a long document written to Jews ("Hebrews" is summarized in the next chapter).

The letters at that time were written on sheets of papyrus that were close in size to sheets of paper we use now. Most of the time, only one sheet was used for a letter. When longer letters were written, they were connected to each other and rolled up as a scroll. Sometimes scribes wrote the letters while that were dictated by the author. Long letters may have had multiple scribes.

The letters usually began with a greeting that included the name of the person sending the letter and who was to receive them. The letters usually ended with a farewell and sometimes greeted others the author knew. Dates were not included, and letters were delivered using travelers who were known by the sender and receiver.

Religious ideas, teachings about correct living, and practical advice were usually included in Paul's letters. He described and interpreted Jesus's teachings and actions, and he discussed what they meant for believers. He also encouraged those who received the letters because they were experiencing hardships because of their new faith.

Paul wrote very long letters that included many concepts about God as he clarified and defended the faith using logical arguments.

This chapter summarizes the main messages of Paul's letters in the order they were probably written.

Letter to the Galatians

The first letter Paul wrote was to the churches in Galatia and discussed controversies about how a Christian is identified. Gentiles had joined the church, and some Jews believed they should obey to all the rules of Judaism, including its food restrictions, circumcision, sacrifices, and separating from others who did not share their beliefs. In the past, Gentiles who converted to Judaism were required to follow the laws of Moses. However, most Gentiles who were becoming Christians did not want to convert to Judaism in addition to following Jesus, and many of them were leaving the church. What made a person a Christians? Was it following the ways of Jesus alone, or must they also follow the rules of Judaism?

Paul used his own experiences to say that following Jesus was enough. God's grace didn't come to him because he was a devout Pharisee who obeyed Jewish laws. Paul knew Peter had met with Gentiles and that "unclean" foods were edible for Christians. Peter approved having Paul preach to the Gentiles and stressed only the need to continue helping the poor. Paul accepted everybody because God no longer showed favoritism toward the Jews. Here is his basic argument:

> A person is not justified (declared righteous and acceptable to God) by following the law, but by faith in Jesus, the Christ. Nobody is made right by obeying the law. I died to the law so that I can live for God. I died with Christ and became a new person because he lives in me. I live by faith in the Son of God who loved me and gave himself for me. If righteousness can be earned through

the law, Christ died for nothing. The law held us together until Jesus came and saved us; having the law proved that we couldn't always keep the law. So there is no requirement to follow the law — we are freed from being slaves to the law. There is neither Jew nor Gentile, neither slave nor free, neither male and female — all are one in the Lord. Non-Jews were adopted into God's family; those who believe and obey Jesus are part of Abraham's ancestors and inherit the promises of God. Rigid views of the gospel pervert the truth and are a form of slavery.

Paul reminded his readers not to disregard the law or think that lawlessness was acceptable. Freedom from the law did not mean freedom to sin. Rather, Christians should be led by God's spirit and not commit immoral acts. Christians should love and serve one another with humility, for the entire law is summed up in one command: "Love your neighbor as yourself."

> Stay away from acts such as sexual immorality, witchcraft and worshipping idols, hatred, arguing, jealousy, extreme anger, selfishness, and drunkenness. The fruit of the Spirit is love, joy, peace, patience, kindness, goodness, faithfulness, gentleness, and self-control. There is no law against these things. If someone is caught in a sin, restore the person gently. Help carry each other's burdens, don't compare your acts with the acts of others, and don't grow tired of doing good to all people, especially other believers.

Letters to the Thessalonians

Paul wrote two letters to the church in Thessalonica, the large capital Macedonia; Silas and Timothy were coauthors. Both letters were written soon after the three men had been driven out of Corinth. The Thessalonica church was mainly composed of Gentiles, and Timothy had told Paul and Silas how well the church was doing.

In the first letter, the authors congratulated the believers on their conversion and growing faith. The church's faithfulness while being persecuted was a good example to the churches in other cities. Three important words — faith, love, and hope — appear early in the letter. Faith produced good works, love led to acts of kindness and mercy, and hope generated grit and endurance during difficult times. The authors also exhorted the believers with practical instructions about how to live.

> Avoid sexual immorality and conduct yourselves in a holy and honorable way. Lead a quiet life and mind your own business. Work so your life wins the respect of outsiders and so you won't have to depend on others. Live in peace with each other. Tell people not to be idle or disruptive, encourage those who are depressed, help the weak, and be patient with everyone. Make sure nobody does something wrong when they are mistreated, and always try to do what is good for each other and all others. Rejoice always, never stop praying, and give thanks in every situation.

The second, shorter letter was written soon after the first letter. The church was being persecuted, and some Christians believed it was a sign that Jesus would soon return to earth. False prophets reinforced this view because many Christians had been killed. Paul's first letter encouraged the believers to be watchful for Jesus and about the dead being raised, which added to their belief that Jesus's return could happen at any time. As a result, some believers had quit their jobs.

Paul explained that Jesus was not returning soon, and it might not happen for a long time. He explained that the time of Jesus's return is unknown, so people needed to go back to work. It was important for the believers to work hard and not be a burden on others, just as the three men had taken care of their own needs. God would eventually punish wicked people.

Letters to the Corinthians

Paul wrote three letters to the believers in Corinth, but the first one was lost, so its contents are unknown. In his second letter (known as First Corinthians), Paul responded to questions in a letter the church had sent him. Corinth was a tough port city with many taverns and people selling their bodies for the pleasure of others, and the church was struggling. Most of the believers were not well educated and came from a lower social class, so they felt inferior to the more educated people in the city. Paul told them that even though they were not wise or noble by human standards, "God chose foolish things of the world to shame the wise and chose weak things of the world to shame the strong."

The people in the Corinth church had many practical questions. They asked how to deal with divisions and lawsuits within the church and with Christians who acted in immoral ways. They had questions about marriage, what foods could be eaten, and how to conduct useful worship services (such as celebrating the Lord's Supper, women in church, and exercising spiritual gifts). Church members also had questions about the resurrection of Jesus and their own resurrection in the future.

Paul pleaded to the church members to be unified rather than be divided based on who taught them. "I planted the seed, Apollos watered it, but God made it grow. I laid a foundation and others build on it. If you fight about what teacher is best, it shows you are still babies in the faith. When you were babies in the faith, I gave you spiritual milk that you could handle. Your divisions show that you aren't ready for solid food."

Paul also clarified what he had said about who Christians should be with and what kind of people to avoid.

> My previous letter said you shouldn't associate with people who committed improper sex acts. I didn't mean you should not associate with people of this world who are immoral, or those who are greedy, thieves, or worship other gods. If that were the case, you would have to leave the world! What I meant was that you must

not associate with those *who claim to be your brother or sister in Christ* but who are sexually immoral, greedy, liars and thieves, or drink too much. We are not to judge those outside the church — God will do that.

Paul explained that being guided by God's spirit was more important than having human wisdom. "If you have the Spirit, you have the mind of Christ." The human body was sacred and the temple of the Holy Spirit. Those committing major sins needed to be removed from the church and excluded from the Lord's Supper.

In regard to marriage, Paul said being single was good because it allowed people to serve God and others more freely. But because of our sexual nature, God blessed marriages because "it's better to get married than burn with uncontrolled passions." Those who get married need to give their bodies to each other, and neither party has power over the other. Paul also gave his opinion (not words from God) about other matters related to marriage and divorce.

Paul said a person can eat anything, but if a person thinks it's not right to eat something and then eats it, they have sinned. Eating becomes a stumbling block to those who have a less-developed faith. Therefore, Christians should not eat something if it causes another person to eat something they think they shouldn't eat. (Most of the meat eaten at the time had been sacrificed to idols.) Paul said, "I'm a Jew with the Jews, but when I'm with others who don't follow rules about what to eat, I eat what they eat. I've become all things to all people so they will be more willing to hear my message. God won't let you be tempted beyond what you can bear. When you are tempted, there is always a way to get out of it."

Paul wrote about how to conduct worship services. Believers needed to make sure they were sharing the Lord's Supper in peace. If there was a disagreement among individuals, they were to resolve it first. Paul also said women should not talk or ask questions during worship if they didn't understand something — they should ask others about it later. Women should also avoid having disruptive side conversations and be quiet unless they were praying and teaching as part of the worship activities.

Paul said that too much time was being spent having people speak in other languages that nobody else understood. This was a gift given by the Spirit to some believers, and it happened during the first Pentecost. But if nobody could interpret what was said, it wasn't useful, and others might think the church was of people who were mentally ill. Everybody had spiritual gifts, such as healing, wisdom, knowledge, faith, understanding if a spirit is good, speaking another language, help, and guidance. Less-dramatic gifts given by the Spirit, such as preaching and understanding the truth about God, were more useful. Paul said, "I speak in tongues more than all of you. But I'd rather speak five good words of instruction among believers than speak 10,000 words in another language."

He spoke about the church as if it was a human body with many parts — everybody had a different function.

> The ear can't say, "Because I'm not an eye, I'm not part of the body." If the whole body were an eye, how could we hear? God created many parts of one body, and all the parts should work together. The parts that seem weaker are indispensable. If one part suffers, everybody suffers.

Paul then wrote that using spiritual gifts was not nearly as important as being a loving person. Paul compared spiritual gifts and love this way:[7]

> If I speak in another tongue but don't show love, I'm just making noise. If I have the gift of prophecy and can understand all mysteries and knowledge, or if I have so much faith that I can move a mountain, but I don't show love, I'm nothing. If I give everything I have to the poor and sacrifice my body but don't love others, I gain nothing.

---

[7] Paul used the Greek term *agape* as the word for love in this passage. The word involves action and sacrifice for others. It does not mean an emotional feeling, friendship (*philia*), or physical love (*eros*).

Love is patient and kind. It isn't jealous and doesn't brag or dishonor others. It's not proud or selfish. It doesn't get angry easily or keep track of when people do something wrong. Love doesn't delight in evil but rejoices with the truth. It bears and believes all things; it is always hopeful and endures all things. When I was a child, I talked and thought like a child. Now that I've matured, I've put away my childish and selfish ways. Love never fails. Prophecies will cease and tongues will go quiet and knowledge will pass away. Faith, hope, and love are the most important, and the greatest of these is love.

Finally, Paul discussed the resurrection of the body, a strange concept to the Greeks that caused some believers to doubt that they would come back to life at some point. Nobody doubted that Jesus came back from the dead. This meant that others could come back from the dead. Jesus defeated death so a person's spiritual body will come back to life. Paul concluded with this mystery:

When we are dead, we will be changed instantly when the last trumpet sounds. The dead will be raised and will live forever. What Hosea said will come true, "Death has been swallowed up in God's victory. Where, O death, is your victory; where is your sting?"

Paul's Last Letter to the Corinthians

Paul made several trips to Corinth to support and teach the believers, and some of his visits were "painful." Opposition to Paul had risen, but the leader of a rebellion had been disciplined. Paul wrote to express relief and joy that the church had dealt with this problem, and he encouraged the believers to allow the rebel leader back into the church. Since being a Christian in the Roman empire was hazardous, he reminded the church of the hope they had in the resurrection of their souls. Christians walked by faith, not by their own sight. They were new creatures because God lived in them — they had moved on from their old ways of acting and thinking. Believers are like pots of clay, shaped by the master potter, that perform different functions as God desires.

Paul spoke about all his qualifications to teach, but he also stressed his own weaknesses, including having a "thorn in the side." Paul never said anything about what bothering him, and he had prayed several times to have the problem taken away. But God said that "my power is shown in human weakness." Paul was good enough just as he was, and his limitations kept him humble — when he was weak, he was strong.

Letter to the Romans

Paul's longest letter was sent to the house churches in Rome that had both Jewish and Gentile believers. He wrote before his first trip to Rome and didn't know many of the Christians in Rome personally, so his writing is more formal than the other letters he wrote.

His letter summarized the basic ideas of the new Christian faith to believers who didn't have this knowledge. He explained the general principles of the faith as if his letter was a legal case. His overall message was that Jesus died and delivered all people from sin, so a relationship with God is available to anybody who has faith in Jesus, the Christ. He used five themes to support this message:

- All people have a sinful nature.
- The death of Jesus was the best and last sacrifice of blood needed to take away the sins of the world and allow all people to be acceptable to God.
- Christians need to be holy and rely on God's Spirit to endure during difficult times. Deeper faith leads to deeper righteousness.
- Jews were initially chosen as God's people, but Gentiles are now included because the Israelites continually rejected God.
- Being a Christian means living in a different way in a sinful world.

People Have a Sinful Nature

The first theme noted that all people have a sinful nature; individuals and society as a whole tend to do evil things. People commit all types of crimes and don't show mercy or fairness to others. They lie, fight, gossip, and think of ways to help themselves, even when they know there are severe consequences for doing so. They are proud and brag about how great they are and are not patient or kind. They hear the law but don't obey it; they don't practice what they preach.

> Nobody is righteous, everybody has turned away from God. We can't be acceptable to God by obeying the law. Our inability to obey the law shows our sinful nature. There is no difference between Jew and Gentile — all have sinned and fallen short of God's standards for righteousness.

Jesus, the Best and Last Sacrifice Needed

The second theme tells how the death of Jesus was the best and last sacrifice of blood needed to take away the sins of the world and allows people to stand justified and righteous before God. The blood shed by Christ permanently stopped God's anger against people's sinful nature, just as the sacrifices of high-quality animals previously removed the sins of the Israelites. But those sacrifices only stopped God's anger temporarily against the Jews. The sacrifice of Jesus applies to everybody.

Abraham was "justified" (righteous) because of his faith. He obediently moved from Mesopotamia to Canaan, and he was ready to kill Isaac, even though God promised him countless descendants. He never lost hope for a son, even when he and Sarah were very old. He wasn't justified by obeying the law — he showed his faith before he was circumcised, which was simply a sign of his faith. A true Jew is somebody who is faithful to God's teachings, not somebody who has the outward characteristics of a Jew or obeys the law. "The sins of one man (Adam) affected all humans; the sacrifice of one man (Jesus) cleansed all humans."

The benefits of being a Christian are free because Jesus paid the price. People only need to have an earnest faith in Jesus to stand clean before God and gain the benefits. These benefits include having peace, joy, and hope, even during difficult times. Sin kills, but Jesus died to give us life.

Christian Holiness

A third theme focused on the processes of becoming mature in the Christian faith. People naturally do things they know they shouldn't do, but God's spirit helps people resist temptation and change their character. "All things work together for good for those who love God. Suffering produces perseverance, which produces character, which produces hope. If God is for us, who can be against us? Nothing can separate us from the love of Christ." Those who are guided by the Spirit aren't relying on their own resources. They are tapping into God's "living water," which gradually transforms them into people who reflect God's nature and character. The Spirit helps Christians become the salt of the earth and the light of the world.

Updating the Promises to the Israelites

The fourth theme related to the issue of how Judaism relates to Christian beliefs. God had chosen the Israelites to be God's representatives on earth — had that changed? Paul knew most Jews didn't believe Jesus was the Messiah and rejected the idea that the kingdom of God had come. Jews expected the Messiah to become a king and overthrow the Romans. As a devout Pharisee, Paul fully understood the laws of Moses and had personal experience that allowed him to tie the ideas of Judaism with the new ideas of Christianity. The new promises are logically linked to the previous promises. A sovereign God could "elect" any group of people to be the chosen people. By focusing on obeying the law rather than having faith in God, the Jews lost their special status as God's chosen people. Now Gentiles who had faith in Jesus were included — adopted into God's family, a branch grafted onto a holy tree to replace dead branches. The Jews were still special to God, but when God included the Gentiles in the kingdom, there were more messengers who could bear fruit and carry the good news of God's saving love and forgiveness to all parts of the world. The Gentiles could also help the Jews understand God's overall plan for the world. God's love and mercy for the human race had not changed at all.

Living as Christians in the World

Paul ends by discussing what it took for a Christian to live in an evil world. Christians are to be obviously different.

> I urge you to offer your bodies as a living sacrifice to God, which is a form of worship. Don't conform to the ways and ideas of this world, but be changed by renewing your mind.
>
> Everybody should use their gifts to the best of their ability. Each person is part of one body, yet we all have different functions and gifts. Some will preach while others will serve or teach; some will encourage or give generously while others will lead or show kindness.
>
> Love must be sincere. Love one another and honor others more than yourself. Be happy in hope, patient during problems, and faithful in prayer. Share with other Christians who are in need and practice hospitality. Don't be proud and think of yourself more highly than you should. Instead, view yourself with realistic eyes.
>
> Bless those who persecute you. Rejoice with those who rejoice; weep with those who weep. Do what you can to live at peace with everyone. Be willing to associate with people in low positions who do simple and dirty work. Hate what is evil; embrace what is good. Don't do evil to those who do evil to you, and do what everybody thinks is right. Don't seek revenge — that is something God will handle. Instead, "If your enemies are hungry, feed them; if they are thirsty, give them something to drink. In doing this, you will heap burning coals on their

head."[8] Don't be overcome by evil, but overcome evil with good.

Submit to the government officials who provide justice. Give to those what you owe them: If you owe taxes or have debts, pay them. Respect and honor those who require it.

Letter to the Colossians

The city of Colossae was 100 miles east of Ephesus and was on a major trade route connecting Asia and Europe. Paul had never been there, but he had visited cities near there and heard about its growing church composed mainly of Gentiles. Paul wrote to the Colossians to address false teachings that the church was facing, teachings that blended Jewish legalism, Greek philosophy, and Oriental mysticism.

The first half of the letter dealt with correct Christian doctrine. He stressed the supremacy of Jesus.

> Jesus is the visible image of the invisible God, the firstborn of all creation. All things on earth and in heaven, visible and invisible, were created by him and for him. He existed before all things, and he holds everything together. He is the head of the body, the church, and is supreme in everything. God's fullness lived in him, and through him all things on earth and in heaven are reconciled to God through the sacrifice of his blood on the cross.

Paul urged his readers to focus on Jesus rather than following strict Jewish practices, philosophies of angel worship, and ideas of self-denial. The blending of these additional elements into the faith took the people's attention away from the idea that Jesus was all Christians need to be right with God.

> Christ died so you don't need to follow the rules of this world that say, "Don't touch this, don't taste this!" These rules are based on human commands and teachings that

---

[8] See the footnote in Chapter 13 in the section related to Proverbs 25 for the meaning of this saying.

appear to be wise with their false humility and harsh treatment of the body but don't have any lasting value.

In the second part of the letter, Paul wrote about how Christians should behave. Believers are to set their sights on doing godly things, not evil things.

> Take off your old self and put on your new self. This means doing away with anger, saying lies about others, bad language, sexual immorality, evil desires, and selfishness. As God's chosen people, show compassion, kindness, humility, gentleness, and patience. Bear with each other and forgive one another, just as Jesus forgives you. Most importantly, love others so you all stay together. Act wisely toward outsiders and make the most of every opportunity. Your conversations should be full of patience and kindness as you talk to others.

Letter to the Ephesians

Paul wrote a longer and more sophisticated letter to the church in Ephesus that was similar to his letter to the Colossians. He sent both letters at about the same time while he was in prison in Rome. He had lived in Ephesus for several years, so he knew his audience well. There was no specific reason for writing other than to keep teaching the church about what it meant to be the church.

While his letter to the Colossians stressed Jesus as the head of the church, his letter to the Ephesians focused on the church as the body of Christ, a collection of chosen people who were adopted into the faith. The general nature of the letter indicates that it was probably meant to be sent to the other churches in the region. Like the letter to the Colossians, his letter had two major parts — one on correct Christian ideas and the other about how to live out the faith in the world.

The first part of the letter states that it was always part of God's larger plan to have all people on earth be in a loving relationship with God, not just the Jews. The three forms of God played a role in the development and continuation of God's overall plan. God the "Father" chose the believers; the Son (Jesus) made people holy through his death, which forgave all the sins of the world; and the Spirit guided people living on the earth. Paul stressed that people had done nothing to earn any special status with God. It was entirely God's grace, a free and undeserved gift that came to believers because of their faith in Jesus.

> You were previously dead in your sins, but now you are alive in Christ — your sins are forgiven. Grace has saved us because of our faith; it is God's free gift, not by what we have done so we can brag about it. We are God's handiwork and have been created to do good works. God prepared us to do this long ago.
>
> Jews and Gentiles are now one group with citizenship in heaven. God's purpose was to create one new humanity out of the two, thus making peace. Gentiles are no longer foreigners and strangers but fellow citizens with God's people and members of God's family which was built on the foundation of the apostles and prophets. Jesus is the chief cornerstone — in him the whole building is joined together and rises to become God's holy temple. In Jesus, you are the church that is being built to be where God's Spirit lives.

Paul saw himself simply as God's servant to help reveal this overall plan to the Gentiles. He didn't want anybody feeling sorry for him while he was in prison. He was doing what he was meant to do. He just wanted believers to understand the amazing love God had for them and to continue growing in their faith and love for one another.

These ideas were developed in the second part of the letter — an extended set of instructions and encouragement to live in peace with one another, despite their diversity, in order for the world to see an example of how people should live as one on the earth.

Showing unity within a diverse group had implications for individuals (how they should live their own lives as new creatures) and for the group (how the diversity of the church should operate in unity). Each person had a different role, just as the different parts of the body help the entire body function. Paul wrote many of the same things he wrote to the Colossians about how Christians should live their lives and how to live in a community of faith. He expanded on his views about the roles within the family.

> Submit to one another out of respect for Christ. Wives, submit yourselves to your husbands as you do to the Lord. Husbands, love your wives like Christ loved the church and gave himself up for her to make her holy. Love your wives as if they were your own body. He who loves his wife loves his own body, just as Jesus loves the church.
>
> Children, obey your parents. Fathers, don't irritate your children. Raise them with training and instruction about the Lord. Slaves, obey your masters with respect and sincerity. Masters, treat your slaves in the same way. Don't threaten them, for our Master in heaven shows no favoritism. Serve others as if you were serving the Lord, who will reward us based on what we do, not whether we are a slave or free.

Paul ended his letter by encouraging the church to be on guard against evil while being strong to keep and expand the faith. Using the analogy of a soldier's armor, he described defensive and offensive tools to fight the devil's schemes. "Our struggle is not against flesh and blood, but against the powers of darkness in this world and against the spiritual forces of evil."

Letter to the Philippians

Philippi was a major city in Macedonia and the first city in Europe Paul visited. It was a prosperous Roman colony, and the Gentiles in the church were Roman citizens who supported Paul financially. He wrote his letter when he was in prison in Rome and is very personal. He gave an update on his travels and thanked them for their financial support. He talked about how he was doing while under house arrest, and he said that being in prison helping spread the gospel — the prison guards and various Roman officials were hearing the good news about Jesus.

Paul encouraged the Philippians to stand firm in their faith and rejoice when they were persecuted for their faith. He wasn't worried about dying — he would gain from it by being even closer to God. He wrote about the importance of being humble and used Jesus as the ultimate example of humility, which was not considered a virtue among the people who lived at that time.

> Be of one mind and don't do anything out of selfish ambition. Be humble and value others and their interests above your own. In your relationships with others, have the same attitude that Jesus had. Even though he was a form of God, he didn't consider equality with God as something he should use to his advantage. Instead, he became a human servant and was obedient to God, dying in a humiliating way on a cross. As a result, God honored him to be in the highest place and gave him the name that is above every name. Everything in heaven, on earth, and under the earth will bow down to him, and everyone will say that Jesus Christ is Lord.

Paul talked about his own credentials as a devout Jew. He could have boasted about his religious background and holiness. But these were now irrelevant; he gave up his privileges in the religious community in order to believe in Jesus and promote the good news. He was still learning and trying to understand Jesus more, even if it meant dying for his faith.

> Don't be anxious about anything. In every situation, present your requests to God by praying with thanks. The peace of God which is beyond our understanding will guard your hearts and minds. Whatever is true, whatever is noble, whatever is right, whatever is pure — if anything is excellent or worth praising — think about these things. I've learned to be at peace in every situation. I know what it's like to be in need and to have plenty, to be hungry or well fed. I can do all things through Christ who gives me strength and what I need.

Paul said a Christian's citizenship is in heaven and believers are ambassadors for the kingdom of God to those living on earth. Christianity represented a new model of thinking and living, and the Spirit transforms and protects believers on their mission in this world.

Letters to Church Leaders

Paul wrote letters during and after he was in prison in Rome to pastors who lived in areas he had visited. Several of the letters were dictated to scribes who were allowed to put Paul's ideas in their own words. This has led some to doubt that Paul was the author. The letters focused mainly on organizing the leadership of the church, teachings about good conduct in the world, and dealing with false teachings.

Titus

Paul wrote a letter to his friend Titus, a Greek Gentile who became a believer during Paul's first trip to Asia Minor. Titus was with Paul and Barnabas when they went to Jerusalem to tell the church leaders about the conversion of the Gentiles, and he was used as an example during the discussion about the need for circumcision among the Gentiles. Titus was left on the island of Crete during one of Paul's trips and eventually became the leader of all the churches on the island.

Paul wrote to guide Titus when he appointed leaders ("elders") to lead the local churches on the island. Elders were to show the fruits of the spirit (e.g., being patient, kind, hospitable, self-controlled, disciplined). They needed to be strong believers: acting with holiness, holding firmly to the Christian message, encouraging others with correct teaching and opposing those who didn't believe it, being faithful to their wives, and not being violent or drinking too much alcohol. In fact, these qualities should be exhibited by all believers, regardless of their position or gender. This would help people respect and admire those who followed Jesus.

Paul told Titus to crack down on the Jews who were saying bad things about Gentile believers who were not following the Jewish customs. He also told Titus to teach all believers not to rebel against the government leaders, to do good whenever they could, and to avoid talking about foolish and useless controversies. Those who caused divisions should be warned several times, and if they continued being divisive, they should be avoided.

Philemon

Paul's shortest letter (one page) was written while he was a prisoner in Rome. He met and converted a slave named Onesimus (meaning "useful") while they were both in prison. The slave belonged to Philemon, a Christian living in Colossae who led a house church. Paul had previously helped Philemon become a believer while they were in Ephesus. Onesimus had taken some of Philemon's money and run away to Rome. Onesimus was being released from prison, and Paul convinced him to return to Philemon and be useful rather than be useless like a missing slave.

Paul's letter encouraged Philemon to take in Onesimus again and treat him as a fellow believer and not punish or kill him as he would do to a typical runaway slave. Paul promised to pay Philemon the money he was owed by Onesimus. Paul implied that Philemon should free Onesimus from slavery and that Philemon owed Paul a favor because of his own conversion.

(Onesimus was freed by Philemon and went on to become the bishop of the church in Ephesus; Philemon became the bishop of the church in Gaza. Both men were eventually killed by the Romans because of their faith.)

Timothy

Paul wrote two letters to Timothy, the half-Gentile Christian from Lystra who was his traveling companion. Although Timothy was young, Paul left him in charge of leading the large and diverse church in Ephesus because of his preaching and teaching skills.

In his first letter, Paul warned Timothy about several Jews who were teaching incorrect ideas about what was required to be a Christian. Their emphasis was on obeying the laws of Moses, not loving others and having faith in Jesus. The law was still useful when it dealt with criminals, liars, rebels, slave traders, and those who practiced sexual immorality.

Paul also wrote about how to organize worship services and the church. He gave instructions about how to pray, how women should dress, and who should speak and teach during worship. He gave Timothy many of the same instructions he gave Titus about the qualifications for the elders (also called bishops), and he discussed the qualifications of the deacons.

He gave Timothy advice about how to maintain his health and noted that paying elders for their work was a good idea. He encouraged him to pursue godliness and show faith, love, endurance, and gentleness to others. Finally, Paul gave him advice about how to deal with believers in every part of life: those who were old and young, married or widowed or single, slaves and their masters, those who were accused of a sin, and the rich and poor.

> Be content with what you have. Those who want to get rich fall into a trap. Many foolish desires are harmful and ruin people, for the love of money causes all kinds of evil. Some who are eager for money have left the faith and have had many problems. Those who are rich in this life shouldn't be proud or put their hope in their possessions that can be uncertain. They should put their hope in God who richly provides everything we need to be happy. Command them to do good and be rich in good deeds, being generous and willing to share. In this way they will store their treasures in heaven.

Paul's second letter to Timothy was written much later when he was in prison again in Rome. He was suffering in a cold prison cell because he was a Christian. Paul believed he would soon be killed by the Romans under Nero, and it was the last record of any of Paul's writings. All Christians were being persecuted at the time and many of his followers had abandoned him, so he was feeling alone.

Although Paul was depressed, he encouraged Timothy to keep the faith and not be afraid of dying because of his faith. Suffering was part of the Christian life, and dying meant being closer to God. Paul warned Timothy about false teachers who spent time quarreling about things that were not important. Those who opposed him should be dealt with gently so they would come to their senses, be sorry, and turn back to the truth.

Paul also told Timothy to continue preaching and teaching from the scriptures, which had made him wise and understand the words and thoughts of God. The scriptures were all useful for teaching, correcting, and training others in holy living. The inspired scriptures help equip Christians for every good work.

Paul ended his last letter by asking Timothy to visit him in prison. Luke was the only person left in Rome who comforted and encouraged him. (There is nothing written about whether Timothy arrived in Rome before Paul was executed.)

CHAPTER 23

OTHER LETTERS TO BELIEVERS
Apostles Send General Letters to the Church

Paul wrote most of the letters in the Bible to fellow believers, but other letters were written by the apostles Peter and John and the two half-brothers of Jesus, James and Judas (calling himself Jude). Another letter was written by an unknown author to Jews in general. This chapter summarizes these letters.

Peter's Letters

Peter wrote two letters to believers. The first letter was sent to Gentile believers in cities that Paul visited who were being attacked verbally and physically for their faith. The main point of the letter was to encourage believers to remain strong in their faith as they suffered in difficult times, just as Jesus did. Believers should love one another, be good citizens, and have good families in order to give a good impression to others. In the end, their efforts would be rewarded in heaven.

> God is pleased when you suffer and endure for doing good. You are a chosen people, a holy nation, and God's special possession so you may speak about Jesus who called you out of darkness into his wonderful light. Your beauty should not come from what you wear — it should be your inner self, the unfading beauty of a gentle and quiet spirit. Always be prepared to give an answer to everyone who asks you why you have hope, but do it with respect and gentleness. Above all, love each other deeply, for love covers many sins. Be alert and sober because your enemy, the devil, prowls around like a roaring lion looking for somebody to devour. Resist him and stand firm in the faith because you know that

the family of believers all over the world is experiencing the same kind of suffering.

Peter's second letter is shorter and focused on a different issue: resisting false teachers and evildoers who influenced the church. The diversity of the early church brought with it new ideas that were not consistent with the teachings of Peter, Paul, and other Christian leaders, and Peter wanted to emphasis the church's basic teachings.

He started by telling believers to grow in their faith. "Make every effort to add to your faith the qualities of goodness, knowledge, self-control, perseverance, godliness, support for others, and love. If you increase these qualities, they will help you be effective and productive." Then he wrote that true prophets always speak for God and from God and don't rely on their own ideas to try to influence the thoughts and actions of others; false teachers tell stories to take advantage of gullible believers.

One of these false teachings was that Jesus would not return and there would not be a final judgment. Peter emphasized again that Jesus would return and be the final judge. Evil would be destroyed with fire, just as evil was destroyed by water in the days of Noah. The day was unknown because "a day is like a thousand years" to God. Eventually the false teachers would be judged harshly.

Letter from James

James was a half-brother of Jesus who initially did not follow Jesus but became a believer after the resurrection. James led the Jerusalem church that Paul addressed when discussing issues related to the Gentiles. His letter was addressed to Jews who lived outside of Palestine. His letter mainly stressed what it meant to follow Jesus and did not say much about Christian ideas.

The letter is basically a manual for correct Christian conduct, so it assumes those who read it were already well-informed Jews who were now Christians. The book rambles in different directions and discusses different topics.

239

Be glad when you face trials, for tests of your faith produces perseverance, which leads to maturity. Those who persevere receive a crown of life …. If you lack wisdom, ask God for it and you will receive it. But when you ask, believe and don't doubt. Otherwise, you won't get what you asked for …. If you are tempted, it's because you have evil desires. These desires give birth to sin. God doesn't do the tempting; only good things come from above. It's in God's unchanging nature to do good and not do evil …. Don't just listen to the word of God — do what it says …. Those who consider themselves religious but don't control their tongue have a worthless religion …. A person with a pure religion takes care of orphans and widows in their distress and is not polluted by the ways of this world …. Don't favor the rich and those who look nice. Love everybody equally. The wealth of the rich will be destroyed because of their self-indulgence …. Don't put too much faith in your own plans. You don't know what will happen in the future. It might happen if God wants it to happen …. Confess your sins to each other and pray for each other so that you may be healed. Prayers of righteous people are powerful and effective.

James's other main message comes in his attack on those who see a difference between people who claim to have faith and those who do good deeds. The two go together: "A person's faith is dead if it is not also accompanied by action. The faith of our ancestors was always shown by what they did."

Letters from Jude and John

Jude was the brother of James and the half-brother of Jesus. Like Peter's first letter, Jude's letter focused on addressing false teachings that were spreading in the church. There is nothing written in this very short book (less than one page long) about his audience and the false teachings. Jude simply speaks strongly against the false teachers who misrepresented the concept of grace and the role of Jesus. These teachers were highly critical of things they didn't understand. Jude listed many examples of God's judgment and said false teachers would be punished one day, just as God punished the false prophets and teachers who had lived among the Jews.

Letters from John

John was a fisherman before becoming one of the original 12 disciples. He wrote a long account about the life of Jesus, and he wrote three general letters to Christians late in the first century AD. He probably lived in Ephesus at the time.

John wrote his first letter to encourage and strengthen the church while false teachings infiltrated the church. The heresy of Gnosticism was developing at the time, which held the belief that all physical things are evil and only the spirit is good. This meant that it was the spirit of Jesus that counted, not his body; some believed Jesus was not even human. This belief led Gnostics to live immoral lives because keeping the law had no consequences. The Gnostics were very proud of their beliefs and looked down on those who didn't believe the way they did.

John opposes each of the Gnostic views. As an eyewitness and close personal friend, John experienced the reality of Jesus's physical life. Jesus was God in physical form. John also stressed righteous living, humility, and loving others. A true Christian believed Jesus was the Messiah and the Son of God, obeyed Jesus's commands, lived a good life, and loved other Christians.

> This is what love is: Jesus Christ died for us. We should be willing to die for our brothers and sisters. If anyone has material possessions and sees a brother or sister in need but doesn't help them, how can the love of God be in that person? Let us not love with words but with actions. Let us love one another, for love comes from God. Everyone who loves has been born of God. Those who do not love do not know God, because God is love. There is no fear in love. Perfect love drives out fear because fear has to do with punishment. We love because Jesus first loved us. Jesus gave this command:

Anyone who loves God must also love their brother and sister.

John's second letter was only a few paragraphs long. He wrote to warn the church about false teachers who influenced the church without its knowledge. John said the church should have nothing to do with such people. John also repeated the two points he made in his first letter: the need for members of the church to obey Jesus's commands and to love each other.

John's third letter was also short. He sent it to instruct a friend about how to handle an unusual situation in the church. A teacher who had been sent by John to support various churches was not accepted by the leader in one of the churches. This leader acted like a bully, controlled people, and even expelled some believers who helped other visiting teachers. John thanked his friend for helping the teachers who had visited, and he indirectly warned the leader that he would soon deal with him in person.

Letter to the Hebrews

Hebrews was written to Jews to convince them that Jesus was superior to all the other heroes of the Old Testament. It was meant to keep Jewish believers from going back to Judaism. Although Hebrews is considered a letter, it's structured like an essay. It begins by discussing how God spoke first through the prophets but now spoke through Jesus.

> God spoke previously to our ancestors through the prophets at many times and in various ways, but in these last days, God has spoken to us through Jesus. He was appointed the heir of all things, and God used him to make the universe. Jesus is the exact representation of God and holds the world together by his words. Now that he purified us from our sins, he sits at the right hand of God in heaven. He is far superior to any angel in heaven.

The author frequently refers to Jesus as being "better than" the heroes of the Old Testament. The author explains how Christ is better than the Old Testament, better than the angels, better than Moses, better than Joshua, better than all the priests, and better than Abraham. The New Covenant — Jesus's sacrifice cleansed people of their sins and provides everlasting life to all of God's people, the church —is better than the Old Covenant. Jesus's sacrifice is better than sacrifices performed under the Old Covenant, and experiencing Jesus is better than experiencing the events on Mount Sinai. Jesus is the great high priest who intercedes for the people to God and is also the Judge.

> The word of God is alive and sharper than any double-edged sword. It judges our hidden thoughts and attitudes. Nothing is hidden from God's sight. Everything is opened and laid bare before God to whom we must give account. We have a high priest who can empathize with our weaknesses. Jesus was tempted in every way, just as we are, but he did not sin.

Jesus came into the world as the ultimate sacrifice; it was impossible for the blood of bulls and goats to take away sins. Sacrifices to eliminate the stain of sin were no longer needed. But the deliverance from sin did not give people permission to use that freedom to keep sinning. Instead, a Christian's focus should be to "encourage one another to show our love and good deeds." Those who have faith in Jesus should be bold and persevere through difficult times and not be timid.

> Faith is the certainty of things we hope for and confidence for what we have not seen. Our faith helps us believe what God has done. It was Abraham's faith that led him to leave his home in Ur and move to Canaan and to know he and Sarah would have a child at a very old age. We had faith in God when Moses led us through the waters to escape the Egyptians. Nearly everybody died before seeing the promised land, but they could see it from a distance and did not doubt because they had faith in God's promises to us.

By faith the walls of Jericho fell, and by faith the prostitute Rahab was not killed because she welcomed the spies. I don't have time to talk about Gideon, Barak, Samson, Jephthah, David, Samuel, and the prophets. Through faith they conquered kingdoms, provided justice, and gained what was promised. They shut the mouths of lions, quenched the fury of the flames, and escaped the edge of the sword. Their weakness turned into strength as they became powerful in battle.

Others were tortured and refused to be released so they would gain an even better resurrection. Some faced jeers, beatings, and imprisonment. They were put to death by stoning, sawed in two, and killed by the sword. They wore the skins of sheep and goats and were poor and homeless, persecuted, and mistreated. They wandered in deserts and mountains, living in caves and holes in the ground.

Since we are surrounded by such a great cloud of witnesses, get rid of everything that stops us and the sin that traps us. Strengthen your feeble arms and weak knees and run the race we face with perseverance. Fix your eyes on Jesus who endured the cross and now sits next to God's throne.

The author ends by telling the Jews to keep living a moral and loving life, showing hospitality to strangers, and remembering those who were in prison and who suffered because they were mistreated.

CHAPTER 24

PREDICTIONS ABOUT THE FUTURE
Mysterious Messages Foresee a Cataclysmic Finale

Jesus had talked about the kingdom of God as if it already existed on earth but also that it was still to come. He said a king would judge people like a shepherd separates sheep from goats, sending sheep to heaven and goats to hell. Jesus spoke privately to his disciples when they asked him about the events at "the end of the age." Jesus told them:

> You will hear about wars and rumors of wars, earthquakes and famines — but these are just birth pangs. There will be tribulations and many will hate you because you follow me. Many will fall away and betray others, and false prophets will lead many astray. The end will come after the gospel is preached to all nations. When you see the Antichrist standing in the Temple, as Daniel predicted, you need to flee as fast as you can. The persecution will be like none other, and if times was not cut short, nobody would survive. False prophets will tell you Jesus has returned and the end is coming, but don't believe them, for these other things must happen first.

The Christians thought Jesus would soon return as a king to save them from abuse and persecution. Their hope was not that they would avoid terrible times but that they would soon be with Jesus. He told parables about being ready for his return — believers needed to be prepared like a pure woman who waited for a possible husband who could show up at any time.

But by the end of the first century AD, it was clear Jesus was not returning anytime soon. The Romans had destroyed Jerusalem and the Temple, and according to the predictions about the return of the Messiah, both needed to exist. Nobody knew when the predictions about when he would return, eliminate evil, and judge all who lived in the world would happen. During his ministry, Jesus told a parable about the coexistence of good and bad.

> The kingdom of heaven is like what happened to a farmer who sowed good seeds of wheat in his field. While everybody slept, his enemy planted weed seeds in the wheat field and left quietly. When the wheat sprouted, the weeds also appeared. The farmer's workers asked him, "Didn't you sow good seed in your field? Where did the weeds come from?"
>
> The farmer replied, "An enemy did this."
>
> The servants asked the man, "Should we pull up the weeds?"
>
> The man answered, "No, if you pull up the weeds, you will also uproot some of the wheat. Let both of them grow together until the harvest. Then I will tell the harvesters to collect the weeds and tie them in bundles that will be burned. Then I will tell them to gather the wheat and bring it to my barn."

So Jesus may not return for a very long time. Meanwhile, believers live alongside those who do not believe as they do. Believers live on earth with their citizenship in heaven; churches are like small colonies that show the rest of the world a bit of what heaven will look like. The kingdom of God has come in part but will be complete when Jesus returns and evil is destroyed.

Many predictions have come true about the Israelites and the Messiah, but there are still a few predictions about what will happen in the future that have not yet happened. These predictions mainly relate to the "end of time" return of the Messiah and the separation of people going to either heaven or hell. Some of these predictions are highly symbolic and full with vivid images, and the prophets who received them from God did not know what they meant. But they wrote them down so others could make sense of them later. Because of the ongoing persecution, Christians were interested in any details they could get about when their pain might end. They endured with hope rather than feeling sorry for themselves.

Near the end of the first century, John, the fisherman who was one of the first disciples, was a pastor in Ephesus. He resisted the Romans that wanted to kill Christians because they did not pledge allegiance to the emperor and worship him (Daniel faced this situation when he did not worship King Nebuchadnezzar). The Romans sent John to live alone on the Greek island of Patmos.

Difficulty Understanding Apocalyptic Literature

When John was on Patmos, he wrote the book of **Revelation** using a popular type of literature at that time that related to the destruction of the world (the apocalypse). Apocalyptic literature used highly symbolic language, such as strange animals and special numbers, and usually lacked important details. The content was hard to understand and could mean many different things. This type of literature had been used by a few Old Testament prophets and New Testament authors.

Christians were being persecuted for not obeying Roman laws that violated the principles of their faith.[9] John wanted to communicate with members of the church from a distance, but it was dangerous for him to be clear in his letters. Since the lives of those receiving the letter could be in danger if the letter was read by Roman officials, John used terms that had double meanings or would only be understood by believers. It was similar to how an athletic team or members of an underground community use secret signs and terms to communicate with each other: his words were in code and were not to be taken literally. For example, he talked about the evils of Babylon, but he was really talking about the evils of the Roman empire. He often used the number seven to symbolize completeness (seven cities and hills, seven seals, seven stars, seven trumpets).

---

[9] In the last decade of the first century, the Roman emperor Domitian severely persecuted the Christians and gave himself the title "Lord and God" and wanted everybody to worship him.

Encouragement to Seven Churches

The first three chapters of Revelation were directed to seven churches in Asia Minor, starting with Ephesus. The cities were connected by a major road, and the letter was meant to be sent to the next church along a circular route.

Persecution had caused believers in each city to compromise their beliefs and actions in order to blend in with nonbelievers. John wrote to encourage them to resist the temptation to worship the Roman emperor and stay true to their beliefs. Believers should have hope because God is in charge and will eventually win the war against evil.

John adjusted his messages to the specific situation that each local church faced. For example, Laodicea was a prosperous city, and the people in its church were lazy and self-sufficient. Although the city was a center for banking, John said the church was spiritually poor; although the city produced beautiful clothes, John said the believers were naked; although the city had a medical school, he said the church was blind. The hot springs in the area were good for bathing, and cold water was refreshing in the heat. The hot water that flowed to the city via aqueducts turned lukewarm by the time it reached them, and lukewarm water was used to cause vomiting. John told those in the church these words from God:

> I know you are neither cold nor hot. Because you are lukewarm, I'm about to spit you out of my mouth! You say, "I am rich, I have acquired wealth and don't need anything." But you don't realize you are pitiful, poor, blind, and naked. I rebuke and discipline those I love.

But despite the church's laziness and pride, John reminded the church of God's goodness. God says, "I stand at your door and knock. If you hear my voice and open the door, I will come in and eat with you." The choice is always there for an individual to respond, without being forced, to the invitation to know God. A central theme of the scriptures is that after sin and judgment, God provides love and grace rather than punishment.

The End of History

After writing to the seven churches, John wrote about visions of the future that came from God as a message to all believers. He described a set of events associated with the end of time when Jesus will return from heaven. There will be "birth pangs" that signal the final events are coming, and then the final events will occur.

John described the final events of history in terms of a "rapture" (Christians going to heaven), a "tribulation" (years of intense persecution of Christians, accompanied by many natural disasters and warfare), a "beast" (an evil power that used its powers against the Christians), the Antichrist (a false prophet identified by the number 666),[10] a final battle between the forces of good and evil at Armageddon (a valley in northern Israel), a "millennium" (1,000 years of peace), and the return of Christ who defeats all the powers of darkness and burns all evil. God's kingdom will then be established in heaven and on earth without any evil being present.

It's not clear how all these characters and events work together. Some people believe that the rapture will come first, then the tribulation, followed by the second coming of Christ and the millennium. Then a final rush of evil occurs, after which Christ comes back a third time and defeats evil in one final battle. Others believe that Christians will experience the rapture *after* the tribulation; after that comes the millennium, followed by the return of Christ and the final judgment. Another view is that we are already in the millennium and the tribulation will come before the rapture.

There is a rationale for each view, and other combinations are possible. But because of the mysteries of the symbolism

---

[10] The meaning of 666 is unknown. Attempts have been made to identify the person using a numbering system associated with the alphabet. Many scholars think it symbolized incompleteness (the number 7 symbolized completeness, so 666 was not quite 777), and it may refer to a Roman emperor. The Dutch thought it related to the year when they lost a major naval battle 1666. Many claimed Adolf Hitler met the conditions of the Antichrist.

and the lack of details about how and when the events will happen, nobody really knows how all these events will unfold. Many scholars believe the events apply in a general sense and can be interpreted within the context of events at multiple times of history, with the key point that Christians should persevere and have hope during times of extreme hardship. In this perspective, the revelations are not meant to predict specific events in the future. For many believers, it's enough to know there is a happy ending despite a painful process.

A sign that the end of time is approaching is the construction of the Temple for the third time in Jerusalem. The Antichrist is predicted to serve in the Temple, only to turn on the Jews and persecute them. Many natural disasters, such as earthquakes, famine, and darkened skies, are predicted to occur in the final days.[11] John confirmed some details that Isaiah and Paul said would happen about the return of Jesus: those who have died will come back to life again as Jesus did, and every creature, dead or alive, will bow and honor Jesus as the King and Lord of the universe.

A number of awful things are predicted to take place before a final battle between good and evil takes place. The good forces are led by a shining king, the "Lion of Judah, the Root of David" (Jesus), who was "worthy to receive power, wealth, wisdom, strength, honor, glory, and praise." Various natural disasters, plagues, wars, and terror will be carried out by evil men.

Evil will grow so strong and widespread in hell's all-out desperate attempt to defeat the forces of good that God will have seen enough, and it will be time for the judgment. A battle among many nations will take place in Armageddon, and the description of the battle closely resembles modern-day warfare — the sounds of thunderous jets, bombs, and

---

[11] The creation of the nation of Israel in 1948 after nearly 1,900 years without a national status has prompted some Christians and Jews to believe it is a sign that the end of time is coming soon. More severe natural disasters and changes in the world's climate support their beliefs.

missiles falling from the sky, flashes of light and rumbling earth, and widespread destruction. Evil forces attack heaven but are defeated by God's army of angels, led by the archangel Michael. Babylon is destroyed because of its immorality, false religions, and the comforts of materialism. Individuals are then judged, and nonbelievers will be crushed like grapes in a winepress. God then throws most of the evil powers into a lake of fire.

Evil still exists but has no influence on the earth, which leads to a long period of peace. This shows people what life can be like without the influence of evil. Later, Satan will be unleashed and evil forces will surround the people of God, but fire will come from heaven. Satan and all remaining forces of evil will be thrown into the lake of fire where they will be tormented day and night for eternity — they will finally get what they deserve.

A New Heaven and a New Earth

Those in heaven will rejoice at the destruction of evil and sing, "Hallelujah, for the Lord, God Almighty, reigns." The holy city of Jerusalem will be restored on earth, and God's dwelling place (heaven) will be among the people. The king says from his throne:

> There will be no more tears in their eyes and no more death or crying or pain — the old things have passed away and I have made everything new! It is done. I am the Alpha and the Omega, the Beginning and the End. To the thirsty I will give free water from the spring of the water of life. These victors will inherit all this. I will be their God, and they will be my children.

The foundation and walls of the holy city are spectacular. There is no sun or moon because the glory of God always provides light; there is no darkness or night. Those whose names are in the book of life will live as the bride of God forever. Just as in the book of Job, the pain and suffering of God's people are eventually rewarded — the perseverance of the faithful results in a happy ending. Spiritual battles have been epic through the ages, but the war comes to an end. There is total victory, and evil is destroyed forever.

John ends by writing that it was Jesus who told him to write about his vision to the church. Jesus says to all, "I'm coming soon. Let those who are thirsty come to me." Amen.

EPILOGUE

Revelation was the last book written by an eyewitness of Jesus's life that was included in the Bible. The Christian movement grew rapidly throughout the Roman Empire thanks in part to the 200 years of peace in the empire at that time and an excellent road system. These made it easier for people to travel safely over long distances. The Jews were scattered throughout the empire after Jerusalem was destroyed in AD 70, and they brought with them an understanding of the God of Abraham, the history of the Israelites, and all the prophets. This made the messages of those spreading the news about Jesus more understandable.

Even though Christianity was an illegal religion and many believers were killed throughout the empire, an account written in about AD 200 said Christians "filled the cities, islands, fortresses, towns, marketplaces, the army itself, tribes, companies, the Imperial Palace, the Senate, the Forum." In other words, Christians were found everywhere.

The spread of Christianity was influenced by the promises of life after death to believers and by the predicted downfall of the Roman Empire. Justin Martyr tried to convince the Roman government that Christians were good citizens, even though they would not worship the Roman gods, but he was killed with some of his disciples in AD 165. Other Christian leaders were persecuted and killed in spectacular and gruesome fashion. Because of the strong persecution against the Christians, most believers at the time thought they were in the midst of the tribulation. The Roman Empire eventually stopped persecuting Christians in AD 313 during Constantine's rule. More than 1,700 years later, Christians are still persecuted and mistreated in some parts of the world.

In 1517, a monk in Germany named Martin Luther raised concerns about the religious practices and ideas of the Roman Catholic Church. His protests led to the Protestant movement, and other religious scholars started new forms of the church. Since that time, many other Protestant groups ("denominations") have formed based on their different religious views. The power of the church was reduced as each believer's interpretation of the scriptures became more acceptable. If people did not agree with what was being taught or anything else that was happening in the church, they just left and went elsewhere or did not continue being part of any church. Meanwhile, the Catholic Church is led by one person (the Pope) and has stayed intact while it continues to change its traditions over time.

In the past 200 years, there has been more interest by some groups of Christians to spread the gospel throughout the world, sometimes as they provide needed services to others, such as education and medical care. Jesus's final words on earth commanded believers to "make disciples of all the nations" (the "Great Commission" found in Matthew 28:19–20). The word *nation* applies to different types of people, not governments, and this command motived many to find groups of people in the world who have not yet heard the messages of Jesus and to communicate these messages to their people in terms they will understand.

In the early 1800s, a preacher named Charles Finney started a revival movement to get people to return to the church and to convert people to Christianity. He used different methods to increase the number of converts. A new way to define a successful Christian and church became the number of people who made a decision to follow Jesus.

In the past 150 years, Protestant churches in the United States have differed significantly in their approach to various social issues, such as slavery and racial relations, and religious issues, such as the truthfulness of the scriptures and how important it is to care for people's physical needs. These differences have led to many divisions within the church. The label *Christian* now means many different things.

Those who call themselves Christian represent about 30% of the world's population, and Christianity is the world's largest religious group. About half of the 2.4 billion Christians are Catholic, and most are found in Africa, Asia, and Latin America. Muslims represent the second largest religious group (about 25% of the world population), and Islam has the fastest growth rate among of the world's major religions.

AUTHOR'S PERSPECTIVE

The early chapters of the Bible describe God's beautiful creation that was damaged by evil forces. People were given the ability to tell the difference between right and wrong and the freedom to choose their own way to live. Those who are selfish and do not follow God eventually harm themselves and others. God always forgives and loves all people even though nobody is perfect. God's support for people often helps those who do not believe, while at the same time, evil in the world affects those who follow God. Life is not always fair and we often don't know what will happen in our lives.

Evil Forces Still Exist

The predictions made in Revelation about the destruction of evil have obviously not yet come true. Many bad things in the world still cause pain, suffering, and death.

Evil forces quietly affect many aspects of life and try to disrupt the forces of good in individuals and in society. Meanness and unfairness are still signs of evil influences.

Paul told those in Ephesus, "Our struggle is against the rulers and authorities and the spiritual forces of evil" (Ephesians 6:12). The ways of evil can be attractive, but Satan poses as "an angel of light" and influences people to follow the wrong path. The end result of evil action is often some form of terrible pain, and nobody knows when the evil in this world will end.

Those who follow and practice the teachings of Jesus represent the kingdom of heaven to others on earth. Just as today's ambassadors to other countries do not obey laws that violate the laws and requirements of their home country, Christians are to live in this world but not violate God's requirements. Individually and as a group, Christians are to be examples of God's love and forgiveness. God's people, the church, are to have a different way of thinking and acting. Christians are God's "exhibit A" to the world about how people should live on earth and promote peace in the midst of conflict.

Being God's Ambassador Is Very Challenging

Being an effective ambassador is not an easy task. Christians are not perfect examples, and the church is constantly being attacked by evil forces that focus their efforts on believers and the organizations they create. One strategy used by evil forces is to reduce the influence and messages of the church. This is done by creating divisions, distractions, and doubts and by making small things important while more important things are ignored. This gets Christians focused on talking about religious ideas instead of acting with love.

Another way evil forces affect the church is by slowly influencing Christians to embrace the culture of non-Christians. Paul warned Christians about this: "Don't let the world squeeze you slowly into its own mold, but be changed by constantly renewing your mind" (Romans 12:2). The world thinks success is defined by a person's wealth, health, and comfortable life. By this definition, many Christians are successful, yet none of these provide lasting happiness or inner joy.

Relatively few believers make much of a significant difference in the world because this requires following God's priorities. Making a difference requires self-sacrifice, sometimes to the point of death. We must all decide what to do with our lives, what to live for and what to die for; our life and death should have meaning. Following Jesus requires people to make sacrifices and help others.

Jesus's parable of the farmer who sowed seeds described in chapter 16 discusses this challenge. Two of the three types of seeds that take root produce no crop. One set refers to those who fall away when things get hard because they are not yet mature in their faith. The other set refers to those who are choked by life's worries, riches, and pleasures.

Doing What Is Required

Christians are called to fight the forces of evil with love and compassion and to promote fairness for all people. God requires people to "act fairly, love kindness, and walk humbly with God" (Micah 6:8). Jesus condemned the Pharisees for making their religion a show but not doing these three things. In fact, Jesus only got angry when he spoke to religious leaders who said one thing but did another, who judged others harshly, and who used religion to further their own interests.

Micah's message is simple, but living it is very hard. It is only possible through the slow and steady process of becoming more like Jesus and by being led by God's spirit to act in ways that provide healing and hope to others. The task is easier when we are supported by those who do these things. The kingdom of God on earth grew rapidly because the early Christians loved others in unusual ways. They were the sheep who fed the hungry, gave a drink to the thirsty, invited the stranger in, clothed the naked, cared for the sick, and visited those in prison. True faith and belief are shown through one's actions, not by what a person says.

Christians who reflect God's character exhibit certain types of "fruit." Paul told the early believers, "The fruit of the Spirit is love, joy, peace, patience, kindness, goodness, faithfulness, gentleness, and self-control" (Galatians 5:22–23). Those who call themselves Christians but who do not exhibit these fruits are not good models to follow. We will know mature Christians by their love for others, not by what they say they believe.

APPENDICES

APPENDIX A
BOOKS IN THE BIBLE

The number of "chapters" in each
book is noted in parentheses.

Old Testament (39 Books)

Genesis (50)
Exodus (40)
Leviticus (27)
Numbers (36)
Deuteronomy (34)
Joshua (24)
Judges (21)
Ruth (4)
1 Samuel (31)
2 Samuel (24)
1 Kings (22)
2 Kings (25)
1 Chronicles (29)
2 Chronicles (36)
Ezra (36)
Nehemiah (13)
Esther (10)
Job (42)
Psalms (150)
Proverbs (31)
Ecclesiastes (12)
Song of Solomon (8)
Isaiah (66)
Jeremiah (52)
Lamentations (5)
Ezekiel (48)
Daniel (12)
Hosea (14)
Joel (3)
Amos (9)
Obadiah (1)
Jonah (4)
Micah (7)
Nahum (3)
Habakkuk (3)
Zephaniah (3)
Haggai (2)
Zechariah (14)
Malachi (4)

New Testament (27 Books)

Matthew (28)
Mark (16)
Luke (24)
John (21)
Acts (28)
Romans (16)
1 Corinthians (16)
2 Corinthians (13)
Galatians (6)
Ephesians (6)
Philippians (4)
Colossians (4)
1 Thessalonians (5)
2 Thessalonians (3)
1 Timothy (6)
2 Timothy (4)
Titus (3)
Philemon (1)
Hebrews (13)
James (5)
1 Peter (5)
2 Peter (3)
1 John (5)
2 John (1)
3 John (1)
Jude (1)
Revelation (22)

APPENDIX B
CHRONOLOGY OF MAIN BIBLICAL CHARACTERS AND EVENTS
(dates are approximate)

Old Testament	
Prehistory	
Adam and Eve	Creation of the world
Noah	Great flood
Patriarchs (1850–1240 BC)	
Abraham and Sarah	Promises to become God's people
Isaac and Rebekah	Isaac blesses Jacob
Esau, Jacob, Rachel, and Leah	Jacob leaves then returns to Canaan
Jacob and his 12 sons	Jacob and his family move to Egypt
Moses and Aaron	Exodus from Egypt, God gives laws
Joshua	Israelites enter and occupy Canaan
Judges and Oppressors (1240–1050 BC)	
Deborah and Barak	Victory over Canaanites based in Hazor
Gideon	Victory over raiders from the east
Jephthah	Victory over Ammonites
Samson	Victory over Philistines
Eli and Samuel	Battles with Philistines
Boaz and Ruth	Foreigner's child precedes future king
Kings (1050–930 BC)	
Saul	First king of Israel with many flaws
David	Most significant Israelite hero and king
Solomon	Wise king expands Israel's territory
Divided Kingdom (930–586 BC)	
Amos, Elijah, Elisha, Isaiah	Israelites in Northern Kingdom eventually enslaved by the Assyrians (722 BC)
Isaiah, Micah, Jeremiah	People of Southern Kingdom (Judah) eventually exiled to Babylon
Exile and Return (586–400 BC)	
Ezekiel and other prophets	Jews settle in Babylonia, many return
Daniel and Esther	Exiled Jews thrive in Babylonia and Persia
Ezra and Nehemiah	Jerusalem and the Temple are rebuilt

New Testament	
Jesus's Birth and Preparation (5 BC–AD 7)	
Mary, Joseph, and Jesus	God becomes a human
John the Baptist	Predictions of the Messiah come true
Jesus's Ministry (AD 25–28)	
Twelve disciples	Miracles attract large crowds
Jewish religious leaders	New ideas challenge existing rules
Roman political leaders	Jesus is killed but comes back to life
Leaders Spread Good News (28–95)	
Twelve disciples	News about Jesus spreads in Israel
Saul (Paul)	Good news is extended to Gentiles
Believers in Asia and Europe	Apostles encourage struggling churches

APPENDIX C
SUGGESTIONS FOR
FURTHER READING

Study Bibles include more information about the Bible to help readers understand the stories and meanings. These versions often include more historical information, maps, glossaries, indexes, word meanings, geographical notes, explanations of the characters and events mentioned in the Bible, and lists of specific types of content (e.g., parables, prophecies, miracles). Some study Bibles include informative articles to provide more context to the Bible stories and ancient times.

More readable **paraphrased translations of the Bible** have been created to help readers understand what was written. The best paraphrases are listed below.

- The *New Testament in Modern English* was written by J.B. Phillips, an Anglican clergyman. This translation was first published in 1958 using British spellings, and some editions do not include verse numbers. Phillips did not translate the Old Testament into more readable text.
- The *Good News Bible* is a translation of the Bible by the American Bible Society. The New Testament was originally published in 1966 using the name *Good News for Modern Man*. The complete Bible was finished in 1976. It uses simplified language that children can read. This book is also known as the *Good News Translation* and is used in many countries and by many denominations.
- *The Living Bible* was created in English by Kenneth Taylor in 1971 and has been translated into many languages. Taylor wrote it so his children would understand the stories text when his family read the book together. An updated version (*New Living Translation*) was published in 1996.
- *The Message: The Bible in Contemporary Language* was written by Eugene Peterson, an American Presbyterian pastor and author. This translation uses modern American ways of talking. A translation of the entire Bible was finished in 2002.

APPENDIX D
GLOSSARY OF KEY TERMS

This appendix explains the key terms (people, geographical sites, concepts) discussed in *The Simplified Short Bible*. They appear alphabetically in the chapter in which they are first mentioned, and they are not repeated if they occur again in another chapter. In some cases, more than one person or location has the same name. For example, there are several people who have the name Joseph, and they are listed separately in the chapter where they are first mentioned.

INTRODUCTION

Canon	The collection of documents that are contained in the Bible
God	Name given to the supreme force in the universe who has three parts; sometimes called Lord
Grace	An undeserved gift or favor
Israel	Canaan, area where the Israelites (Jews) lived
Israelites	God's chosen people of Israel
Lord	Another word for God
Palestine	Current name for Canaan, the Promised Land ("Holy Land")
Prayer	A form of human interaction with a divine power
Spirit	One part of God (Holy Spirit)

PART 1: OLD TESTAMENT

Chapter 1	The Beginning
Abel	Second child born to Adam and Eve, killed by Cain
Abram/Abraham	Man who lived in Ur and moved to Canaan with his wife, Sarai/Sarah; first father of the Jews
Adam	First man created by God who lived in the Garden of Eden with Eve

Angels	Cosmic beings that can be good or evil and sometimes interact with humans
Asher	Son of Jacob and Zilpah
Beersheba	Desert-like city in southern Canaan and birthplace of Isaac
Bilhah	Rachel's maid and Jacob's wife who had two sons (Dan and Naphtali)
Cain	First child born to Adam and Eve who killed his brother Abel
Canaan	Land promised to Abram and now called Palestine ("Holy Land")
Covenant	Agreement made between God and the people of God
Dan	Son of Jacob and Bilhah
Dinah	Daughter of Jacob and Leah
Egypt	Large empire located southwest of Palestine and an area frequently visited by the Israelites during times of crisis
Esau	Older son of Isaac and Jacob, lost birthright and blessing to his brother Jacob, married foreign wives and left home to live in Edom
Eve	First woman created by God, lived in the Garden of Eden with Adam
Flood	Cataclysm used by God to destroy all humans, which ended with a rainbow, signifying God will never destroy all humans again
Gad	Son of Jacob and Zilpah
Garden of Eden	Idyllic home of Adam and Eve before they sinned
Hagar	Egyptian servant of Sarah who gave birth to Ishmael (Abraham was the father)
Haran	Area in northern Mesopotamia that was the home of Rebekah, Laban, and his daughters Rachel and Leah
Isaac	Son of Abraham and Sarah ("son of promise") who had two sons (Esau and Jacob)
Ishmael	Son of Abraham and Hagar who lived east of the Jordan River
Issachar	Son of Jacob and Leah
Jacob	Younger son of Isaac who obtained Esau's birthright and blessing and who had 12 sons and a daughter with his four wives

Joseph	Son of Jacob and Rachel who became a leader in Egypt
Judah	Son of Jacob and Leah
Laban	Rebekah's brother, Rachel's father, and Jacobs' father-in-law
Leah	One of Jacob's wives who had six of his sons
Levi	Son of Jacob and Leah
Naphtali	Son of Jacob and Bilhah
Noah	Faithful man who built an ark to save all living creatures from a massive flood
Rachel	Wife of Jacob who had two sons (Joseph and Benjamin)
Rebekah	Wife of Isaac who had two sons (Esau and Jacob)
Reuben	Son of Jacob and Leah
Sarai/Sarah	Wife of Abram/Abraham
Satan	Evil angel leader that was expelled from heaven and the "prince of this world" who loses the final battle with God for the control of the universe (also called the devil)
Simeon	A son of Jacob and Leah
Ur	City in southern Mesopotamia and south of Babylon where Abram and Sarai lived before moving to Canaan
Zebulun	Son of Jacob and Leah
Zilpah	Wife of Jacob who had two sons (Gad and Asher)

Chapter 2	**Jacob Returns to Canaan**
Benjamin	Son of Jacob and Rachel and Jacob's youngest son
Edom	Mountainous region east of the southern end of the Salt Sea (also known as Seir, meaning "rough") where Esau went to live
Ephraim	Younger son of Joseph and his Egyptian wife, was blessed by Jacob
Goshen	Fertile area in northern Egypt where Israelites settled after leaving Israel during a famine
Israel	Name given to Jacob after fighting with an angel before meeting Esau
Israelites	Descendants of Jacob
Manasseh	Older son of Joseph and his Egyptian wife

Nile River	Major river running northward through Egypt
Pharaoh	An Egyptian king
Potiphar	Leader of Pharaoh's bodyguards
Shechem	City in the hills of central Israel near Samaria

Chapter 3	**Life in Egypt**
Aaron	Moses's older brother who became the first High Priest
Exodus	The departure and travels of the Israelites from Egypt after years of harsh treatment
Hebrew	Language spoken by the Israelites; a word used to indicate something Jewish
Jethro	Midianite priest who helped Moses
Midian	Southeastern area of the Sinai Peninsula and area east of the peninsula where Moses initially went to escape the Egyptians
Moses	Son of Levite parents and younger brother of Aaron; he was adopted by Pharaoh's daughter, led Israelites out of Egypt and through the wilderness, and authored several books of the Bible
Passover	Celebration of the night when God passed over the homes of the Israelites and killed the firstborn children of all other families living in Egypt just before the exodus
Wilderness	Name given to areas on and near the Sinai Peninsula after the Israelites left Egypt; a general term to describe desolate lands

Chapter 4	**The Israelites Leave Egypt**
Ark of the Covenant	An ornately covered box that contained holy relics of the Jews
Joshua	Leader who went with Moses to Mount Sinai and was one of the spies who said Canaan could be conquered and later led the successful invasion of Canaan
Levites	Descendants of Levi who became priests or workers to support religious activities
Manna	Sweet cracker-like substance ("bread") that appeared on the ground in the morning during the Israelites' days in the wilderness

Mount Sinai	Highest mountain on the Sinai Peninsula, located near the southern end of the peninsula, where Moses met God and got the 10 commandments
Red Sea	Large body of water between Egypt and Arabia with two northern branches (Gulf of Aqaba and Gulf of Suez)
Repent	The act of acknowledging wrong and then "turning" in another direction to pursue correct and more appropriate action
Sabbath	The last day of the week, a day of rest
Tabernacle	A network of movable tents and courtyards where God dwelled before the construction of the Temple in Jerusalem
Ten Commandments	Commands from God given to Moses on Mount Sinai
Year of the Jubilee	The year after seven cycles of seven years (every 50 years) when debts are canceled; a term used in the writings of Isaiah that announced the arrival of the Messiah

Chapter 5	**Life in the Wilderness**
Caleb	One of the two spies who said the Israelites could conquer Canaan and was allowed to enter Canaan
Jericho	Large walled city near the northwest corner of the Salt Sea
Nazarites	People who dedicate themselves to serve God for a specific amount of time and agree not to shave their head or consume any form of a grape or touch a dead person
Salt Sea	Large salty body of water where the Jordan River ends (Dead Sea)

Chapter 6	**The Occupation of Canaan**
Ai	City close to Jericho where several battles took place
Cities of refuge	Six cities run by the Levites that provided asylum and protection for anyone who unintentionally killed a person (manslaughter) until their case went to trial
Gibeon	Area north of Jerusalem whose people tricked the Israelites into making a peace agreement

Hazor	Powerful city in northern Canaan
Hebron	City located about 25 miles south of Jerusalem
Phoenicia	Area north of Palestine along the Mediterranean coast
Rahab	Prostitute who hid two Israelite spies in Jericho, mother of Boaz
Shiloh	City with religious significance in northern Israel

Chapter 7	**Israel Struggles in Canaan**
Ammonites	Descendants of Ben-ammi (son of Lot) who lived east of the Jordan River
Baal	Main local God of the non-Jews living in Canaan
Barak	Man who lived in northern Canaan who fought with Deborah to defeat the army of Hazor
Bethlehem	Town near Jerusalem and birthplace of Jesus
Boaz	Husband of Ruth, father of Jesse, and grandfather of David
David	Son of Jesse who killed Goliath, lived in Jerusalem as Israel's second king, and the father of Solomon
Deborah	Woman prophet and judge who led the battle with Barak to defeat the army of Hazor
Delilah	Samson's girlfriend who got him to reveal the secret of his strength
Gideon	Unusual prophet who used a fleece to confirm God's call to fight the Midianites
Jephthah	Unusual leader from Gilead who defeated the Ammonites but tragically killed his only child
Midianites	People who lived in the Midian region (north of the Red Sea)
Naomi	Mother-in-law of Ruth and relative of Boaz (Ruth's husband)
Obed	Son of Boaz and Ruth and father of Jesse
Orpah	A daughter-in-law of Naomi (the other was Ruth)
Othniel	Judge and military leader and Caleb's younger brother who defeated Israel's norther enemies
Philistines	People living in Philistia, a nation located on the coast of the Mediterranean Sea (southwest Canaan)

Prophet	A person who speaks God's truth to others, often to those in power, and may make predictions about the future
Ruth	Moabite daughter-in-law of Naomi who married Boaz
Samson	Flawed Jewish hero known for his strength coming from his long hair

Chapter 8	**Crowning a Unifying King**
Hannah	Mother of Samuel
Jesse	David's father and the grandson of Boaz and Ruth
Jonathan	Saul's son and close friend of David
Samuel	Important prophet and judge when Israel selected its first king
Saul	First king of Israel; the Hebrew name of Paul

Chapter 9	**King David and King Solomon**
Bathsheba	Wife of Uriah who became David's wife and Solomon's mother
City of David	Another name for Jerusalem where David served as king
Damascus	The most important city in Syria, northeast of Palestine
Jeroboam	Official who worked for Solomon who became the first king of the Northern Kingdom
Nathan	Prophet who confronted David about his affair with Bathsheba
Phoenicians	People who lived in Phoenicia
Rehoboam	Solomon's son who became the first king of the Southern Kingdom
Solomon	Son of David and Bathsheba who became a wise king of Israel and built the Temple in Jerusalem and authored several books of the Old Testament
Temple	Buildings and courtyards in Jerusalem where the Jews honored and worshipped God
Uriah	Bathsheba's husband whose death in battle was planned by David
Zion	Another name for Jerusalem because of its hill called Mount Zion

Chapter 10	The Divided Kingdom
Ahab	King in the Northern Kingdom, husband of Jezebel
Ahaziah	King in the Southern Kingdom, son of Jehoram
Amos	Prophet in the Northern Kingdom
Babylon	Major city in Mesopotamia (near the current city of Bagdad)
Elijah	Main prophet in the Northern Kingdom
Elisha	Prominent prophet in the Northern Kingdom after Elijah disappeared
Gentiles	People who are not Jewish
Hosea	Prophet to the Northern Kingdom
Immanuel	A name given to the Messiah ("God with us")
Isaiah	Major prophet who wrote to both parts of the divided kingdom
Israel	Name given to the Northern Kingdom
Jehoram	King in the Southern Kingdom who shared his reign with his father Jehoshaphat
Jehoshaphat	King in the Southern Kingdom who shared his reign with his son Jehoram
Jezebel	Evil wife of King Ahab
Manasseh	Longest reigning king in the Southern Kingdom and son of Hezekiah
Micah	Prophet to the Southern Kingdom
Naaman	Syrian who was healed of a skin disease by Elisha
Samaria	Area in northern Palestine inhabited largely by non-Jews

Chapter 11	Both Kingdoms Fall
Edomites	People who lived in Edom (an area southeast of Canaan)
Habakkuk	Prophet in the Southern Kingdom
Hezekiah	King in the Southern Kingdom
Jeremiah	Prophet to the Southern Kingdom
Jews	Another word for the Israelites (not Gentiles)
Joel	Prophet to the Southern Kingdom
Jonah	Prophet to the Assyrians who avoided God's call by going to Spain
Josiah	King in the Southern Kingdom

Mesopotamia	General area with fertile land along the Tigris and Euphrates Rivers (currently in Iraq)
Nahum	Prophet in the Southern Kingdom
Nineveh	Capital city of Assyria
Obadiah	Prophet in the Southern Kingdom
Samaritans	People who lived in Samaria and were despised by the Jews
Zedekiah	Last king of the Southern Kingdom
Zephaniah	Prophet in the Southern Kingdom

Chapter 12	**Life in Exile, Then Restoration**
Abednego	Faithful man trained in Babylon and one of three Jews who survived burning in a furnace
Aramaic	Widely-used Syrian dialect that was used in the Near East to conduct business and diplomacy; a language used in Palestine in addition to Hebrew
Artaxerxes	King in Person, son of Xerxes
Cyrus the Great	Persian king during the time when the Israelites were in exile
Daniel	Religious and political leader who lived in Babylon and survived being thrown to the lions
Esther	Jewish wife of the Persian King Xerxes
Ezekiel	Unusual Jewish prophet who lived in Babylon
Ezra	Jewish leader who lived in exile in Babylon who got permission for the Jews to return to Palestine
Haggai	Prophet to the Jews who returned to Palestine and advocated for the rebuilding of the Temple
Haman	Prime minister in Persia who tried to get rid of all the Jews
Magi	Priests of the Zoroastrianism faith
Malachi	Prophet to those living in the rebuilt city of Jerusalem and the last prophet who lived during the Old Testament period
Meshach	Faithful man trained in Babylon and one of three Jews who survived burning in a furnace
Mordecai	Uncle of Esther who lived in Persia

Nehemiah	Jew who served as the Persian king's cupbearer and returned to Jerusalem to rebuild its walls and gates
Shadrach	Faithful man trained in Babylon who was one of three Jews who survived burning in a furnace
Xerxes	Persian king during the time of Esther and Mordecai
Zechariah	Prophet to the Jews who returned to Palestine and advocated for the rebuilding of the Temple
Zoroastrianism	Persian religion

Chapter 13	**Unique Books in the Old Testament**
Bildad	One of the characters in Job who tells Job why he is suffering
Elihu	One of the characters in Job who tells Job why he is suffering
Eliphaz	One of the characters in Job who tells Job why he is suffering
Job	Main character in the book of Job who suffers greatly even though he is faithful to God
Psalms	Old Testament book of poetry; a type of Jewish poetry (Psalm)
Proverbs	Old Testament book of wisdom literature; a type of wise sayings
Tarshish	A city in Spain where Jonah fled instead of going to Nineveh
Zophar	One of the characters in Job who tells Job why he is suffering

PART 2: NEW TESTAMENT

Chapter 14	**The Messiah Arrives**
Alexander the Great	Greek leader who conquered much of the world and helped spread the influence of Greek culture before the time of Jesus
Andrew	One of the first disciples of Jesus, a fisherman and Simon's brother
Bartholomew	One of the 12 disciples (also known as Nathaniel)
Caesar Augustus	Roman emperor at the time of Jesus's birth who ordered a census

Capernaum	City on the Sea of Galilee in northern Palestine where Jesus lived during his ministry
Christ	Greek word for Messiah, another word for Jesus
Disciples	People who learn from a teacher; men who traveled with Jesus
Essenes	Jews who withdrew from the world and lived simple lives near the Salt Sea
Gabriel	Angel who revealed John's birth to Zechariah and Jesus's birth to Mary
Galileans	People who lived in northern Palestine and were viewed with contempt because they often married non-Jews and disliked outsiders who lived in their communities
Gospel	"Good news" about Jesus' free gift of eternal life
Greek	Language spoken and written in Greece and throughout and beyond the Mediterranean region during the time of Jesus; a person from Greece
Hanukkah	Jewish celebration to remember the victory over the Greeks in 142 BC
Hellenists	Jews who followed Greek traditions
Herod	Roman king in charge of Palestine at the time of Jesus's birth
Herod Antipas	Roman governor of Galilee when Jesus was alive
Herodians	Jews who followed Roman traditions and beliefs
James	Fisherman and brother of John who was one of the 12 disciples of Jesus and later authored a book contained in the Bible
Jesus	Son of Mary and Joseph and a human form of God who was born in Bethlehem and who was given many names and fulfilled the Old Testament predictions of the Messiah (Christ)
John	Fisherman and brother of James who was among the first disciples of Jesus and who wrote several books contained in the Bible
John the Baptist	Unusual prophet and peer of Jesus who prepared the Israelites for the ministry of Jesus
Joseph	The father of Jesus

Luke	Gentile doctor and traveling companion of Paul who wrote a book (Luke) about the life of Jesus and a book (Acts) about what happened among the disciples after Jesus left the earth
Mary	Mother of Jesus
Messiah	The Anointed One who was predicted to save the Jews from their oppressors (Christ in Greek)
Nazareth	Town in Galilee 70 miles north of Jerusalem and hometown of Jesus
Peter	First disciple chosen by Jesus who became the leader of the church (also known as Simon and Simon Peter)
Pharisees	Influential Jewish religious leaders who adhered closely to the laws of Moses
Philip	One of the 12 disciples of Jesus who later preached in various places in Palestine
Rabbi	Jewish religious teacher or scholar
Romans	People who led a vast empire that lasted for more than 500 years throughout much of Europe, northern Africa, and parts of southwest Asia
Rome	Largest city in Italy and the center of the Roman Empire
Sadducees	Small group of influential Jewish religious leaders who stressed morality rather than obeying religious rules
Sanhedrin	A diverse group of Jewish leaders who watched over the religious life of the Jews and had the powers to punish Jews
Scribes	People who wrote important documents (often religious in nature) and were experts in the law
Sea of Galilee	A very large lake in northern Israel (also known as Lake Tiberias)
Simeon	An old man who God promised would see the Messiah
Simon	Disciple also named Peter or Simon Peter
Synagogue	Place of worship for the Jews and those who believe in Judaism
Zechariah	Priest who married Elizabeth and became the father of John the Baptist at an old age

Zealots	Jews who rebelled against foreign powers that occupied Palestine and were willing to fight and die for their cause
Chapter 15	**Acts of Jesus**
Abyss	A very deep and vast space, a word that describes hell
Apostle	A messenger of God
Beelzebul	Another word for Satan and the devil
Cana	Sight of a wedding where Jesus turned water into wine
Joanna	Woman who managed Herod's household and supported Jesus and the disciples financially
Judas	One of the 12 disciples and half-brother of Jesus who wrote the book Jude
Judas Iscariot	Man with financial expertise who was a disciple and betrayed Jesus to the Jewish leaders
Lazarus	Good friend of Jesus who was raised from the dead
Martha	Sister of Mary Magdalene and Lazarus
Mary Magdalene	Woman who helped Jesus, sister of Lazarus and Martha, and the first person to see Jesus after his resurrection (often called Mary)
Matthew	Jewish tax collector, also known as Levi, who became one of the 12 disciples of Jesus
Nain	Town in Galilee where Jesus raised a man from the dead
Nicodemus	Religious Jew who secretly met Jesus and helped bury him after the crucifixion
Parable	A simple story told to convey an important message
Resurrection	When a person comes back to life after being dead
Rich young ruler	Man who asked Jesus what he must do to have eternal life
Simon the Zealot	One of the original 12 disciples of Jesus
Susanna	Woman who supported Jesus and the disciples financially
Thomas	The disciple who doubted that Jesus came back to life
Zacchaeus	Jewish tax collector who climbed a tree to see Jesus

Chapter 16	Teachings of Jesus
Golden Rule	Part of the Sermon on the Mount (Matthew 7:12) that Jesus said summarized the message of the Old Testament
Good Samaritan	Parable told by Jesus about a Samaritan who took care of a man who was attacked on a dangerous road after devout Jews did nothing to help the man
Prodigal Son (Prodigal Father)	Parable about a man who has two sons, the younger of which asks for his inheritance early and squanders it on wild living, but is lavishly welcomed home later by a loving father
Sermon on the Mount	Longest consecutive set of teachings by Jesus early in his ministry, which includes "the Beatitudes" and the Lord's prayer (the full text is found in Matthew 5–7)

Chapter 17	Arrest, Trial, and Execution
Barabbas	Rebel Israelite who was released instead of Jesus
Gethsemane	Garden where Jesus prayed before his arrest and where his arrest occurred
Golgotha	Hill in Jerusalem where Jesus was killed on a cross ("place of the skull")
Joseph	A man from Arimathea who allowed Jesus to be buried in his new tomb
Lord's Supper	Commemorative "meal" consisting of bread and wine which Christians take with other believers to remember Jesus's body and blood given for his followers (also known as the Last Supper with Jesus and his disciples a few hours before Jesus was arrested)
Pontius Pilate	Roman governor of Judea when Jesus was alive

Chapter 18	Life After Death
Emmaus	Village near Jerusalem where Jesus talked to two men after his resurrection
Joses	One of the sons of Mary, the mother of Jesus (she also had sons named James, Simon, and Judas)
Matthias	Man selected to be the twelfth disciple to replace Judas Iscariot

Witness	A person who observes an event and sometimes tells others about it (martyr in Greek)
Chapter 19	**The Apostles Respond and Scatter**
Ananias	1. Man who sold land but lied about the sale price; 2. Man in Damascus who helped Saul (Paul) regain his sight
Antioch	City on the coast at the northeast corner of the Mediterranean Sea where believers were first called Christians (currently in Syria)
Asia Minor	Region located in current day Turkey
Barnabas	Jewish Christian who traveled and preached with Paul
Caesarea	Major port city on the Mediterranean coast
Church	A group of Christians, word used to describe all Christians
Cornelius	Roman soldier who sent for Peter, resulting in new ways of thinking about the Gentiles and Jewish rules
Deacons	People chosen to help run the supporting functions of a church
Dorcas	Elderly Christian woman who was raised from the dead by Peter
Gamaliel	Pharisee who convinced the Sanhedrin not to kill the apostles
Joppa	Town on the Mediterranean coast where Peter raised Dorcas from the dead before Cornelius sent for him
Lydda	Town where Peter healed a man paralyzed for eight years
Paul	Pharisee who persecuted Christians until his dramatic conversion and later became the main evangelist to Gentiles (also known as Saul, his Hebrew name)
Pentecost	After Jesus's ascension, the day when the Spirit gave believers the ability to speak in another language; a day celebrated by Christians
Sapphira	Wife of Ananias who sold land but lied about the sale price
Saul	Paul's Hebrew name

Shavuot	Major Jewish festival held 50 days after the second day of Passover (also the day Christians celebrate Pentecost)
Simon	A tanner who lived in Joppa where Peter stayed before visiting Cornelius
Stephen	One of the original deacons who was martyred after speaking to the Sanhedrin
Tarsus	Coastal city in southern Turkey and home of Saul/Paul
The Way	Term initially given to the religious movement based on the teachings of Jesus

Chapter 20	**Paul's Travels**
Apollos	Jewish scholar and Christian from Alexandria, Egypt
Aquila	Jewish tentmaker who traveled with Paul and preached in Corinth and Ephesus, married to Priscilla
Artemis	Fertility goddess in Ephesus
Athens	Major city and capital of Greece
Berea	City in Macedonia (north of Greece) where Paul, Silas, and Timothy preached to a well-educated Jewish population
Corinth	A port city near Athens where Paul preached and lived 18 months
Corinthians	People who lived in Corinth
Council at Jerusalem	Jewish Christian leaders who debated the requirement of circumcision by Gentile Christians
Derbe	City in Asia Minor where Paul and Barnabas preached
Ephesians	People who lived in the city of Ephesus
Ephesus	Major city on the western coast of Asia Minor (near current Izmir)
Galatia	Region in central Turkey where Paul preached and sent letters
Galatians	People who lived in the region of Galatia
Hermes	One of the gods in the ancient Greek religion
Iconium	City in Asia Minor where Paul and Barnabas preached
Jason	Man who hosted the apostles in Thessalonica and was thrown in jail

Lydia	Business woman who became a Christian in Philippi
Lystra	City in Asia Minor where Paul and Barnabas preached
Macedonia	An area north of Greece
Mark	Jewish Christian who traveled with Paul and Barnabas and later with Peter; he wrote the first book about Jesus's life
Perga	City on the southern coast of Turkey
Philippi	A major city in Macedonia
Philippians	People who lived in Philippi
Pisidian Antioch	City in Asia Minor where Paul and Barnabas preached
Priscilla	Jewish tentmaker who traveled with Paul and preached in Corinth and Ephesus and was married to Aquila
Silas	Traveling companion of Paul
Thessalonians	People who live in the Macedonian city of Thessalonica
Thessalonica	Large capital city of Macedonia
Timothy	Traveling companion of Paul, Silas, and Luke who later became the bishop of Ephesus
Zeus	The supreme god in the ancient Greek religion

Chapter 21	**From Jerusalem to Rome**
Agrippa	Roman king in Palestine who Festus consulted about Paul's case
Crete	Very large Greek island in the Mediterranean Sea
Felix	Roman governor in Caesarea who heard the case against Paul and held him in prison
Festus	Roman governor in Caesarea who replaced Felix and heard Paul's appeal to be tried in Rome (also known as Porcius Festus)
Malta	Small island near Italy's southern coast where Paul's ship wrecked while he traveled to Rome
Nero	Roman emperor who killed Christians during the first century AD

Chapter 22	Paul's Letters to Believers
Colossae	City in Asia Minor near Laodicea whose Christians received a letter from Paul
Colossians	People who lived in Colossae (located in central Turkey)
Fruits of the Spirit	Paul's list of the strong evidence that God's spirit is alive in a person (Galatians 5:22–23)
Love chapter	Part of Paul's letter to believers in Corinth (1 Corinthians 13)
Onesimus	Runaway slave who became a Christian while in prison, returned to his master (Philemon), and became bishop of Ephesus
Titus	Greek gentile who traveled with Paul and Barnabas and became the leader of the church on the island of Crete

Chapter 23	Other Letters to Believers
Gnosticism	Belief that all matter is evil and only the spirit is good
Hebrews	Name of a New Testament book written to the Jews
Philemon	Gentile converted by Paul who led a house church in Colossae, who accepted his runaway slave (Onesimus) at Paul's request

Chapter 24	Predictions About the Future
Antichrist	False prophet who deceives the Jews during the final tribulation
Apocalypse	Events related to the end of times
Armageddon	Site of a final battle described in Revelation (Hebrew for "mountain of Megiddo")
Beast	An evil power that opposes Christians in Revelation
Domitian	Roman emperor who considered himself to be a god
Laodicea	Wealthy city in Asia Minor

EPILOGUE	
Great Commission	Jesus' command for his followers to make disciples in all nations

Appendix E
SCRIPTURE REFERENCES

The quoted sections of this book are paraphrases of the scriptures that are found in versions of the Old and New Testaments. Most quotes are closest to the New International Version (NIV) of the Bible and are listed in the order they appear in this book. Exact quotes are indicated by an asterisk (*) and are short phrases that are used in many versions.

Chapter	Bible Book	Chapter	Verse
1	Genesis	12	2–3
1	Genesis	22	12, 17–18
1	Genesis	27	28–29
2	Genesis	45	4–11
2	Genesis	46	3–4
3	Exodus	2	7
3	Exodus	3	4–22
3	Exodus	4	1–4, 6–17, 22–23
3	Exodus	5	1
4	Exodus	19	3–6
4	Exodus	20	1–17
4	Exodus	21	12–18, 23–24
4	Exodus	22	18–25, 29–30
4	Exodus	23	1–4, 8–10
4	Exodus	32	26
4	Leviticus	17	11
5	Numbers	6	24–26*
5	Numbers	11	14–15
5	Numbers	13	17–20
5	Numbers	14	8–9, 11–12, 15–20, 29–34
5	Numbers	16	29–30
5	Numbers	33	51–53, 55–56
5	Deuteronomy	4	25–27, 29–31
5	Deuteronomy	6	4–5
5	Deuteronomy	9	5–6
5	Deuteronomy	11	18–19, 26–29
5	Deuteronomy	30	2, 6, 10–12, 15–16, 19
6	Joshua	24	14–15

7	Judges	16	28
7	Ruth	1	16–17
7	Ruth	2	10–13
8	1 Samuel	1	11, 17
8	1 Samuel	10	24
8	1 Samuel	15	22–23
8	1 Samuel	16	7
8	1 Samuel	17	34–36, 45–46
8	1 Samuel	18	7
9	2 Samuel	7	9–10, 12–16
9	2 Samuel	12	1–14
10	1 Kings	18	27, 36, 39
10	2 Kings	6	16–17
10	Hosea	12	6
10	Isaiah	1	11, 13, 15–17
10	Isaiah	28	16–17
10	Isaiah	40	31
10	Isaiah	42	16
10	Isaiah	43	1–2, 19
10	Isaiah	53	3–5, 7, 9–12
10	Isaiah	57	21
10	Isaiah	58	1–10
10	Isaiah	61	1–3
10	Isaiah	2	2–4
10	Micah	6	8
10	Micah	7	18
11	Jeremiah	1	4, 7–8
11	Nahum	1	3, 7
11	Habakkuk	2	4
11	Lamentations	3	22–23, 25
12	Jeremiah	29	5–7
12	Ezekiel	36	22–27
12	Ezekiel	37	24
12	Daniel	2	27–28, 47
12	Daniel	3	16–18
12	Daniel	6	16, 22
12	Haggai	2	4–7, 9
12	Zechariah	2	4
12	Zechariah	7	9–14

12	Zechariah	8	16, 23
12	Esther	3	8–9
12	Esther	4	16
12	Malachi	3	1–7
12	Malachi	4	6
13	Proverbs	3	35
13	Proverbs	1	7, 20–23, 33
13	Proverbs	4	23–27
13	Proverbs	6	6–11
13	Proverbs	10	1–5, 8–9, 12–13
13	Proverbs	15	1–4
13	Proverbs	22	1–2, 6, 9, 16
13	Proverbs	25	21–22
13	Ecclesiastes	1	2*, 9, 14*
13	Ecclesiastes	3	1–8
13	Job	1	1, 3, 21
13	Job	2	9, 10
13	Job	19	25–26
13	Job	27	4–6
13	Job	38	4–5, 19, 24–25
13	Jonah	4	2–3, 8–11
13	Song of Solomon	8	6
13	Psalm	1	1–6
13	Psalm	23	1–6
13	Psalm	100	1–5
14	Luke	1	13–19, 28*, 30–33, 35–36
14	Luke	1	42, 45, 69–77
14	Matthew	1	20–23
14	Luke	2	10–12, 14
14	Luke	2	29–31, 34–35
14	Matthew	2	15
14	Luke	2	48–49
14	Matthew	3	2, 3
14	Luke	3	4–5, 7–9
14	John	1	23
14	Luke	3	11, 14
14	Luke	3	16–17
14	John	1	29
14	Matthew	3	14–15, 17

14	Matthew	4	3–4
14	Luke	4	3, 4, 6–12
14	Matthew	4	6–10
14	Matthew	4	17
14	Luke	4	18–19, 21
14	Luke	4	23–29
14	Luke	4	34–35
14	Luke	5	5
14	Luke	5	8
14	John	1	46–47
15	John	4	9–26, 29
15	John	3	2–21
15	Luke	7	43–50
15	John	12	8
15	Luke	18	22–27
15	Luke	19	8–10
15	John	2	4, 10
15	Matthew	9	5–6
15	Mark	2	9–11
15	Luke	7	6–8
15	Matthew	8	10, 13
15	Mark	8	24
15	John	5	8*, 14
15	Luke	8	45–48
15	Matthew	15	24–28
15	Matthew	12	25–28, 31
15	Matthew	8	29, 32
15	Luke	8	28, 30
15	John	11	21–22, 25–27, 39, 41–43
15	Luke	5	31–32, 34–38
15	John	2	16–20
15	Luke	20	3–4
15	Matthew	14	28, 31
15	Matthew	8	26
15	Luke	10	5*
15	Matthew	11	3–5, 10, 18–19
16	Matthew	15	7–9, 17–20
16	Mark	7	6–18, 21–23
16	Matthew	23	25–26

16	Luke	11	39, 41
16	Mark	2	25–27
16	Matthew	12	3–7, 11–12
16	Luke	6	9
16	Luke	10	27–37
16	Luke	15	4–10
16	Luke	15	22–24, 29–32
16	Luke	14	16–24
16	Matthew	20	12–16
16	Matthew	18	23–35
16	Matthew	13	3–8, 18–23
16	Matthew	5	3–10*
16	Matthew	5	11–16, 21–24, 27–30, 38–47
16	Matthew	6	1–4, 19–20, 25–27, 33–34
16	Matthew	7	1–5
16	Matthew	7	12–27
16	Matthew	7	7–11
16	Matthew	11	25–30
16	John	8	19, 31–32
16	John	6	30–31
16	John	6	32–40, 51
16	John	6	53–58
16	John	6	68–69
16	Matthew	10	37–38
16	Luke	14	26–33
16	Matthew	10	16–23, 28, 32–33, 39
16	Matthew	25	21, 26–27, 34–45
16	Luke	18	10–14
16	Matthew	23	4–7, 23, 27–36
16	Luke	11	46, 52
16	Luke	20	45–47
16	Matthew	21	31–32, 38–43
16	Mark	12	13–17
17	John	6	35
17	John	11	25
17	John	10	1–18
17	John	11	47–50
17	Zechariah	9	9
17	Matthew	21	9*

17	John	13	8
17	John	13	12–15
17	Luke	22	19–20
17	Matthew	26	26–28
17	Mark	10	42–45
17	Matthew	26	2, 31–34
17	John	13	33–35, 37–38
17	John	14	2–12, 16–19, 26
17	John	15	1–8, 18–20, 25
17	John	16	33
17	Matthew	26	39–42, 45–46, 52–56
17	Matthew	26	63–68
17	Matthew	27	9
17	Matthew	26	73
17	Matthew	27	11, 13
17	Matthew	27	17–18, 20–23
17	John	19	7, 11
17	John	18	36–38
17	Luke	23	14–15, 21
17	John	19	14–15, 30
17	Matthew	27	24–25, 29, 40–43
17	Luke	23	34, 39–43, 46
17	Matthew	27	46, 54
17	John	19	25–27, 36–37
18	Luke	24	5–7
18	John	20	13–16
18	Luke	24	17–24, 26
18	Luke	24	36, 38–39
18	John	20	25–29
18	Luke	24	44–49
18	Matthew	28	18–20
18	John	21	15–17*, 19*
18	Acts	1	7–8, 11
19	Acts	2	22–24, 30–32, 36, 38, 40
19	Acts	3	6, 12–16, 22–23
19	Acts	4	9–12
19	Acts	5	9
19	Acts	5	28–32, 35–39
19	Acts	6	1–4

19	Acts	7	56
19	Acts	9	4–6, 15, 17
19	Acts	8	32–33
19	Acts	10	15, 28–29, 34–36, 42–43
19	Acts	11	17
20	Acts	13	46–47
20	Acts	14	11*, 15–17
20	Acts	15	7–11, 14–20
20	Acts	16	17–18
20	Acts	16	28, 31
20	Acts	17	22–23
20	Acts	19	13–15, 28, 34
20	Acts	20	35
21	Acts	22	25
21	Acts	23	6, 11
21	Acts	26	17–18
21	Acts	28	26–28
22	Galatians	5	14, 16–23
22	Galatians	6	1–4, 9–10
22	1 Thessalonians	4	3, 11–12
22	1 Thessalonians	5	13–18
22	1 Corinthians	1	27
22	1 Corinthians	3	1–6, 10
22	1 Corinthians	5	9–13
22	1 Corinthians	7	9
22	1 Corinthians	2	16
22	1 Corinthians	9	19–23
22	1 Corinthians	10	13
22	1 Corinthians	14	18–19
22	1 Corinthians	12	16–24, 26
22	1 Corinthians	13	1–13
22	1 Corinthians	15	51–52, 54–55
22	Romans	3	11–12, 20, 22–23
22	Romans	5	12–17
22	Romans	8	28, 31, 38
22	Romans	5	3–4, 12, 17
22	Romans	12	1–21
22	Romans	13	1–7
22	Colossians	1	15–20

22	Colossians	2	20–23
22	Colossians	3	5–10, 12–14
22	Colossians	4	5–6
22	Ephesians	2	1–6, 8–9, 11–22
22	Ephesians	5	21–29
22	Ephesians	6	1–9
22	Ephesians	6	12
22	Philippians	2	2–11
22	Philippians	4	6–8, 11–13
22	1 Timothy	6	6–10, 17–19
23	1 Peter	2	9, 20
23	1 Peter	3	3–4, 15
23	1 Peter	4	8
23	1 Peter	5	8, 9
23	2 Peter	1	5–8
23	James	1	2–7, 13–17, 22, 26–27
23	James	2	1–4, 8–9, 20–24
23	James	4	4, 13–15
23	James	5	1–5, 16
23	1 John	3	16–18
23	1 John	4	7–8, 18–21
23	Hebrews	1	1–4
23	Hebrews	4	12–15
23	Hebrews	10	24
23	Hebrews	11	1, 3, 8, 11, 13, 16, 26–40
23	Hebrews	12	1–2, 12
24	Matthew	24	6–23
24	Matthew	13	24–29
24	Revelation	3	15–17, 19–20
24	Revelation	5	5, 12
24	Revelation	19	6
24	Revelation	21	4–7
24	Revelation	22	12–13, 17, 20
Epilogue	Matthew	28	19–20

APPENDIX F
ALIGNMENT WITH BIBLE BOOKS

The chapters of this book provide the main points of the Bible books shown in the table below (chapter numbers are noted when applicable). Those who read all the Bible books listed will have read the entire Bible.

Chapter	Bible Books
1	Genesis 1–31
2	Genesis 32–48
3	Genesis 48–50, Exodus 1–12
4	Exodus 13–40, Leviticus
5	Numbers, Deuteronomy
6	Joshua
7	Judges, Ruth
8	1 Samuel
9	2 Samuel, 1 Kings, 1–2 Chronicles
10	2 Kings, Amos, Hosea, Isaiah, Micah
11	Jeremiah, Joel, Zephaniah, Obadiah, Nahum, Habakkuk, Lamentations
12	Ezekiel, Daniel, Haggai, Zechariah, Esther, Ezra, Nehemiah, Malachi
13	Proverbs, Ecclesiastes, Job, Jonah, Song of Solomon, Psalms
14	Luke 1–5, John 1, Matthew 1–4
15	Luke 5–10, 18–21; John 2–5, Matthew 8–9, 11–12, 14–15, 17
16	Luke 11–21, John 6–9, Matthew 5–7, 10–25, Mark
17	Luke 22–23, John 10–19, Matthew 26–27
18	Luke 24, John 20–21, Matthew 28, Acts 1
19	Acts 1–11
20	Acts 12–20
21	Acts 21–28
22	Galatians, 1–2 Thessalonians, 1–2 Corinthians, Romans, Colossians, Ephesians, Philippians, Titus, Philemon, 1□–2 Timothy
23	1–2 Peter, James, Jude, 1–3 John, Hebrews
24	Matthew 13 and 24, Revelation

APPENDIX G
MAPS

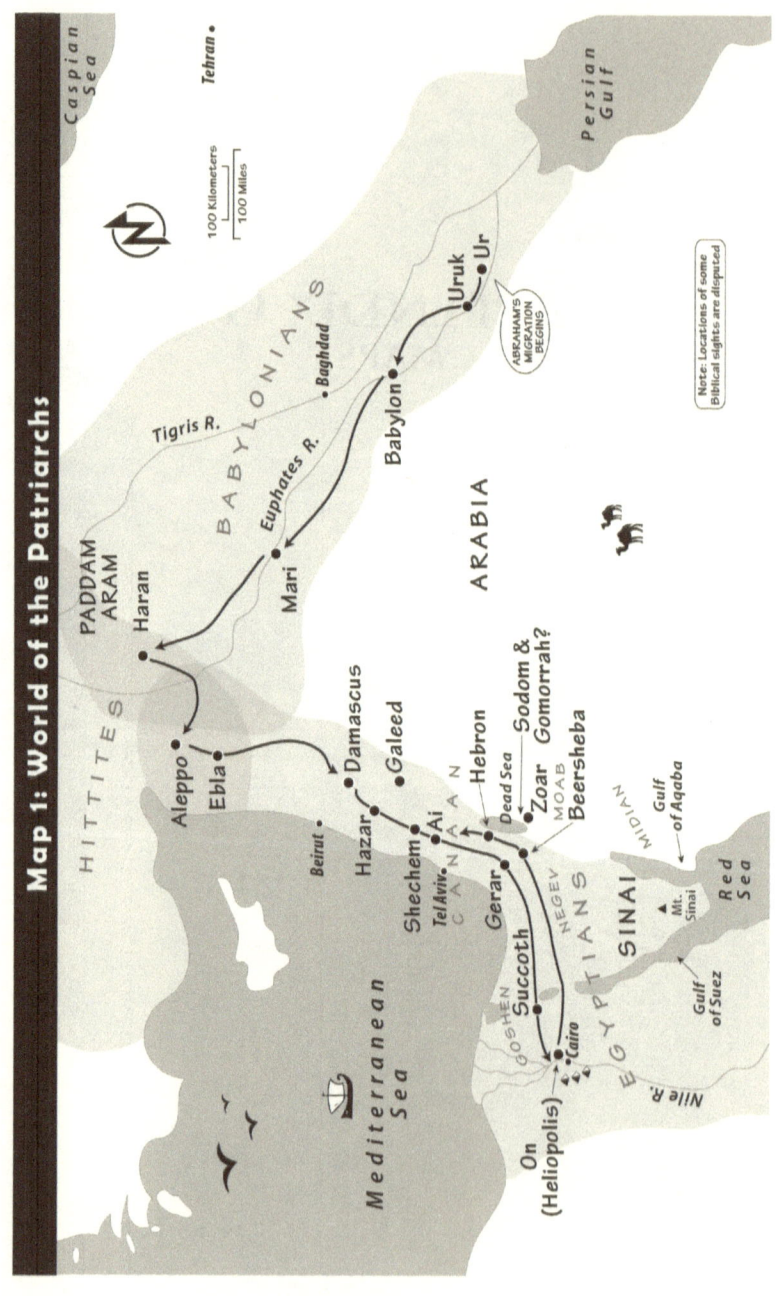

Map 1: World of the Patriarchs

Map 2: Moses & the Exodus

50 Kilometers
50 Miles

HITTITES

Beirut •

Damascus •

Mediterranean
Sea

Sea of
Galilee

Nazareth •

Jordan R.

Jabbok R.

ISRAELITES
ENTER
CANAAN

C A N A A N

Tel Aviv •

Jericho • ▲Mt.Nebo

Jerusalem •

MOSES
DIES

Salt
(Dead)
Sea

Gaza •

Hebron

PHILISTINES

Arnon R.

Nile
Delta

EXODUS
BEGINS

Beersheba •

DESERT OF ZIN

MOAB

Ramses •
(Tanis)

CROSSING
OF THE
RED SEA?

GOSHEN

Succoth

Kadesh-
Barnea

NEGEV

Mt.
Hor

Bitter
Lakes

WILDERNESS
OF SHUR

Mtns. of
Edom

Heliopolis

EGYPT

Kibbroth-
hattaavah?

EDOM

• Cairo
• Memphis

WILDERNESS
OF PARAN

Nile River

• Marah

DESERT OF SIN

SINAI

Ezion-geber

MIDIAN

Elim

Dophkah?

Gulf of Aqaba

Rephidim?

• Hazeroth?

Mt. Sinai
(Horeb)

Gulf of Suez

MOSES
RECEIVES THE TEN
COMMANDMENTS

Note: Locations of some
Biblical sights are disputed

— Traditional Exodus Route
• Ancient Cities – Heliopolis
• Modern Cities – *Cairo*
Civilizations – EGYPTIANS

Red Sea

Map 3: The 12 Tribes & Conquest of Canaan

Damascus •

Mt.
▲ Hermon   *Pharpar R.*

Tyre •

PHOENICIA

*Mediterranean
Sea*

ASHER

NAPHALTI

Dan •

• Hazor

Merom ✳

EAST
MANESSEH

N

Sea of
Galilee

• Golan

10 Kilometers
10 Miles

ZEBULUN

Varmuk R.

Megiddo •
Taanach •

ISSACHAR

MANESSEH

Jordan River

Jabbok R.

Shechem • ▲ Mt.
Ebal
▲ Mt.
Gerizim

Valley
← of Achor

Tel Aviv
Joppa •

EPHRAIM

GAD

AMMON

DAN

Bethel •

Emmaus •

BENJAMIN

Jericho •
• ✳
Gilgal

Mt.
▲ Nebo

Gibeon ✳
Bethlehem •

• Jerusalem

Ashkelon
•

PHILISTIA

JUDAH

REUBEN

Gaza
•

• Hebron

Salt
(Dead)
Sea

Arnon R.

En Gedi •

MOAB

AMALEC

• Beersheba

SIMEON

• Zoar

Zered R.

WILDERNESS
OF ZIN

EDOM

NEGEV

• Kadesh-
Barnea

✳	Major Battles
•	Ancient Cities – Shechem
•	Modern Cities – *Tel Aviv*
	Nations – PHILISTIA

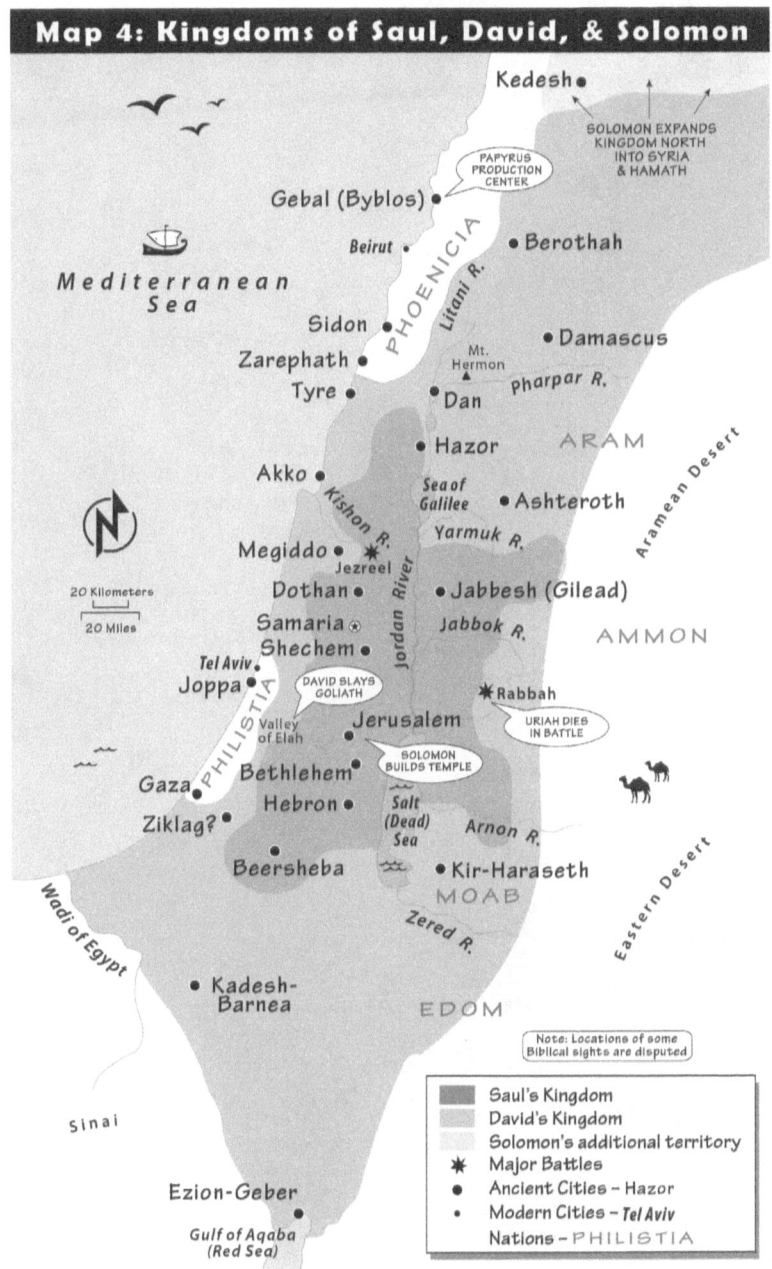

Map 4: Kingdoms of Saul, David, & Solomon

Kedesh

SOLOMON EXPANDS KINGDOM NORTH INTO SYRIA & HAMATH

PAPYRUS PRODUCTION CENTER

Gebal (Byblos)

Beirut

Berothah

Mediterranean Sea

PHOENICIA

Litani R.

Sidon

Zarephath

Tyre

Mt. Hermon

Damascus

Pharpar R.

Dan

Hazor

ARAM

Akko

Kishon R.

Sea of Galilee

Ashteroth

Yarmuk R.

Aramean Desert

Megiddo

Jezreel

Dothan

Jordan River

Jabbesh (Gilead)

Jabbok R.

AMMON

20 Kilometers

20 Miles

Samaria

Shechem

Tel Aviv

Joppa

PHILISTIA

DAVID SLAYS GOLIATH

Jerusalem

Rabbah

URIAH DIES IN BATTLE

Valley of Elah

SOLOMON BUILDS TEMPLE

Gaza

Bethlehem

Hebron

Salt (Dead) Sea

Arnon R.

Ziklag?

Beersheba

Kir-Haraseth

MOAB

Eastern Desert

Zered R.

Wadi of Egypt

Kadesh-Barnea

EDOM

Note: Locations of some Biblical sights are disputed

Sinai

▓	Saul's Kingdom
▓	David's Kingdom
▓	Solomon's additional territory
✳	Major Battles
●	Ancient Cities – Hazor
•	Modern Cities – *Tel Aviv*
	Nations – PHILISTIA

Ezion-Geber

Gulf of Aqaba (Red Sea)

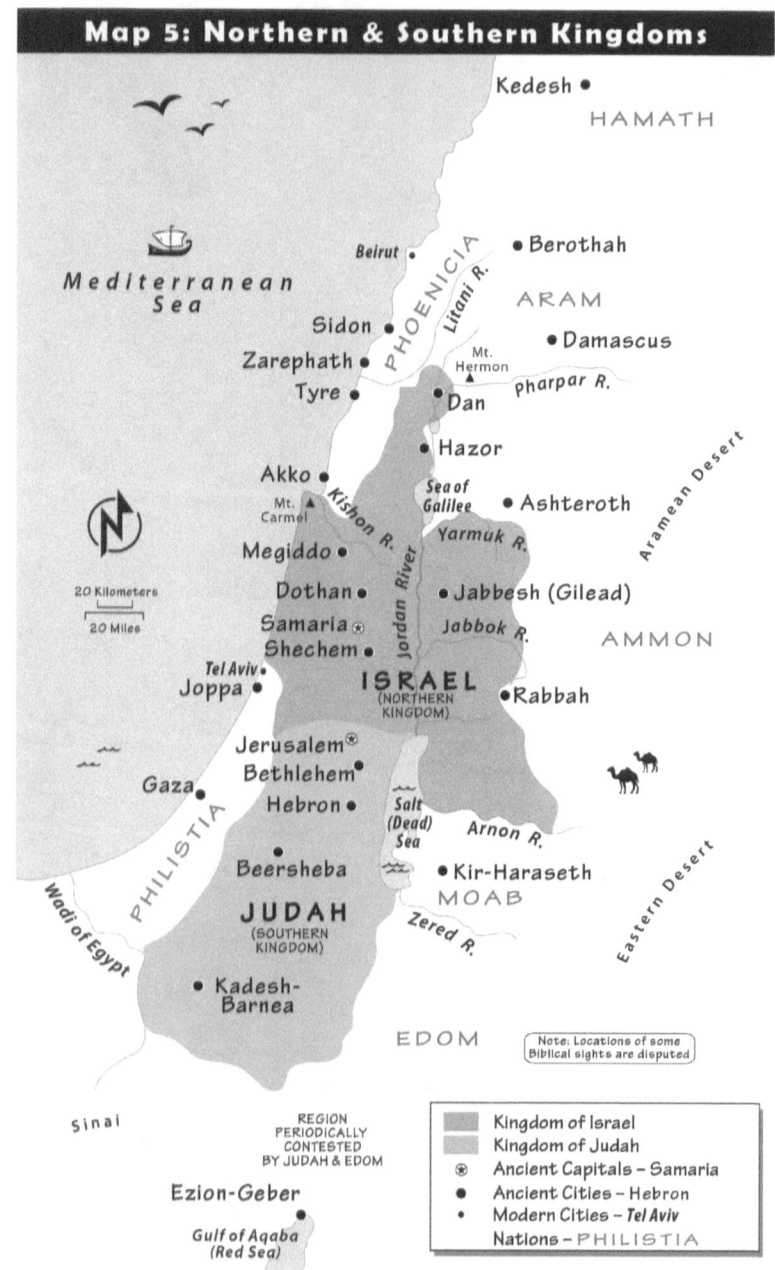

Map 5: Northern & Southern Kingdoms

Kedesh •

HAMATH

Mediterranean Sea

Beirut •
PHOENICIA
Litani R.
• Berothah

ARAM

Sidon •
Zarephath •
Tyre •
Mt. Hermon
• Damascus
Pharpar R.
• Dan

• Hazor

Akko •
Mt. Carmel
Kishon R.
Sea of Galilee
Yarmuk R.
• Ashteroth

Aramean Desert

Megiddo •
Dothan •
Jordan River
• Jabbesh (Gilead)
Jabbok R.
Samaria ⊛
Shechem •
ISRAEL
(NORTHERN KINGDOM)

AMMON

20 Kilometers
20 Miles

Tel Aviv •
Joppa •
• Rabbah

Jerusalem ⊛
Bethlehem •
Gaza •
Hebron •
Salt (Dead) Sea
PHILISTIA
Arnon R.

Beersheba •
• Kir-Haraseth
MOAB
JUDAH
(SOUTHERN KINGDOM)
Zered R.

Eastern Desert

Wadi of Egypt

• Kadesh-Barnea

EDOM

Note: Locations of some Biblical sights are disputed

Sinai

REGION PERIODICALLY CONTESTED BY JUDAH & EDOM

Kingdom of Israel
Kingdom of Judah
⊛ Ancient Capitals – Samaria
• Ancient Cities – Hebron
• Modern Cities – *Tel Aviv*
Nations – PHILISTIA

Ezion-Geber

Gulf of Aqaba (Red Sea)

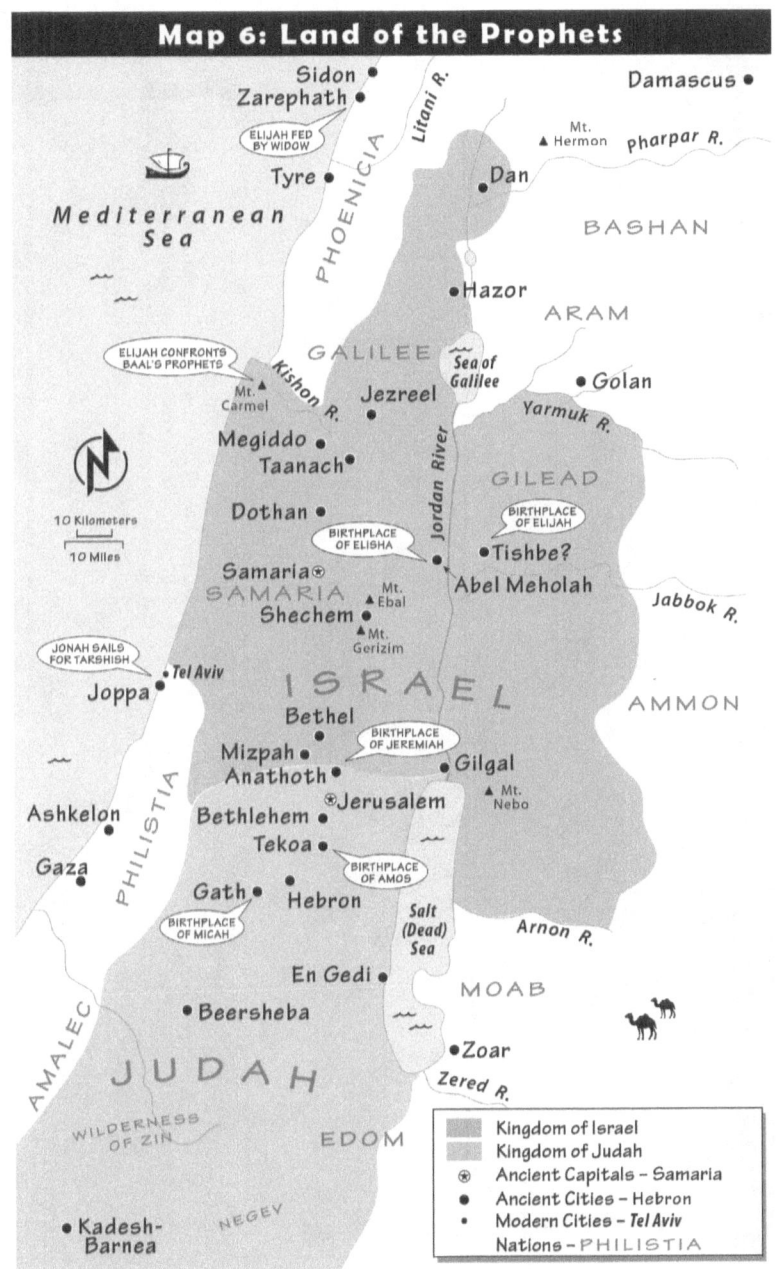

Map 6: Land of the Prophets

Sidon
Zarephath
ELIJAH FED BY WIDOW
Tyre
Mediterranean Sea
PHOENICIA
Litani R.
Dan
Mt. Hermon
Pharpar R.
Damascus
BASHAN
Hazor
ARAM
ELIJAH CONFRONTS BAAL'S PROPHETS
GALILEE
Kishon R.
Sea of Galilee
Mt. Carmel
Jezreel
Golan
Yarmuk R.
Megiddo
Taanach
GILEAD
Dothan
Jordan River
BIRTHPLACE OF ELISHA
BIRTHPLACE OF ELIJAH
Tishbe?
10 Kilometers
10 Miles
Samaria
SAMARIA
Mt. Ebal
Shechem
Mt. Gerizim
Abel Meholah
Jabbok R.
JONAH SAILS FOR TARSHISH
Tel Aviv
ISRAEL
AMMON
Joppa
Bethel
Mizpah
Anathoth
BIRTHPLACE OF JEREMIAH
Gilgal
Mt. Nebo
Ashkelon
PHILISTIA
Bethlehem
Jerusalem
Gaza
Tekoa
BIRTHPLACE OF AMOS
Gath
BIRTHPLACE OF MICAH
Hebron
Salt (Dead) Sea
Arnon R.
En Gedi
MOAB
AMALEC
Beersheba
Zoar
Zered R.
JUDAH
WILDERNESS OF ZIN
EDOM
NEGEV
Kadesh-Barnea

Kingdom of Israel
Kingdom of Judah
⊛ Ancient Capitals – Samaria
● Ancient Cities – Hebron
• Modern Cities – *Tel Aviv*
Nations – PHILISTIA

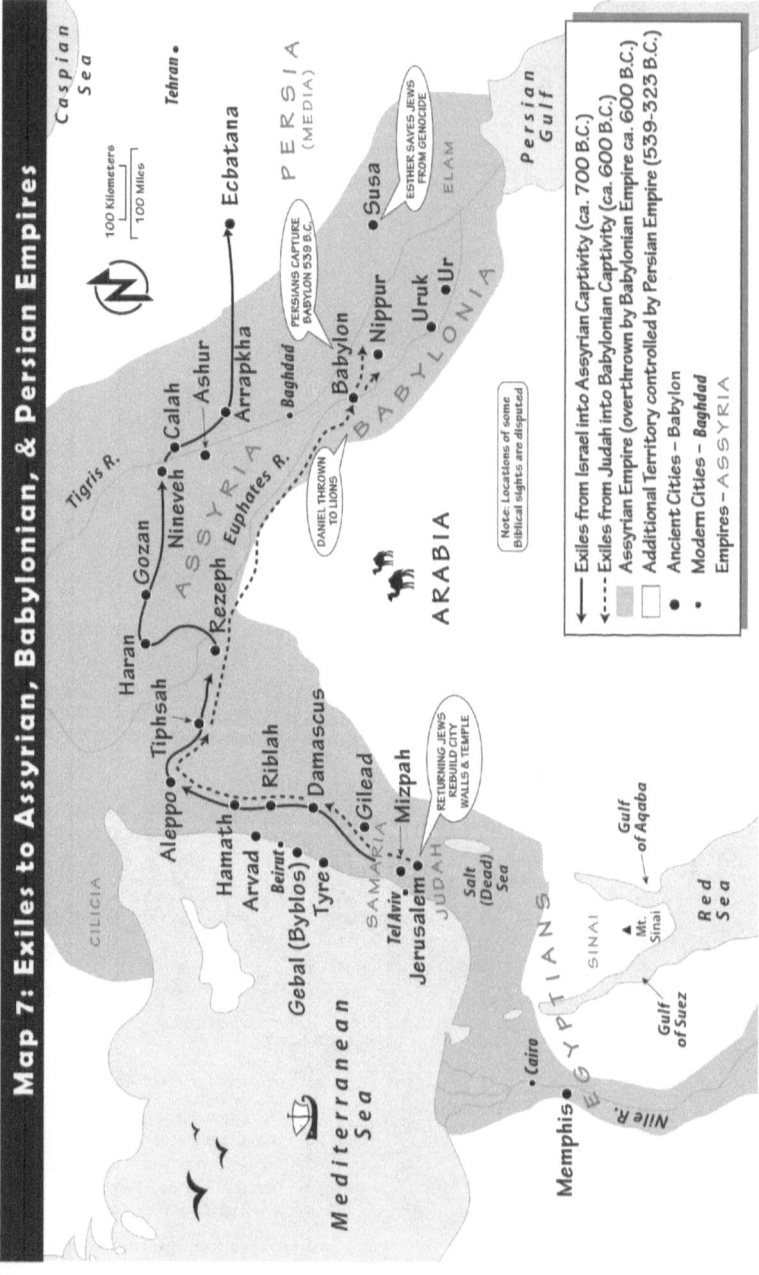

Map 7: Exiles to Assyrian, Babylonian, & Persian Empires

Map 8: Jesus' Ministry in Palestine

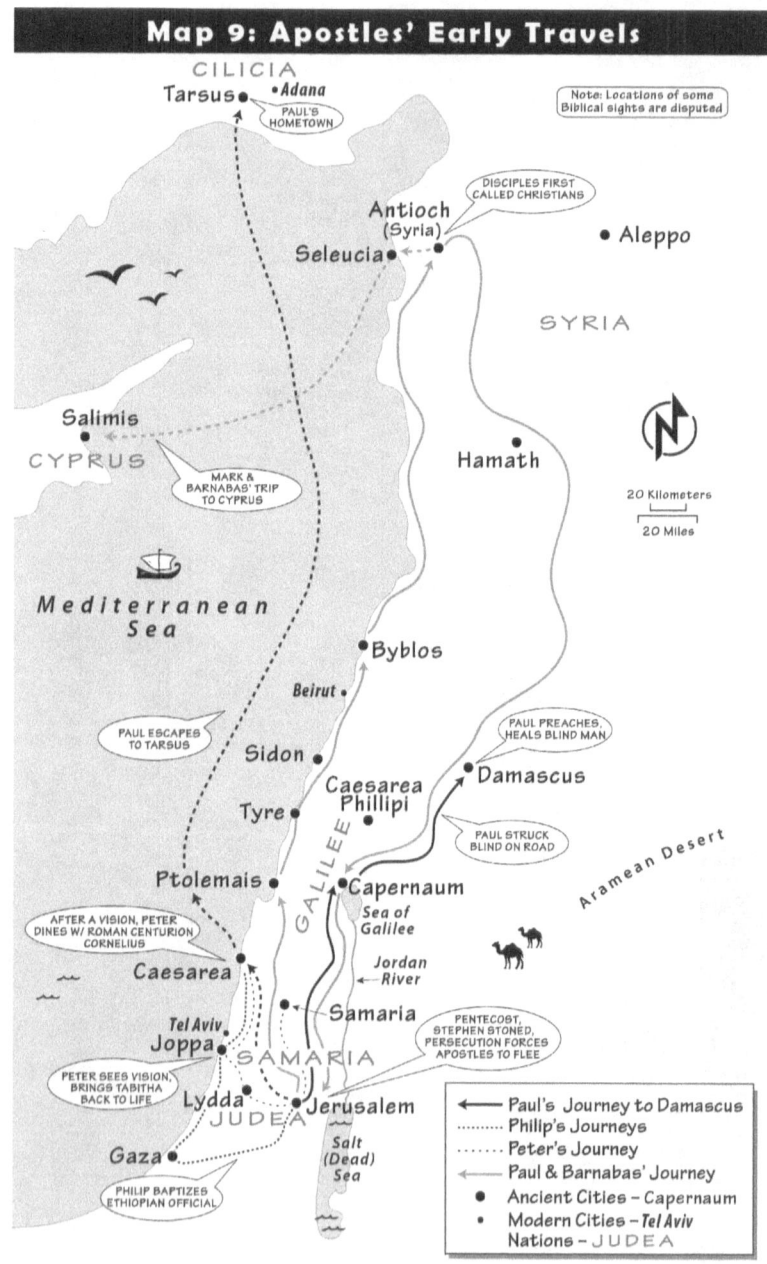

Map 9: Apostles' Early Travels

CILICIA
Tarsus • •*Adana*
PAUL'S HOMETOWN

Note: Locations of some Biblical sights are disputed

DISCIPLES FIRST CALLED CHRISTIANS

Antioch (Syria)
Seleucia •

• Aleppo

SYRIA

Salimis •
CYPRUS

MARK & BARNABAS' TRIP TO CYPRUS

Hamath •

20 Kilometers
20 Miles

Mediterranean Sea

• Byblos
Beirut •

PAUL PREACHES, HEALS BLIND MAN

PAUL ESCAPES TO TARSUS

Sidon •
Tyre •

Caesarea Phillipi

• Damascus

PAUL STRUCK BLIND ON ROAD

Ptolemais •

GALILEE

Capernaum
Sea of Galilee

Aramean Desert

AFTER A VISION, PETER DINES W/ ROMAN CENTURION CORNELIUS

Caesarea

Jordan River

Tel Aviv
Joppa •

Samaria

PENTECOST, STEPHEN STONED, PERSECUTION FORCES APOSTLES TO FLEE

PETER SEES VISION; BRINGS TABITHA BACK TO LIFE

SAMARIA

Lydda •
JUDEA
Jerusalem

Gaza •

Salt (Dead) Sea

PHILIP BAPTIZES ETHIOPIAN OFFICIAL

◄─── Paul's Journey to Damascus
.... Philip's Journeys
.... Peter's Journey
◄─── Paul & Barnabas' Journey
• Ancient Cities – Capernaum
• Modern Cities – *Tel Aviv*
Nations – JUDEA

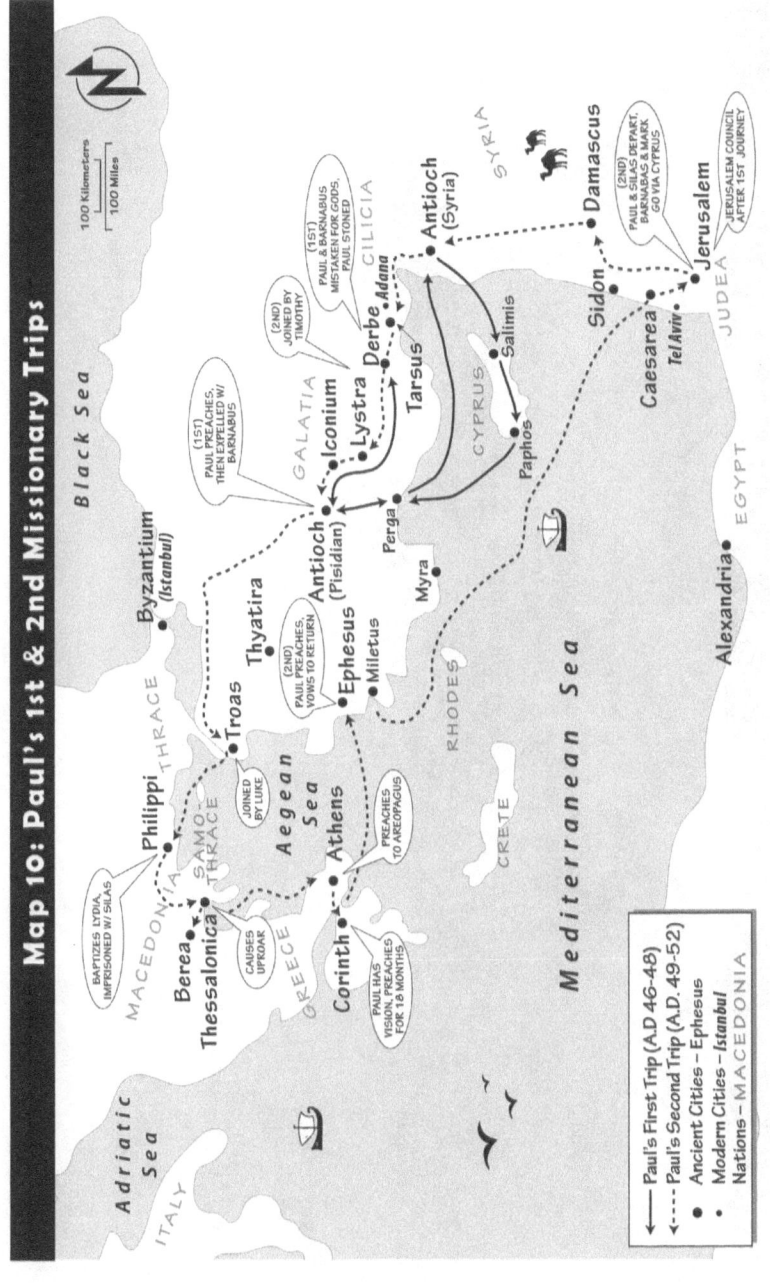

Map 10: Paul's 1st & 2nd Missionary Trips

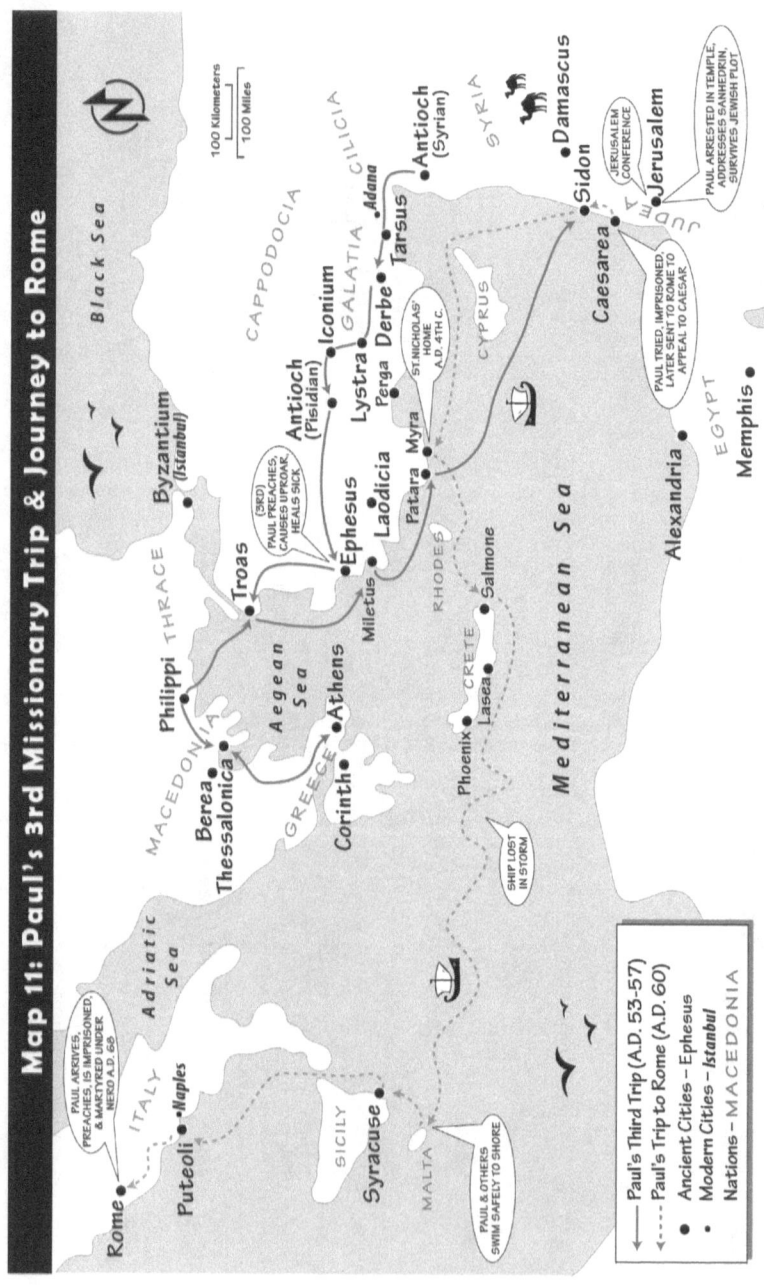

Map 11: Paul's 3rd Missionary Trip & Journey to Rome

www.ingramcontent.com/pod-product-compliance
Lightning Source LLC
Chambersburg PA
CBHW021611120626
46545CB00001B/171

*9 7 8 1 9 6 4 0 6 0 0 9 5 *